Lines and Lyrics

Lines and Lyrics

An Introduction to Poetry and Song

||||||||||||||||||||||||||||||||||||||||||||||||||||||||||||||||||||||||||||||||||||

Matt BaileyShea

Yale

UNIVERSITY PRESS
New Haven and London

Copyright © 2021 by Matt BaileyShea.
All rights reserved.
This book may not be reproduced, in whole or in part, including illustrations, in any form (beyond that copying permitted by Sections 107 and 108 of the U.S. Copyright Law and except by reviewers for the public press), without written permission from the publishers.

Yale University Press books may be purchased in quantity for educational, business, or promotional use. For information, please e-mail sales.press@yale.edu (U.S. office) or sales@yaleup.co.uk (U.K. office).

Set in Merope type by Tseng Information Systems, Inc.,
Durham, North Carolina.
Printed in the United States of America.

Library of Congress Control Number: 2021931596
ISBN 978-0-300-24567-7 (hardcover : alk. paper)

A catalogue record for this book is available from the British Library.

This paper meets the requirements of ANSI/NISO Z39.48-1992 (Permanence of Paper).

10   9   8   7   6   5   4   3   2   1

For Chelsea, Kilian, and Rory

CONTENTS

Note to the Reader   ix

Introduction: Why Study Lyrics?   1

1. Diction   9
2. Meter   32
3. Rhyme   64
4. Lines and Syntax   96
5. Address   126
6. Form   146
7. The Complete Song   179

Conclusion: Some Thoughts About Poetry, Meaning, and Word Painting   210

Appendix: Transcribing Lyrics   217

Notes   227

Further Reading   237

Acknowledgments   241

Credits   243

Index   249

Note to the Reader

This is a book that encourages close, attentive listening to songs. It will be difficult to follow the ensuing discussion without having a direct connection to the music. To help make everything as accessible as possible, I have created a Spotify playlist called "Lines and Lyrics" (available at https://open.spotify.com/playlist/2Idu5dQlDgFe94qm2WUIG6). Throughout the book, I'll refer to this playlist. When I want to direct your attention to a specific moment in the middle of a song, I will reference a specific timestamp (e.g., Spotify playlist, track 42, 2:17).

All the songs under discussion can be accessed by alternate online platforms, such as YouTube, but the times might not be exactly synced with the Spotify playlist. This should not cause much confusion, however. Listening to any versions of the songs while following along with the book will make the reading experience more valuable and more rewarding.

Lines and Lyrics

INTRODUCTION ||||||||||||||||||||||||||||||||||||||||||||||||||||||||||||||

Why Study Lyrics?

> We were born before the wind
> Also younger than the sun
> Ere the bonnie boat was won
> As we sailed into the mystic.

Many readers will recognize these lines as the opening of Van Morrison's "Into the Mystic" from the 1970 album *Moondance*. The song is widely viewed as a classic; it still gets played regularly on rock radio stations around the globe. It is *not*, however, great poetry. Imagine if Morrison, rather than writing a song, had tried to publish these lyrics as a poem. He probably would have suffered many rejections. Poetry editors no doubt would have cringed at the faux mysticism, the clichéd sentimentality, and the borderline meaninglessness of its verses. These words come to us not as a written poem, however, but as a song. And the words, shaped into melody, are beautiful (Spotify playlist, track 1).

In a 1978 *Rolling Stone* interview, Morrison adopted a familiar anti-intellectual, rock & roll posture when asked about his lyrics, arguing that people take them too seriously and that the words might even be "irrelevant."[1] Anyone interested in studying his songs, then, might follow suit and simply set aside the lyrics and focus on other things: the harmonies, the texture, the rhythm and meter, the vocal timbre. Why bother engaging in serious interpretation of the lyrics if they are no more than a vehicle for a catchy tune?

We should be careful, however, not to adopt such a dismissive attitude. What happens, for instance, if we *do* take a closer look at the lyrics? There is actually quite a bit to savor. The opening line is heavy on alliteration: The *w*'s at the edges of the line—"we," "were," and "wind"—flank the *b*'s in the middle ("born before"). There is nothing especially ingenious about this (alliteration comes easily), but it chimes nicely with the third line, which retains those internal *b*'s—"bonnie boat"—and brings back the *w*'s as well ("was won"). There

1

are other pleasing recurrences as well. We might notice the rhyming syllables: "young," "sun," and "won" or "born before." And we might recognize the way the first three lines all share the same basic structure: seven syllables with the same pattern of accent (TUM, ta-TUM, ta-TUM, ta-TUM). There is a lilting, breezy quality to the lyric that reinforces the pastoral beauty of the melody—a simple folk-like tune over a two-chord base.[2]

But notice also some of the striking *differences*. The word "mystic," for example, is unlike any other sound in the lyrics thus far. It has no rhyming or alliterative partner. And its two syllables stand out in contrast to the other concluding, single-syllable words: "wind," "sun," "won," "*mystic*." That final word punctuates a line that is different from the others in size and accent. It has eight syllables, and although we could force it into the same four-stress pattern as the previous lines—"**as** we **sailed** in**to** the **mys**tic"—a more natural reading would be much lighter and quicker, with only two strong accents: "as we **sailed** into the **mys**tic." The contrast is significant: it provides a change of pace that aligns well with the conclusive turn of phrase in Morrison's melody, which relaxes, for the first time, into a stable tonic as the final note (the "tonic" is the resting point at the beginning and end of a musical scale).

Perhaps more vital, however, is the way this serene, quasi-mystical language contrasts with the song's first climactic outburst: "I want to rock your gypsy soul." This line, occurring about one minute and twenty-five seconds into the song, must be heard to be appreciated. It is a perfect microcosm of Van Morrison's vocal talent. Like the opening lines, it is not great poetry, but it *is* powerfully effective as a lyric. The entire song appears to be addressed to a lover, but the effusiveness of this moment is markedly different from the odd past-tense voice of the opening, which might be imagined as a strange, first-person-plural narrator ("we were . . . we sailed . . ."). This climax is something else entirely: a far more direct, present-tense exclamation with a contemporary phrase—"rock your gypsy soul"—that draws on the previous old-world diction but with a more modern spin. It is the first point in the song at which Morrison vaults into a distinctly higher vocal and emotional register, and the contrast with the earlier lyrics reinforces the musical shift.

Simply put, and despite Morrison's protestations to the contrary, the words to this song *matter*. The sounds of the words matter. The patterns of accent matter. The phrasing, the connotations, the narration and address all contribute to the musical effect of the entire song. I would hope that this would be an obvious point. How could the words of a song *not* matter? Bob Dylan, after all, won the Nobel Prize for Literature. And yet skepticism about the role of language in song often persists, perhaps even for good reason.

Consider the devil's advocate position. To begin with, songwriters themselves, like Morrison, often draw attention to the irrelevance of their lyrics. Indeed, they sometimes do it *in the lyrics themselves*. Here, for instance, are the opening lines of the song "Hook," a 1994 hit by Blues Traveler (Spotify playlist, track 2):

> It doesn't matter what I say
> As long as I sing with inflection
> That makes you feel that I'll convey
> Some inner truth or vast reflection.

Many readers, no doubt, will recognize a flash of truth in these lyrics. Who among us has not enjoyed a song, perhaps one we have heard many times, without really processing the lyrics? How many listeners, when hearing the opening verse of "Tumbling Dice" by the Rolling Stones—the biggest hit from one of their greatest albums, *Exile on Main Street* (1972)—could comprehend more than a quarter of Mick Jagger's words? The bluesy inflection is clear; the lyrics are not (Spotify playlist, track 3).

Rock & roll songwriters, moreover, are not the only ones to draw attention to the potential insignificance of lyrics. Ira Gershwin, one of the greatest lyricists of the Tin Pan Alley tradition, once wrote a song called "Blah, Blah, Blah," used in the 1931 film *Delicious*. The first verse concludes with the lines "I've studied all the rhymes that all the lovers sing / Then just for you I wrote this little thing." Next comes the song's chorus (Spotify playlist, track 4, 0:30):

> Blah, blah, blah, blah moon
> Blah, blah, blah above
> Blah, blah, blah, blah croon
> Blah, blah, blah, blah love

The joke hits its mark because it exposes something that many people already suspect, that all a popular song needs are a few clichéd rhymes and a pretty tune.

Is the situation any different in the hallowed halls of Western classical music, where genius composers write songs to the poetry of Shakespeare, Goethe, and Whitman? Surely the words in these songs must play a vital role, given that they were written by some of the greatest poets of Western literary history. But the devil's advocate has an easy, rapid response: many fans of classical music enjoy songs in French, German, and Italian without understanding the languages at all. Furthermore, certain composers seem to excel when setting unremarkable poems; some of the best songs by Schubert and Mahler involve masterful settings of mediocre poetry. And consider the case of Eric Whitacre's "Sleep" (2000), a choral piece that was composed as a setting of Robert Frost's "Stopping by Woods on a Snowy Evening." After a few initial performances, Whitacre learned that the famous poem was still under copyright and the Frost estate would not grant permission for its use. In order to save his music, Whitacre asked a friend and collaborator, Charles Anthony Silvestri, to write a replacement text using the same meter and rhyme scheme as the Frost poem, along with the general theme of sleep (inspired by Frost's final stanza). The piece went on to become a massive success; it has received millions of views on YouTube and has been performed by countless vocal ensembles (Spotify playlist, track 5). For our devil's advocate, the lesson is clear: the greatness of Frost's poem was entirely unnecessary; all that was needed was something vaguely similar—a well-executed "shadow poem"—to make the music work.

Such skepticism about the value of lyrics is understandable, perhaps even defensible. But the central premise of this skepticism—the idea that the words of a song could easily be exchanged for any other words without damage—would ring false (and appallingly so) for most music lovers. Imagine telling Kendrick Lamar fans that his hip-hop rhymes were essentially irrelevant, that all that mattered was the beat. Imagine telling Joni Mitchell fans that all the songs they sing along to would work just as well if the lyrics were replaced with something else. Or take the Beatles—their lyrics are sometimes silly and inconsequential, like those of many other pop songwriters, but who would want them any other way? Beatles fans cherish those lyrics like old friends. They love them for what they are, not for what they could be.

So yes, skepticism about song lyrics is understandable. But this is not a book for the skeptics. This is a book for people who find themselves moved and fascinated by the words of a song, whether a hip-hop verse, a Broadway show stopper, or an expert setting of a poem by Emily Dickinson. Even more, this is a book for people who are so enchanted by the combination of words and music that the simple act of listening is not enough; this is for people who want more, who want to ask questions about songs, ponder the choices of the artists involved, and track every creative shift in tone, metaphor, and meaning. In short, this is a book for people who enjoy interpretation, people who relish the study of song in all its particulars: form, rhythm, meter, melody—and lyrics too.

Interpreting song, however, is not easy. It requires skill and training in two different disciplines: poetic analysis and music analysis. This creates an obvious problem: musicians typically lack the skills of the poet and poets typically lack the skills of the musician. How many music scholars can speak coherently about historical variations in the Petrarchan sonnet? How many poets can speak about enharmonic reinterpretation in chromatic music? The challenges are especially unavoidable with the art song repertoire. How, for instance, do we approach Benjamin Britten's settings of John Donne when they combine highly sophisticated music with staggeringly complex poetry?

My goal for this book, then, is that it be the kind of guidebook that I wish I had had when I was a student. Although there are many superb introductions to poetry and several excellent scholarly introductions to song, I know of nothing that effectively introduces both in a single text. Moreover, a combined introduction to poetry and song is not simply a convenience—"two for the price of one"—it is a necessary way to grapple with the complex combination of words and music. Recognizing stress patterns, for instance (iambs, trochees, dactyls, and so forth), is important when reading poems; but those stresses play a different role in song, where specific rhythmic and dynamic values determine how each word will be articulated. A similar situation arises with the issue of lineation. The structure of lines is as crucial in Shakespeare's eighth sonnet as it is in Stravinsky's setting of that sonnet ("Music to hear"). But the melodic flow of the lines in the song is strikingly different from any natural poetic reading. Every issue in poetry, in other words, has an important corresponding status in song, but always transformed, always different.

For repertoire, I have decided to focus almost entirely on songs with English texts. Like many music scholars, I have a deep affection for the German Romantic vocal tradition. And it troubles me to set aside other languages as well (the songs of Debussy and Fauré, the great Italian arias). But appreciating poetry requires linguistic fluency; readers will need to be able to identify subtle nuances in sound, meaning, and syntax. And though the focus on English-language songs necessarily discards a great many foreign-language masterpieces, it nevertheless rewards us with an expansive and rich tradition, from John Dowland to Bob Dylan.

This particular pairing—Dowland and Dylan—reflects yet another important choice about repertoire: I will be drawing examples from both art songs and popular music. There has been considerable discussion, especially in recent years, about whether pop lyrics—rock, hip hop, country, and so forth—can rise to the level of poetry. (Dylan's Nobel Prize reanimated what had already been a heated debate.) But the question of whether pop lyrics qualify as poetry is not my central concern. Like many people, when I read the lyrics of a pop song *as if it were a published poem*, I often find them unsatisfying and sometimes downright silly. I get the overwhelming feeling that the words are being asked to play a role that they were not meant to play, and this, of course, is usually true—most lyrics are conceived with a specific musical context in mind. But luckily, there is no reason for us to decisively separate lyrics from music. Why would we? Words that seem clumsy on the page might be expressed with remarkable elegance in song. Words that seem clichéd as poetry might seem startlingly original as melody. For that reason, the question Do pop lyrics qualify as poetry? is far less compelling than a different question: How can the study of poetry better help us appreciate song?

Needless to say, the answer to this question will be different when we are looking at Ruth Crawford's settings of Carl Sandburg from what it will be when we look at, say, a song by Bruce Springsteen. With Crawford, there was a preexisting poem, and the relevance of poetic analysis is therefore obvious. But even if a Springsteen song lacks a specific source poem, its lyrics will probably feature language that is obviously "poetic" (using rhyme, metrical patterns, metaphors, lineation, and much else). There is thus no substantive reason to avoid frequent shifts between contrasting styles, genres, and historical periods. Indeed, my examples will mirror, in many ways, contemporary listening habits, veering from song to song without strict stylistic homogeneity.

This, I believe, is one the book's most important attributes. It directly contrasts seventeenth-century song with modern hip hop. T. S. Eliot lands side by side with Johnny Cash. Anne Sexton is paired with Outkast. The music of "classical" composers, such as Aaron Copland, Edward Elgar, and Sofia Gubaidulina, locks arms with music by Pink Floyd, Patti Smith, and Queen. None of this is done for the sake of shock value, nor is it done for the sake of marketing ("music for all tastes!"). It is done, rather, out of an earnest and, I think, legitimate belief that we can learn a great deal by identifying commonalities in different genres of songs while also recognizing their obvious differences.

The book's eclecticism also enhances its value as a scholarly introduction, one that assumes no prior knowledge of complex music or poetic analysis. Each of its six principal chapters takes a specific poetic concept as a starting point. They move from basic, fundamental features toward issues of greater complexity, highlighting first crucial elements of sound (diction, meter, and rhyme), then broader topics, such as lineation, address, and form.

Naturally, this approach is not comprehensive. Poetry, like music, offers too much to attend to. We can listen to the sound of words, the patterns of accent, or the balance of rhymes. We can think about style, tone, voice, and address. We can study form and syntax, rhythm and pacing, meter and metaphor. The possibilities for scholarly inquiry are vast and growing—the best poetry allows for countless points of approach. And the greatest writers command our attention with an unbounded palette of artistic devices: repetitions and interruptions, shifts in diction and shocking non sequiturs, apostrophes, exclamations, and competing voices.

When a composer decides to set a poem to music, she or he can transform most of these features by drawing from a different set of sonic possibilities: melody and harmony, texture and timbre, dynamics and dissonance—too much to list, and too much to process in a single hearing. It can be dizzying to consider all the options, but this book affords an entry point: an initial step toward a better understanding of music and language. It offers a chance to dwell on the details of our most beloved songs: Van Morrison's voice, the gypsy souls, a carefree sail into the mystic.

CHAPTER ONE ||||||||||||||||||||||||||||||||||||||||||||||||||||||||||||||||

Diction

> The porcupine sips a quill of mercy.
> —Robert Lowell, translating Eugenio Montale
>
> baby, baby, baby, oh!
> —Justin Bieber

Let's begin with the porcupine. A reader who encounters Robert Lowell's translation of Eugenio Montale's "News from Mount Amiata" may puzzle over its wonderfully strange conclusion: "the porcupine sips a quill of mercy."[1] What do these words mean? Why would a porcupine "sip" mercy? In what sense might mercy be contained in a quill?

These are reasonable questions to ask, but let's set aside problems of interpretation for a moment and focus first on the individual words. The English language, like all languages, is the product of history and cultural change. The Norman conquest of 1066 resulted in a clash between two different linguistic traditions: the Germanic language of the Anglo-Saxons and the Latinate vocabulary of the French invaders. As centuries passed, the language transformed and evolved into modern English, in which we find in Lowell's translation a thrilling alchemy: Latinate words such as "porcupine" and "mercy" fuse with Germanic words like "sips" and "quill."

These are potent combinations, and quite pleasurable to read. As the scholar Helen Vendler might say, the words "seem purposefully magnetic toward each other, rather than accidentally related." But what accounts for their aural effect? This is a difficult question to answer because there is always something slightly ineffable in the sonic beauty of great poems. I suspect, however, that it has something to do with the way certain recurring sounds are passed from one word to another. Notice, for instance, the three *p*'s in "<u>p</u>orcu<u>p</u>ine si<u>p</u>s." And notice how those three sounds are then interlaced with three sibilant *s* sounds in "<u>s</u>ip<u>s</u>" and "mer<u>c</u>y." The word "quill" shares the same vowel

9

as "sips," but it begins with a more sharply articulated consonant, which in turn provides a nice contrast to the softer sound of "mercy" at the line's end. The meaning of the words is important, of course, and a full appreciation of this line would require deep engagement with everything leading up to it. But the sounds themselves are symptomatic of what modern English affords us—the frequent presence of words from different traditions that can nevertheless be blended with exciting, resonant juxtapositions. To enjoy English poetry is to bask in the disparate beauty of the language itself.[2]

When we speak about poetic diction we are referring to a poet's choice of words. As with Lowell's translation, this might involve juxtapositions of words with very different histories. Long, complex, Latinate words, such as "insatiable" or "transference," might commingle with short, punchy, Germanic words like "spit" and "pluck." Emily Dickinson gracefully pairs words from each tradition when she describes an "impetuous bird" and nature's "admonition mild," and we often hear echoes of such juxtapositions in the work of modern songwriters, such as David Bowie, who describes a stream's "warm impermanence" in one of his most celebrated songs ("Changes").

But we can also think about poetic diction as something indicative of broader stylistic traits. Poets might strive for something like the elevated, rapturous tone of Percy Bysshe Shelley's "Adonais" (1821):

> The leprous corpse, touched by this spirit tender,
> Exhales itself in flowers of gentle breath;
> Like incarnations of the stars ...[3]

Or they might choose more colloquial speech, as we find in Anne Sexton's "Praying on a 707" (1972):

> Mother,
> each time I talk to God
> You interfere.
> You of the bla-bla set.[4]

Often writers will shuttle between high and low speech, a technique that Paul Simon describes as fundamental to his songwriting approach: "That's what I was trying to learn to do ... to be able to write vernacular speech, and then intersperse it with enriched language, and then go back to vernacular."[5] The possibilities for modern poets are incalculable because the English language is stunningly complex and constantly changing. Poets might choose words that are familiar or obscure, outdated or startlingly novel. In isolation, most words lack real power. But when artfully combined, they can be gripping, innovative, provocative, and enchanting.

When we read great poetry, we will be moved to ask questions about diction: Why this word and not that? Why use high poetic language here and a lower, more colloquial style there? When we analyze songs, we will want to ask similar questions, but other issues will also arise. Most important, we will want to think about what it means to *sing* certain words instead of others. Lowell's translation of Montale—"The porcupine sips a quill of mercy"—is wonderful to read. But would it make a good lyric? Perhaps it would (to my knowledge, no composer has attempted to set that translation to music), but it lacks the intuitive sound of words written for song.

For that, we might shift our attention to Justin Bieber, whose hit song "Baby" includes the chorus quoted at the outset of this chapter:

(And I was like) baby, baby, baby, oh!

As can be heard on the Spotify playlist, track 6 (0:44), the vocabulary here is childishly simple, which is entirely appropriate for a teen-pop love song. But the simplicity of the language need not mean that the specific words are unimportant. The word "baby," for instance, is a term of endearment with two syllables, the first of which is accented relative to the second (BAY-bee). There are many other words that fit the same criteria, but how well would they work with Bieber's melody?

Before addressing that question, we should recognize that the word "diction" has at least two meanings, both of which I want to embrace in this chapter. It can mean either the choice of words in speech and writing, as when we say, "Shakespeare's diction is puzzling to me," or the style of enunciation in speech and song, as when we say, "Her diction is crisp and clear." With both those definitions in mind, consider what happens if we sing Bieber's chorus but replace "baby" with "darlin'." In some ways, the exchange is suitable. "Darlin'" is also a term of endearment with two syllables and an accent on the first. But sing the alternate version and you are likely to agree that it is not an improvement (And I was like darlin', darlin', darlin', oh!). Perhaps the most obvious problem has to do with cultural connotations. This is a song sung by a teenage boy and marketed primarily to a teen audience. (Bieber was sixteen when the song was released in 2010.) "Darlin'," in that context, is an absurdity—it's a word that people are more likely to associate with country music than bubblegum pop.

But awkward cultural connotations are not the only problem. To sing the word "darlin'" requires different vocal mechanics from those required to sing "baby." "Darlin'," quite simply, is a mouthful. It is trickier to articulate in this song, especially compared to "baby," with its bright vowels and repeated *b*'s. It is not that "darlin'" *can't* be sung here. But it doesn't *feel* right, especially with Bieber's melody. It requires awkward vocal mechanics, which can quickly become a problem for vocalists. Opera singers spend years training themselves to move fluidly among languages like French, German, and Italian, and they do this not simply because they want to pronounce the words correctly, but because different types of words ask the singer to do different things with lips, tongue, and throat. Changes in vocabulary require changes in vocal technique—they require practice and exercise.

We could try other words in place of "baby"—alternative terms of endearment like "sweetie" or "honey," or specific names, like "Lucy" or "Kendra," but all these alterations will have a significant impact not just on the connotations of the song but on the fundamental sound of the song itself. Try singing "sweetie" in Bieber's song, for instance, and compare the airy sound of the *sw* with the sharper *k* in "Kendra." You can sing the same notes with both words, but they don't *feel* the same when we sing them nor do they *sound* the same when we hear them. Our physical engagement with the language matters (a point that the music theorist Stephen Rodgers has made convincingly in recent research).[6] Bieber's lyrics are not great poetry, but, like those of any other successful song, they indicate an awareness of sound and the human voice. They indicate an awareness of the basic attributes of the English language.

A Brief Introduction to English Phonemes

There are twenty-six letters in the English alphabet, but there are at least forty-four common "phonemes"—the small, distinct sounds that help us distinguish one word from another. Some letters can be used to represent multiple sounds, as happens with the letter *a* when used in "bay," "band," "bad," and "ball." Sometimes different letters are used to produce the same sound, as happens with the *a* and *o* in "ball" and "doll." Moreover, the specific sounds that we hear in ordinary speech can change depending on dialect. Someone born and raised in London will use a different set of phonemes from someone born and raised in Alabama. How, then, do we grasp the full range of potential sounds in poetry and song?

Linguists have created helpful phonetic alphabets in which each phoneme has its own symbol, usually rendered in brackets, such that, for example, the symbol [ʊ] would represent the vowel sound in "bull" and [ʌ] would represent the vowel sound in "hum" (these are the symbols used in the International Phonetic Alphabet [IPA]). The details of these taxonomies can become quite complicated—and I have no intention of accounting for all of them here—but there are, nevertheless, certain broad categories that are vitally important for anyone interested in understanding the essential sounds of English words.

Plosives

Plosives are the sounds of consonants like *b, d, t, p,* and *k*. They involve a temporary blockage in the airflow that can be achieved by using the tip of the tongue (as happens with the *t* in "talk"), the lips (as happens with the *p* in "puncture"), or the back of the tongue (as happens with the *k* in "kitten"). The burst of sound that follows this blockage is, to an extent, "explosive," and it can be used effectively in both poetry and song. Listen, for instance, to the song "Boy in the Bubble" by Paul Simon, and note the accelerated staccato that Simon creates when he sings about "the boy in the bubble and the baby with the baboon heart" (Spotify playlist, track 7, 2:30). The plosives turn the voice into a kind of percussion, almost like a drum fill, excitedly pulsing its way toward the phrase's exclamation when Simon sings "I believe!"

Fricatives and Sibilants

Fricatives are produced by forcing air through a narrow channel—creating a kind of friction—which we do when we pronounce the *f* in "fin," the *v* in "vixen," or the *th* in "thimble." Notice that fricatives can be conjured in multiple ways: "fin" typically involves lower lip against teeth, whereas "thin," which also typically involves teeth, adds the touch of the tongue. These sounds are similar to sibilants, which require slightly different vocal mechanics but result in a similar forced-air friction: the *s* in "snake," the *z* in "zombie," the *zh* in "vision," and the *sh* in "shadow."

Robert Lowell concludes his masterpiece "For the Union Dead" with a cluster of *f*'s, *s*'s, and *v*'s, which sounds nearly reptilian in its indictment of modern America:

> The Aquarium is gone. Everywhere
> Giant finned cars nose forward like fish;
> a savage servility
> slides by on grease.[7]

But fricatives need not have a sinister quality (indeed, they rarely do). In the song "Scenario"—a classic track from A Tribe Called Quest's *The Low End Theory* (1991)—the rapper Dinco D produces a string of tongue-twisting fricatives that functions primarily as a display of vocal dexterity, a grand conclusion to his one and only verse: "Funk flipped flat back first this foul fight fight fight laugh yo, how'd that sound? (ooh!)" (Spotify playlist, track 8, 2:14). These unrelenting *f*'s have a distinctly musical effect: they chop up the vocal flow into a series of discrete, accented chunks, similar to Simon's "Boy in the Bubble," but in "Scenario" the fricative *f*'s create something different: a textured quasi-percussion that sounds more like the brushes of a jazz drummer than the piercing attacks of a traditional drumstick.

Nasals

Nasals are the sounds of *m*'s and *n*'s and the *ng* that we find in words like "sing." The sound is produced when air is blocked in the mouth but escapes through the nose. It is the sound we make when we hum, ponder a problem ("hmm"), or savor our food ("mmm"). In "Out of the Cradle Endlessly Rocking," Walt Whitman sometimes gathers these sounds into rhapsodic visions that ring out with exceptional beauty:

> The aria sinking,
> All else continuing, the stars shining,
> The winds blowing, the notes of the bird continuous echoing,
> With angry moans the fierce old mother incessantly moaning.[8]

The sonic features here are so arresting—so "musical" in their repetitive enchantments—that the effect is almost hypnotic. Readers may not be consciously aware of the specific nasal sounds that are repeated, but they will probably fall under the spell of the poetry's intoxicating hum regardless.

Liquids

Liquids are vowel-like consonants that can appear when the tongue imposes a partial blockage, as happens with the *r* in "mother" and the *l* in "lie." These liquids often have a softness to them that can be especially appealing for love songs and lullabies. Listen, for instance, to the contrast between the lulling *l*'s and the plosive *b*'s when Bob Dylan sings "Lay, lady, lay / lay across my big brass bed" (Spotify playlist, track 9, 0:12).

The softness of the *l*'s in this passage is important, especially in contrast to the *b*'s, but it is crucial to remember that *every* sound in music and poetry is affected by its placement in a broader context. All words are affected by meaning, rhythm, form, and much else. Just as fricatives are not necessarily snakelike and sinister, so too are liquids not always lovely. The elegant *r*'s and *l*'s in Keats's address to Georgiana Augusta Wylie ("To G. A. W.") sound beautiful:

> Haply 'tis when thy ruby lips part sweetly,
> And so remain, because thou listenest.⁹

But the effect of the *r*'s and *l*'s is quite different when they occur in "The Second Coming" of Yeats:

> And what rough beast, its hour come round at last,
> Slouches toward Bethlehem to be born?¹⁰

Vowels

Vowel sounds are essential in all language, of course, but they are especially crucial in song. A singer cannot isolate and expand a single plosive into a sonorous, melodic pitch. For that, vowels are required. Whereas a *p* trails off quickly with a puff of air, the syllable "pah" can be stretched out and sustained, with the vowel resounding loudly across even the widest auditoriums. Indeed, singers frequently emphasize vowel sounds so strongly compared with their surrounding consonants that they radically transform the sounds of words. Listen, for instance, to a passage from Reginald Goodall's 1975 recording of Wagner's *Die Walküre* (act 1, scene 3), which is sung in English using a translation by Andrew Porter (Spotify playlist, track 10). Most people, I suspect, would find these words unrecognizable on a first listen. The tenor, Alberto Remedios, sings the words "Yes, loveliest bride / I am that friend; / Both weapon and wife I claim." If we already know the text, these words will be perceptible. But without knowing the words in advance, the melody comes across largely as an inscrutable string of vowels that might as well be another language (if you attempt to transcribe other sections from this performance, you will quickly notice the difficulty). This is not always the case—Wagner's music presents special problems, especially when singers must project their voice to the back of a large concert hall—but even in the operas of Benjamin Britten, where we usually hear the words clearly, the experience of listening is often markedly different from the experience of hearing the words read aloud. Consider the following passage, from a stunning act 2 aria in Britten's *Peter Grimes*:

> Who can decipher
> In storm or starlight
> The written character
> Of a friendly fate—

Speak these words aloud and they are likely to sound quite different from the eerie monotone of the tenor Alan Oke singing them in the Spotify playlist (track 11, 0:54). The consonant sounds are highly distinctive in a poetic reading, but they fall away to some extent when translated into operatic song. They are still there—we still hear each consonant briefly articulated—but the vowels take center stage, in this case beautifully sustaining a single melodic pitch in the tenor's high range. This is not to say, of course, that individual performers do not control the degree to which they emphasize the consonant sounds. Many recordings of this passage are available, and readers are encouraged to compare the differences in articulation—the way, for instance, different tenors might roll the *r* at "written" and "friendly," or the degree to which they might emphasize the sibilant *s* in "storm" and "starlight." But even when the consonants are heavily accented, it is the vowels that primarily carry the tune.

How then, do we better understand these vowels? For people untrained in linguistics, classifying vowels is difficult because vowels incorporate a great many physical and perceptual parameters. A full understanding requires a deep dive into a sea of complex categories. For our purposes, a few broad distinctions are important:

1. Tongue position: Where do you typically place your tongue when speaking or singing certain vowels? Is it high and to the front, as when singing "eek"? Or low and to the back, as when singing "ah"? Notice how your tongue frequently moves between high/low, front/back, and middle positions with nearly every sentence you speak.
2. Roundedness: Are your lips rounded when articulating vowels, as when singing "ooh"? Or are they unrounded, as when singing "aw"?
3. Length: When speaking vowel sounds naturally, do you tend to hold the vowel for a relatively long time, as in words like "bee"? Or do you articulate them more quickly as in words like "bit"?
4. Perceived vowel height: You can sing the words "bee" and "boo" on the same pitch (middle C, for instance) and yet still experience the former as sounding "higher" or "brighter" than the latter. This has to do with certain acoustical properties of language. In their introductory

text *A Course in Phonetics*, Peter Ladefoged and Keith Johnson invite readers to whisper the following sequence of words and note the perceptible "falling" sound: "heed, hid, head, had, hoed, hawed, hood, who'd."[11]

All these properties are relevant to the way artists choose their words. In a 2007 *New York Times* article, Sheldon Harnick, the lyricist of *Fiddler on the Roof*, emphasizes how important it is to be thoughtful about which vowels to use when pairing words with sustained, climactic notes. As he points out, "Singers have trouble with the letter 'e' because [it] narrow[s] the throat" whereas a vowel sound like "ah" allows the singer to open wide ("you can really swing the note").[12] These concerns about "singability" are related not only to vowels in the abstract but also to how they are inflected by other surrounding phonemes. I already discussed how alterations to the words in Justin Bieber's "Baby" can cause discomfort ("baby" versus "darlin'"). But notice how much more damaging it is to take the word "baby" and add a plosive to the end of each vowel. If you sing the melody with the following nonsense words—"(and I was like) bait-beat, bait-beat, bait-beat, ohh!"—you will quickly recognize how those added *t*'s drastically shorten the vowels, destroying the fluidity of the tune and making it incredibly awkward to sing. Though the vowels are essentially the same, they have been deeply constrained and altered by the new context.

The relative brightness or coolness of vowels can also have a powerful effect on a poem or song's general sonic atmosphere. Keats, for instance, begins his sonnet "To Sleep" with the line "O soft embalmer of the still midnight." Those initial vowels are wonderfully "chilled" in a way that immediately reinforces the implications of the words ("O soft embalmer"). When Benjamin Britten sets this poem to music in his *Serenade for Tenor, Horn, and Strings*, op. 31, he has the tenor sing a repeated high D for these initial vowels (not unlike the sound we heard in *Peter Grimes*; see the Ian Bostridge recording on the Spotify playlist, track 12). But the high pitch need not contradict our experience of the vowels as sounding "low." What matters most is that Britten lets us hear each vowel sound distinctly. The slow tempo and the monotone repetition, along with Keats's "cooling" vowels, encourages us to drift away into the music's soporific haze. (The effect is especially clear when Bostridge slides down in pitch at the 0.26 mark when he sings the low vowel of "gloom.")

For a similar "cooling" effect, but in a very different context, consider the 2014 hit song "Say Something (I'm Giving Up on You)" by the band A Great Big World (Spotify playlist, track 13, 0:15). The melody of the chorus features accented vowel sounds that descend with a mournful mimicry of the text: "**Say** something **I'm** giving **up** on **you**." As the literary critic Adam Bradley points out in *The Poetry of Pop*, the words "say," "I'm," and "up" coincide with strong beats in the music.[13] The word "you" does not, but it draws our attention because it is both the final word of the phrase and the target of the direct address. To my ears, there is a drooping, darkening quality to those vowels—"ay," "ah," "uh," and "ooh"—which is coordinated with a pitch descent in the melody. All these factors contribute to the overall melancholy effect, along with the slow tempo, the vocal timbre, and the desperate implication of the lyrics.

Case Studies from Poetry and Song

There are no bad words or good words; there are only words in bad or good places.
    —Winifred Nowottny, *The Language Poets Use* (1962)

In the remainder of this chapter I present a short series of analytical "snapshots" from various poems and songs. Some of them focus on small, isolated moments. Others discuss broader changes that happen over time. As should be clear, the role of diction in poetry and song is so dependent on context that it can be difficult to make useful generalizations. What matters most is simply to open our ears to the details—the shifting sounds, rhythms, and textures of poetic language, whether read aloud from the printed page or transformed into recorded song.

The Right Words at the Right Time: T. S. Eliot and Johnny Cash

Poets and songwriters tend to have especially sensitive ears. They will quickly recognize if a word sounds out of place in a given passage. And they will often struggle with countless revisions in order to find the right word for the right moment. We rarely have access to what specific artists were thinking during the creative process, but we can nevertheless give careful thought to the *effects* of a particular revision, the way a substitution of one word in place of another can change the sound of a song or poem. We already considered this, to an extent, with the hypothetical variations of Justin Bieber's "Baby." But let's now look at two *actual* alterations: one by T. S. Eliot, and another by Johnny Cash. Needless to say, these artists have little in common. Eliot, though born in America, is known for his reserved British sensibility; Cash is famous for his hard-living "man-in-black" persona. They both, however, faced a strange, minor conundrum at a certain point in their respective careers: namely, how to manage an artistic description of feces?

For Eliot, this became a pressing question while working on his poem "Sweeney Among the Nightingales." The poem concludes with a description of birds defecating on the shroud of Agamemnon. In Eliot's words, they

> ... sang within the bloody wood
> When Agamemnon cried aloud
> And let their liquid droppings fall
> To stain the stiff dishonoured shroud.

This is artful language, but it is not the final, published version of the poem. Eliot shared an early draft with his friend and mentor Ezra Pound, a poet with an impeccable ear for English diction. Not content with the word "droppings," Pound suggested a change that Eliot later accepted:

> And let their liquid *siftings* fall
> To stain the stiff dishonoured shroud.[14]

We don't know exactly why Pound objected to "droppings," nor do we know precisely why Eliot accepted the word "siftings" in its place. Perhaps they both agreed that the poem required a more original, unusual choice of words (had anyone described bird shit as "siftings" before?). Perhaps they felt that "droppings" made the subsequent word somewhat redundant (what else could "droppings" do but "fall"?). Quite likely, they simply appreciated the sound of "siftings" in this context: the way the short vowel sound of "sift" resonates with "liquid," "stiff" and "dis-," or the way the s of "siftings" nicely prepares the subsequent alliteration of "stain" and "stiff." They might also have appreciated the "descent" of accented vowels that drops down into the final word of the line: "let," "liquid," "sift," and "fall." All these factors contribute to making the substitution sound "right," and although it represents only a small moment in Eliot's poem, it significantly alters the balance of sounds. It changes the music of the poem for the better.

Cash's situation is radically different, but indicative, perhaps, of a similar concern for sonic quality. Late in life, he recorded a version of the song "Hurt" by Nine Inch Nails (2002). Trent Reznor's original lyric for the second verse reads as follows:

> I wear this crown of shit
> Upon my liar's chair.

Cash changed the lyric to "crown of thorns." As with Eliot's alteration, I have no knowledge of why Cash made this change. Perhaps he wanted to avoid profanity and thereby make the song more radio-friendly. Perhaps he simply forgot the words. Whatever the case may be, the *effect* is significant. The two words—"thorns" and "shit"—sound remarkably different. As is clear in the recording, Reznor sings "shit" as an insidious whisper, leaning, for a moment, on the fricative *sh* sound and then snapping it shut with the plosive *t* (Spotify playlist, track 14, 2:36). This works well within the context of his whispery, sinister performance of this verse. But whether it would work as well sung in Cash's aged, gravelly baritone is dubious. "Crown of thorns" is, of course, a cliché. Many rock and heavy metal songwriters have put themselves in the position of a suffering Christ figure, whether ironically or not. And neither option—"crown of thorns" or "crown of shit"—is especially dazzling on the page (this is not the stuff of great poetry). But in Cash's rendition, the word "thorns" sounds especially fitting (Spotify playlist, track 15, 1:46). It is a one-syllable word, but it is rich with complex phonemes. The *r* sound in particular repeats the pained *r*'s of many surrounding words: "wear," "crown," "liar's," and "chair" (not to mention the crucial words of the chorus: "empire," "dirt," and "hurt"). And the *th* of "thorns" also matches the *th* of "thoughts," which occurs at an analogous point in the subsequent lines ("full of broken thoughts / I cannot repair"). All these words are sung by Cash with a strained sense of remorse, an almost desperate and weary fragility. As with the alteration in Eliot's poem, the word "thorns" is a small, subtle change, but it resonates in a way that affects the balance of the entire song.

The Dark Cloths of W. B. Yeats

When Cash made his recording of "Hurt," he maintained the basic harmonic and melodic structure of Reznor's original song. And Reznor, as the original author of both words and music, would have been able to adjust either as he saw fit. But what happens when a composer chooses a preexisting text and attempts to match it with original music? How does one best translate the poetic diction into song? Below is a poem by William Butler Yeats called "He Wishes for the Cloths of Heaven." What kind of music would best suit these words?

> Had I the heavens' embroidered cloths,
> Enwrought with golden and silver light,
> The blue and the dim and the dark cloths

> Of night and light and the half light,
> I would spread the cloths under your feet:
> But I, being poor, have only my dreams;
> I have spread my dreams under your feet;
> Tread softly because you tread on my dreams.[15]

A musician reading this poem aloud might immediately appreciate the way the poem's diction interacts with a fascinating rhythmic complexity. Notice, for instance, that the poem's language and rhythm might have been much more regular, and much less interesting, if the poem had opened like this:

> Had I the heavens' embroidered cloths,
> Enwrought with golden and silver light,
> I'd build us wings like summer moths
> To shoot like stars across the night.

Among other deficiencies, these alternate lines create predictable rhymes that sound forced—cloths, moths / light, night—and they relentlessly uphold a four-beat poetic meter: ta-TUM, ta-TUM, ta-TUM, ta-TUM ("I'd build us wings like summer moths"). The actual poem is much more compelling. The third line in particular sets the poem on a wonderfully different course. It surprisingly ends with the same word as line 1 ("cloths"), which then initiates a pattern of alternately identical line endings that will be maintained for the rest of the poem: cloths, light, cloths, light / feet, dreams, feet, dreams. Many other repetitions occur as well—for example, the repetitions of "tread" and "spread"—but one thing that *does not* repeat in Yeats's poem is a predictable metric pattern. Rather than beating out a consistent "ta-TUM, ta-TUM" rhythm, the third line offers something new: "the blue and the dim and the dark cloths" (ta-TUM, ta ta TUM, ta ta TUM TUM). The line gracefully skips along into its closing double stress, with the richly textured sounds of "dark cloths."

These features could accurately be described as "musical," but how might a composer translate them into *actual* music? Let's consider two different approaches, with a special focus on the treatment of the poem's third line. Thomas Dunhill's 1911 setting can be heard on the Spotify playlist, track 16. Dunhill is not an especially well-known British composer, but his setting was quite popular and it is still frequently performed.[16] John Tavener's setting from 1983 is much more modern (Spotify playlist, track 17). Both composers, however, pay close attention to the sounds of each individual word in the poem, even if they do so in strikingly different ways.

22   Diction

The most interesting feature of Dunhill's setting is the way it seems to mask (but only partially) the complexities of the poem. On one hand, it packages the text as a pastoral folksong in the tradition of the great English and Irish airs such as "Danny Boy" and "Drink to Me Only with Thine Eyes." But on the other, it includes unusual phrase rhythms and surprising key changes that reflect many of the inbuilt tensions of Yeats's poem. The poem almost seems to push *against* the simple intentions of Dunhill's setting and has to be reaccommodated on the fly.[17] I do not mean this as a criticism of Dunhill, however. There are certain moments that sound slightly awkward, but I ultimately find the tensions charming, and I assume the effect is calculated.

This is especially evident in Dunhill's setting of that wonderful third line, "the blue and the dim and the dark cloths" (shown with annotations in example 1.1). The melodic line up until that point moves in a controlled, wavelike pattern, gradually curving up and down in an easy tenor range. But as the poetic rhythm speeds up, the melodic line suddenly shoots upward. As shown in the example, the melody is heading in the direction of what will ultimately become the song's vocal climax, a highpoint that is achieved at the phrase "tread softly." But here, early in the song, the momentary ascent is stifled at the phrase "dark cloths." Those crucial words shift the song back to a lower register and slow it down with a half note at "dark," the longest rhythm of the song thus far. Dunhill, in other words, cleverly translates this key moment into music by using the phrase "dark cloths" to temporarily restrain the persona's increasingly agitated imagination.[18]

Such moments suggest that Dunhill was aware of—and capable of accentuating—the nuances of Yeats's diction. But he never *revels* in the sounds of the words. Only when repeating the word "softly" toward the end of the song does he truly allow the singer to languish in the rich phonetic sounds of the poem. When we listen to Tavener's setting, we hear a song in which every individual word seems an occasion to dwell and bask in the beauty of the poem's enchanting vocality.[19] (Heidi Grant Murphy, the soprano in this recording, brilliantly takes advantage of this, as can be heard in the breathy *h* sounds when she sings "had" and "heaven.") The melody seems to flow with a trancelike improvisation, slowing down and speeding up in seemingly random ways, in which even some of the poem's simplest function words, like "the" or "and," can be extended and expressed with exquisite detail. A critic might argue that this approach focuses on poetic diction *too* much. The song moves at such a slow, carefree pace and so frequently meanders into reveries with various words that

Example 1.1. Thomas Dunhill, "The Cloths of Heaven," interrupted ascent at "dark cloths"

we might lose our sense of the complete poem in the process. But no matter how "loose" the vocal line might sound, Tavener's choices are not random; on the contrary, they are based on a systematic compositional scheme that is the opposite of improvisatory.

Tavener wrote this song using the twelve-tone method, a strategy pioneered by the Viennese composer Arnold Schoenberg in the mid-1920s. In Tavener's song, the melodic phrases cycle through all twelve notes of the Western chromatic scale in a specific order. The first vocal phrase orders the twelve notes as shown in example 1.2 (the 0:41 mark of the recording).

Tavener then alters the sequence in various phrases by either reversing it (playing it backward), inverting it (playing it "upside down"), or inverting it and *then* playing it backward. The choice of notes is highly structured, but the rhythm for each melody is also predetermined; it repeats a simple sequence of four rhythmic units that become progressively longer: quarter note (one beat), half note (two beats), dotted half note (three beats), and whole note

24   Diction

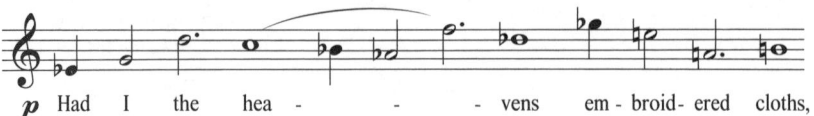

Example 1.2. John Tavener, "He Wishes for the Cloths of Heaven," opening twelve-tone row

Example 1.3. "He Wishes for the Cloths of Heaven," interrupted ascent at "dark cloths"

(four beats). With some phrases Tavener uses that exact ordering—moving from the shorter rhythms to the longer ones—but in other phrases he uses the reverse (longer rhythms to shorter rhythms).

This is a strict method, and it means that many elements of the song result from a pre-compositional plan, even if they sound improvisatory.[20] But although each phrase in the song must, by design, be exactly twelve notes long, none of the lines in Yeats's poem reaches twelve syllables in length. The result is that in every line, Tavener has to choose one or two words to extend with multiple notes for a single syllable (what musicians refer to as melisma). As shown in example 1.2, the first phrase extends the word "heavens." The third phrase—similar to the Dunhill setting—extends the word "dark" (example 1.3, the 1:51 mark of the recording).

What this means, of course, is that both Tavener and Dunhill draw attention to the arresting diction of "dark cloths," even if they do so in radically different ways. In Dunhill's melody, those words restrain the ascending energy of an earlier melodic line by shifting into a lower range. Tavener's melody also leaps down to the word "dark," and it also offers a correction of sorts: the melodic line until this point has fallen into a reverie that begins to lose all sense of the poem's natural accents. It extends unaccented words, such as "the," longer than certain accented words, such as "dim," a procedure that arguably obscures rather than accentuates the poetic meter. But the way the melody lingers at "dark cloths" helps rebalance the relationship between words and music, with the singer giving appropriate emphasis to Yeats's crucial double stress. On the surface, Tavener's song is strikingly different from Dunhill's, but in each the diction of the poem motivates a similar melodic and rhythmic event.

Grave Visitations: Patti Smith's "Dancing Barefoot"

The melodic effects that Dunhill and Tavener employ at the phrase "dark cloths" involve small, isolated moments. But what happens when significant changes occur in diction over the course of a complete song? As the poet and literary critic James Longenbach points out, the drama of great poetry often "depends on our experience of one kind of diction resisting another, giving way to another."[21] Such tensions are common in Shakespeare and his successors in poetry, but they also frequently emerge in the lyrics of rock songs. Consider, for instance, "Dancing Barefoot" by Patti Smith. This song was released in 1979, and although it never achieved widespread popularity, it has been deeply influential for many musicians. *Rolling Stone* magazine placed it at no. 331 on its list "The 500 Greatest of Rock Songs of All Time," and it has been covered by several highly successful bands, including U2 and Pearl Jam. One of the fascinating aspects of the song is the way the diction changes dramatically from section to section. The lyrics begin as follows (Spotify playlist, track 18):

> She is benediction
> She is addicted to thee
> She is the root connection
> She is connecting with he

Note the extravagant strangeness of this language. It pairs distinctly Latinate words, such as "benediction" and "connection," with antiquated and ungrammatical pronouns ("thee ... connecting with he"). The words seem to emanate from an unearthly priestess set back in the shadows. She chants about the fate of "she" and "he," but with a sense of ominous detachment, singing a dark, minor-key melody that dives down in recurring loops.

Things begin to change, however, at the start of the song's "pre-chorus" (the 0:25 mark). A first-person narrator suddenly appears with a string of monosyllabic words that are simple, familiar, and direct: "Here I go and I don't know why ..." As the diction changes, so too does the melody, immediately reversing course and charting a strong upward drive. This sounds like a completely different personality, a different character, possibly the "she" who has already been introduced in the verse as the victim of an addictive spell. And notice that the shift in diction also introduces new sounds. The climax of this initial ascending phrase is the word "why," a piercing vowel in this context, strikingly set against the accompanying harmony and unlike any vowel sound we have heard thus far.

These contrasts return at the song's end, but with more radically direct juxtapositions. At the 3:27 mark, the song concludes with Smith's voice split in two. One voice sings the ascending melody of the pre-chorus, except now repeatedly intoning the words "Oh God I fell for you." This is a return to the monosyllabic directness that we heard in the earlier pre-chorus, but it now includes the crucial pronoun "you," the song's first turn toward direct address. Against this music, we hear another voice, also the voice of Patti Smith, reciting poetic lines that mix self-consciously "elevated" diction with simpler and more direct language. The song ultimately circles back to something similar to the voice from the song's beginning, a return to the pronouns of "he" and "she":

> Grave visitations
> What is it that calls to us?
> Why must we pray screaming?
> Why must not death be redefined?
> We shut our eyes we stretch out our arms
> And whirl on a pane of glass
> An afixiation a fix on anything the line of life the limb of a tree
> The hands of he and the promise
> That she is blessed among women.

There is a degree of circularity in this return to "he" and "she," but there is also a sense in which everything simply spins outward with an entropy that never fully resolves the song's multiple voices. We are given no clear answers, no "fix on anything." We hear a kaleidoscope of changing diction matched with a variety of shifts in the music, and the song's resolution, if there is any, comes from the loose hint of a returning voice, rather than a neat, narrative conclusion.

Diction, Declamation, and "Anti-Melody"

The disruptive shifts in "Dancing Barefoot" reflect a long tradition of similar moves in English poetry. And although sharp twists and turns in poetic diction can be exhilarating to read, composers often struggle when translating these effects into song. Consider John Donne's Holy Sonnet No. 3, which Benjamin Britten set to music in 1945. The poem begins with relatively simple, easily singable words:

> O! might those sighs and tears return again
> Into my breast and eyes, which I have spent.[22]

Britten capitalizes on this simplicity with a slow, mournful tune that lingers on the plaintive vowels of "O" and "sighs" and "tears" (Spotify playlist, track 19). But later in the sonnet, the diction lurches into an entirely different universe of sounds. The speaker—a pitiable figure who professes to have expended a lifetime of tears in vain—laments that his plight is even worse than that of other sinners, a rough cast of characters that includes

> Th' hydroptic drunkard and night-scouting thief
> The itchy lecher and self-tickling proud.

As poetry, this language is thrilling, but it does not lend itself easily to song. Unsurprisingly, Britten's music erupts at this point into loud piano tremolos and a belting, declamatory outburst, conceding, perhaps, that the words are best translated more as a contemptuous tantrum than anything truly melodic (see the 2:18 mark of the recording). A sensitive listener will recognize that this music is based on the same musical gestures as the previous melody (compare the upper and lower part of example 1.4), but Britten rewrites the passage in a way that obscures the relation. He captures the shocking change in diction by transforming the earlier plaintive melody into something almost "antimelodic," unlike anything else that we hear in the song.

By stripping away all melodic niceties, Britten draws special attention to the changes in the poetry. A more extreme version of this would be to reduce the melody to a flat monotone. To understand how that might work, compare another song by Britten, his "Nocturne," from *On This Island*, which sets a poem by Auden, with the song "Lethe" by Rebecca Clarke, which sets a poem by Edna St. Vincent Millay. Both songs draw attention to remarkable changes in diction at the ends of their respective poems, and both do so by allowing their melodies to flatline on a single repeated note. The musical effects, however, and the language they set, are quite different.

Millay's "Lethe" ends with a tercet:

> Immerse the dream.
> Drench the kiss.
> Dip the song in the stream.[23]

The verbs at the start of each line become progressively simpler, from the two-syllable Latinate "immerse" to the one-syllable (but phoneme-rich) "drench," to the simplest of the three: "dip." In Clarke's song (Spotify playlist, track 20, 2:20), she sets the last line with a static monotone, each simple Germanic word uttered with the same quiet pitch. It has a beautiful, eerie effect, and the ex-

Example 1.4. Benjamin Britten, "O Might Those Sighs and Tears," recurring melodic material

pressiveness of this gesture is especially acute when comparing it with the song's opening tercet:

> Ah, drink again
> This river that is the taker-away of pain,
> And the giver-back of beauty!

This single sentence, with its high-flown rhetoric, contrasts sharply with the three short sentences of the poem's conclusion. Millay's language is almost ecstatic at the opening, describing, but not yet embodying, the utter oblivion of the river Lethe. In Clarke's song, the opening music features repetitive chromatic descents that are indicative of a descent toward nothingness, but they do not yet capture the sense of numbness that will come at the song's conclusion. For that, we have the final tercet, with its change of diction and melodic emptiness—a melodic flattening that mirrors the poetic movement toward simplicity: "dip the song in the stream."

W. H. Auden's poem "Nocturne" involves another kind of shift at its end. The poem begins with two six-line stanzas, each featuring a basic rhyme scheme: *aabbcc*. The third and final stanza initially follows the same pattern, and the tone and style of the language are simple and familiar (it sounds, in many ways, like a song lyric—almost like something Bob Dylan might have written):

> While the splendid and the proud
> Naked stand before the crowd
> And the losing gambler gains
> And the beggar entertains:
> May sleep's healing power extend
> Through these hours to our friend.[24]

This might have been the conclusion of the poem, but it is not; an additional five lines stretch the stanza beyond all former proportions:

> Unpursued by hostile force,
> Traction engine, bull or horse
> Or revolting succubus;
> Calmly till the morning break
> Let him lie, then gently wake.

In these closing lines the phrase "or revolting succubus" is especially conspicuous. It is the first and only line that extends a rhyming pattern into a group of three ("force," "horse," and "succubus") and the word "succubus" is the only slant rhyme at the end of a line (it ends with a *similar* sound to "force" and "horse," but is not a perfect rhyme, as is every other end-rhyme in the poem). This unusual rhyme scheme underscores the startling change in diction when the word "succubus" breaks from the simple, almost folksy language that precedes it.

Britten prepares for this change by locking in on a single monotone for all three lines that lead to the word "succubus" (Spotify playlist, track 21, 2:43). The effect is not entirely dissimilar to what we heard at the end of Clarke's "Lethe." Both songs create an ominous atmosphere by having the voice intone a repeated low note while a repetitive piano bass rumbles beneath. In Clarke's song, the sound is less sinister—more suggestive of blank waters than something evil. Britten's sound is more explicitly nightmarish in its evocation of the succubus (despite the poem's prayer that this creature will *not* pursue the ailing friend). Most important for our purposes, however, is that in both cases the monotone melody puts a spotlight on the poetic diction. It grows simpler in the Millay poem and more complex—and horrifying—in the Auden.

▰ The power of a poem's language depends on context. The words "dark cloths" have little of value in and of themselves, but in the context of Yeats's poem, they become rich with sound and meaning. Even an unusual word like "succubus" is not inherently poetic until a poet arranges it in a particularly compelling way. A poem's diction, in other words, constantly interacts with its other aspects, including its rhythm, lineation, and overall form. I will consider these other attributes of poetry and song in great detail later, but we must not lose sight of the simple importance of the words themselves. Anyone can describe the sight of trees hanging over a river, but few would paint the picture that Robert Browning does in stanza 20 of "Childe Roland to the Dark Tower Came":

> Low scrubby alders kneeled down over it;
> Drenched willows flung them headlong in a fit
> Of mute despair...[25]

Similarly, Pink Floyd, in "Shine on You Crazy Diamond," might have written a song about their former lead singer, Syd Barrett, with mundane, clumsy, and forgettable language. But they chose instead words that are distinct, memorable, and evocative, even if they don't pack the same punch as Browning's: "You wore out your welcome with random precision ... Come on you raver, you seer of visions."

Fans of poetry and song sometimes obsess too much about meaning. They want to know what a poem or song is "about," as if the words are nothing more than useful tools to convey thoughts and ideas, and lyrics no more than a code we are meant to crack. I explore this topic more extensively in the conclusion to this book, but even at this point we can recognize the simple truth that words in song offer much more than their dictionary meanings. We return to poems and songs again and again not just to discover their broad themes but also to reexperience their *sounds*. Words become rhythms. They create accents. And as we will see in the next chapter, they play a fundamental role in determining a crucial poetic and musical phenomenon—the perception of meter.

CHAPTER TWO |||||||||||||||||||||||||||||||||||||||||||||||||||||||||||||||||

Meter

There is no escape from metre; there is only mastery.
—T. S. Eliot, "Reflections on *Vers Libre*" (1917)

This is a chapter about beats and rhythms. It is a chapter about the motor that powers the scherzo of Beethoven's Ninth Symphony, the pulsing enchantments of Edgar Allan Poe's "The Raven," and the "two, three, four" count-off before Outkast's "Hey Ya" hits its stride. It is a chapter about the head-bobbing, toe-tapping, physical engagement that almost every human on earth feels when listening to the patterned sounds of music and poetry. In short, this is a chapter about meter.

Meter is just as crucial for Lady Gaga as it is for Langston Hughes, but the commonality only goes so far. If you pick up a book about poetic meter, you will learn about iambs, trochees, and other metrical feet. If you pick up a book about musical meter, you will learn about hypermeasures and hemiolas. The same essential concept, in other words, results in a surprisingly different set of questions, concepts, and terminology. What this means is that if we want to understand how meter might operate in song, we need to begin with basic foundational issues in each discipline.

Meter in Music

In music, an awareness of meter typically begins with the awareness of beats. Imagine a metronome ticking off a series of regular, equally spaced clicks. These clicks—or pulses—are a form of measurement like inches or centimeters; they mark units of time that allow musicians to organize and arrange their sounds into predictable and coherent phrases ("meter" derives from *metron*, the Greek word for measurement). When I use the word "beat" throughout this chapter, I am referring to the regular, recurring, equally spaced pulses that people often tap along to when listening to a song. This definition needs to be distinguished from the looser meanings that "beat" has accrued in popular culture, wherein the word often refers to something more complex, such as a complete drum and bass pattern (as when someone says, "This song has a great beat"). Beats, in the narrower sense of "toe-tapping pulses," are not particularly complex. They can be fast or slow, but it would be strange to think of them as good or bad. Much like any other unit of measurement, they mainly exist to help musicians build and arrange something bigger. And one of the simplest ways to create something bigger is to begin grouping beats into *patterns of accent*.

To better understand this, imagine snapping your fingers once every half second. Assuming each snap was equally loud, you would hear a series of recurring, undifferentiated pulses. Since nothing organizes these snaps into smaller or larger groups, they have no *meter*—they consist of a blank, monotonous series of beats. For *metrical patterns* to emerge, there would need to be some differentiation. There would need to be *accents*. This can be achieved easily by alternating a foot stomp with a finger snap: STOMP, snap, STOMP, snap. The resulting pattern is uncomplicated—an accented beat followed by an unaccented beat—but simplicity in meter is not a weakness; thousands of songs are built on the sturdy foundations of simple alternating patterns. And though chords and melodies can fly off in countless directions, metrical accents provide an anchor that keeps them tethered, allowing us to anticipate and predict where and when they might land.

The "STOMP, snap" pattern involves groups of two, but pulses can easily be grouped otherwise. To create groups of three, we would simply alter the pattern such that each STOMP is followed by *two* snaps (all equally spaced): STOMP, snap, snap / STOMP, snap, snap. This is the basic meter of a waltz. Such groupings are sometimes referred to as "triple meter," which distinguishes them from the more common "duple meter" (groupings of two). In the Spotify playlist, track 22, you can hear the quiet triple meter of "(You Make Me Feel Like) A Natural Woman" by Aretha Franklin. The groupings of three create a lilting, waltz-like effect, with an unmistakable "STOMP, snap, snap" pattern in the background through much of the song. Contrast that with track 23, which features the shamelessly heavy-handed duple meter of Billy Squier's "The Stroke," a song that deploys the "STOMP, snap" pattern with all of the brash audacity of a glam-rock anthem.

In popular song, these recurring groups of twos and threes typically happen at moderate speeds—something that we can easily sync with bodily movement (usually between 60 and 120 beats per minute [bpm]). But songs also involve many other layers that move at an entirely different pace, faster or slower than the recurring beat. Listen, for instance, to the opening of "Dancing on My Own," a 2010 hit by the Swedish singer Robyn (Spotify playlist, track 24). Like all dance music, the goal of this song is to trigger a physical response, but it would be nearly impossible for a dancer to move his or her body at the pace of each individual note in the song's opening seconds; they occur at a speed that is far too fast to intuitively align with bodily movement. After about eight seconds, however, a drum pattern enters with pulses that move at a much more manageable, head-bobbing pace. This, of course, is the simple "STOMP, snap" pattern that we find in countless other pop songs, and it helps organize everything else into hierarchical groups.

As shown in example 2.1, we can identify three prominent levels (among others): the "beat level"—the "STOMP, snap" pattern—represented in the middle of the figure; the *individual* rapid-fire bass notes, which *subdivide* the beats into smaller groups of four, moving at a much faster pace, as shown at the lower level; and the moments when the bass notes change—F# to C# to B—which parses the music into slower-moving groups of four, four, and eight beats, respectively (represented on the higher level).

These patterns are all quite common. Most popular music involves hierarchical groupings that are based on either multiples of two (for example, two, four, eight, and sixteen) or multiples of three (three, six, and twelve). But musicians can also arrange pulses into larger, less familiar patterns, such as groupings of five, seven, ten, or eleven. Listen, for instance, to the song "Everything in Its Right Place" by Radiohead (Spotify playlist, track 25) and try to count the beats that occur in each recurring loop. For most non-musicians, this will probably be extremely difficult, in part because the song does not have a loud percussion track to help listeners count beats, and in part because the pattern involves an unusual *ten-beat* grouping. Even if the listener is not consciously aware of that oddity, she or he might recognize that something unusual is happening—a metrical strangeness that contributes to the weird, psychedelic effect of the music.[1]

Meter, then, depends on patterns of accent. But accents are complicated because they can be achieved in a variety of ways. Probably the simplest thing a musician can do is to make something louder than something else (for example, STOMP versus snap). But there are other ways to generate accents as well. Low and high sounds are often accented relative to sounds in the middle range (which explains why the low sounds of kick drums and bass guitars often establish metrical patterns). Long-held notes are often perceived as accented relative to shorter notes, as happens with the sustained fourth note in

Note Changes SLOW	F#			→	C#			→	B			→
Beat Level MEDIUM	STOMP	snap	STOMP	snap	STOMP	snap	STOMP	snap	STOMP	snap	STOMP	snap
Beat Subdivisions FAST	F#(x4)	etc.	etc.	etc.	C#(x4)	etc.	etc.	etc.	B(x4)	etc.	etc.	etc.

Example 2.1. Robyn, "Dancing on My Own," metric hierarchy

the opening of Beethoven's Fifth Symphony ("ta-ta-ta TUM"). And we can also create accents by introducing new events, such as a new chord, a new manner of articulation, or a change in instrumental timbre. When chords change in popular song—often every two, four, or eight beats (as happens in "Dancing on My Own")—the new event draws attention to itself and sounds distinctly accented relative to everything else.

Since songs often include multiple layers of music, we hear a great many accent patterns happening simultaneously, sometimes in alignment with one another, sometimes in conflict with one another. To make matters even more confusing, we often perceive pulses and accent patterns even when they are not explicitly present. To understand how that can happen, consider the waltz pattern: STOMP, snap, snap / STOMP, snap, snap. If that were repeated several times, occasionally leaving out one of the stomps, it might sound something like this: STOMP, snap, snap / STOMP, snap, snap / (silence), snap, snap / STOMP, snap, snap. In that moment of silence, we do not hear an accented beat, but we *expect* to hear an accented beat, and in some sense our mind *supplies* that missing accent. It exists as a virtual accent: we recognize its presence even when it is unarticulated.

This effect—our ability to perceive regular patterns of accent even when they are not constantly present—is essential to our enjoyment of music. Songs typically establish a consistent metrical pattern, but musicians often contradict and resist that pattern by occasionally placing an accent in the "wrong" place. We call such events syncopation and they are fundamental to our enjoyment of almost every genre of song, from Billie Holiday's blues to Beyoncé's pop. Our bodies become entrained to a regular accent pattern (the basic meter of the song), and we frequently take pleasure in the way musicians expertly challenge our predictions by anticipating, delaying, or altogether evading the articulation of an expected beat.

Example 2.2 shows a process whereby *real* accents in music—things that actually produce soundwaves—can set up a hierarchical pattern, with the dots above representing the relative degrees of accent (more dots = stronger accent).[2] These then generate a perception of *virtual* accents, which might not coincide with the *real* accents. At the top of the example, the black dots represent real accents, places where we genuinely hear percussive attacks. In the lower levels of the example, the gray dots represent virtual accents, the places where we *expect* strong or weak accents in the measure. One of the most crucial things to understand about these virtual accents is that they are based on

The drums create an accent pattern in which the first beat is the most accented, the third beat is the second-most accented, and the second and fourth beats are unaccented relative to the others (shown with black dots).

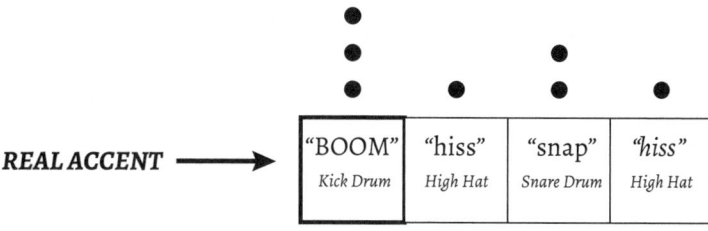

Once a pattern is established, we expect it to continue, and perceive "virtual" accents even when real accents aren't present. The gray dots above the silent beat show a virtual accent even though the "boom" isn't present.

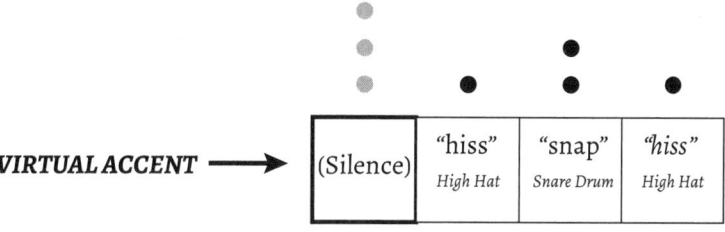

At some point, a real accent, such as a kick drum "boom," might contradict virtual accents. We expect the second beat to be weak (hence, one dot), but the kick drum surprises us with an accent in the "wrong" place. This is syncopation.

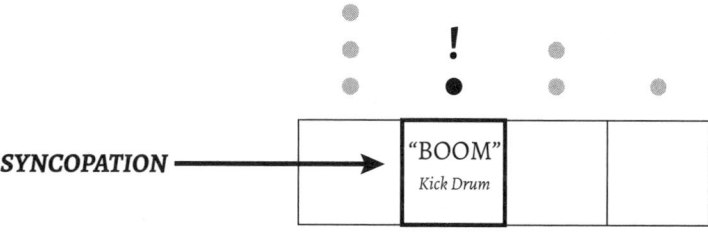

Example 2.2. Real accents, virtual accents, and syncopation

expectations, which are established in part by actual sounds in the music (like a drum pattern), but also by our cultural awareness of common metrical patterns in general. Our expectations, in other words, are affected not only by what we hear in a given song but also by what we have *already heard* in many other songs. It takes very little time, then, for our brains to assume that a piece of music is organized according to a familiar hierarchical structure. At some point, however, a real accent—a loud vocal note, a snare drum hit, or a sudden chord change—might challenge or contradict the virtual accents, creating a syncopation. When this happens, the syncopation can sometimes sound like a forceful imposition of musical will—a resistance to the restraints of a recurring metrical scheme.

Listen, for instance, to Chris Stapleton's "Nobody to Blame" (Spotify playlist, track 26) and compare the vocal rhythms in the verse to the rhythm in the chorus. In the verses, the vocal accents are generally anchored to the recurrent beats of the bass and drums (they have syncopation, to be sure, but not used to excess). In the chorus (the 0:52 mark), Stapleton begins with a strongly accented syllable that occurs just *after* the beat, articulating the pronoun "I" with a displaced, offbeat howl: "(beat) *I* know right where / (beat) *I* went wrong."

Meter in Poetry

If most music is organized according to a grid of equally spaced beats, is that also true of poetry? Is there any recurring pulse in the following lines by Emily Dickinson?

> My life closed twice before its close;
> It yet remains to see
> If Immortality unveil
> A third event to me.³

The poem begins with a line that sounds similar to what we heard in the Yeats poem in chapter 1: ta-TUM, ta-TUM, ta-TUM, ta-TUM (my **life** closed **twice** be**fore** its **close**). This is not unlike our musical pattern of stomps and snaps, except that the order of accent is reversed. But remember that the "STOMP, snap" pattern in music was organized according to a series of equally spaced pulses (or "isochronous" pulses). And when we speak naturally, we do not deploy phonemes and syllables with the precision of a metronomic grid. If we did, our speech would sound robotic. Imagine reciting the first line of Dickinson's poem with each syllable spaced *exactly* one half-second apart: my / life /

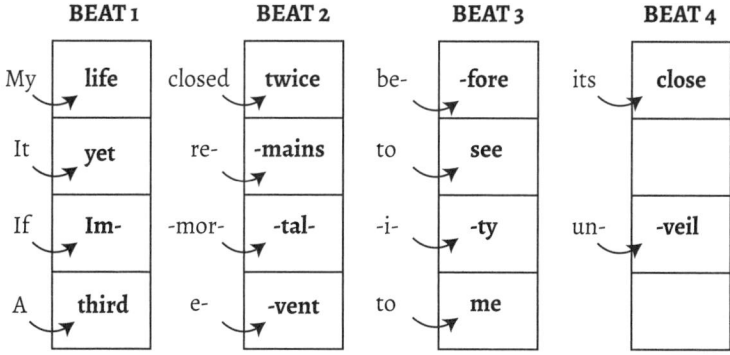

Example 2.3. A four-beat pattern in Emily Dickinson, "My Life Closed Twice Before Its Close"

closed / twice / be-/ fore / its/ close. This would sound stilted and unnatural, nothing like normal speech; the two syllables of "before," for instance, are not normally held for the same length of time; the first syllable, when spoken naturally, is significantly shorter than the second.

But Dickinson's poem *is not* normal speech. And although it sounds bizarre to read it with metronomic regularity, we can nevertheless recognize something "musical" in its patterns of accent. I have already mentioned the "ta-TUM" pattern that can be heard through most of the poem. But notice also that these first four lines—like much popular music—can be grouped according to a four-beat pattern, even if the beats are not precisely equally spaced (example 2.3).

This particular poetic pattern is known as common meter, and it was much used in the Protestant hymns that Dickinson would have heard frequently in western Massachusetts, hymns that originated in sixteenth-century England. Each line begins with an unstressed syllable that leads into the first beat (which is why in the example the first syllable appears *before* the box). In music, these are often referred to as *upbeats* or *pickups*, but both poets and musicians also refer to them as anacruses. In a musical setting, the phrases would rest at the end of the second and fourth lines, which explains the "empty" fourth beats in the example. Thus, although we would not want to *read* Dickinson's poetry with robotic regularity, many of her poems can easily be *sung* with beat-based consistency, whether with sincere, hymn-like melodies or—as often happens in online videos—with performances that match her poetry to popular tunes like "The Yellow Rose of Texas" or the *Gilligan's Island* theme song.

Dickinson's poems are often marvelously bizarre—they frequently resist metric expectations in fascinating ways—but they can also be remarkably "songlike." And all poems can vary in the degree to which they do or do not evoke a sense of regular, organized beats. Light verse, for instance, such as limericks and nursery rhymes, are especially singable; we often recite them by adhering closely to a regular beat. Some modern poetry, on the other hand, can sound especially irregular and unmetered, with few outward signifiers of "musicality." But ultimately, both music and poetry can exist on a spectrum between isochronous, beat-based groupings and non-isochronous, unmetered groupings. Compare, for instance, the obsessively regular pulses at the opening of Beethoven's Ninth Symphony, second movement (Spotify playlist, track 27) with the loose, unpredictable patterns of Luciano Berio's *Sequenza I* for solo flute (Spotify playlist, track 28). With Beethoven, the regular, toe-tapping pulse is unmistakable; with Berio, such toe tapping is all but impossible; the music continually disrupts and complicates any perception of a familiar beat. In poetry, a similar spectrum exists. A poem like Edgar Allan Poe's "The Raven" becomes almost chantlike in its beat-based obsession:

> **Deep** into that **dark**ness **peer**ing, **long** I **stood** there **won**dering,
>
> **fear**ing,
>
> **Doubt**ing, **dream**ing **dreams** no **mor**tal **ev**er **dared** to **dream**
>
> be**fore**.[4]

But these steady beats are nowhere to be found in the free verse opening of Frank O'Hara's "The Day Lady Died":

> It is 12:20 in New York a Friday
> three days after Bastille day, yes[5]

What this suggests is that certain poems, like "The Raven," will align well with beat-based music, while others, such as O'Hara's poem, will align more naturally with unpredictable, unmetered rhythms. And much of the reason has to do with the presence or absence of familiar metrical patterns.

Metrical Verse

When speaking English, we accent certain syllables relative to others. We say "bacon" with an accent on the first syllable and "tonight" with an accent on the second. There can be variation, of course, depending on dialect and context, but for the most part all English speakers learn to put accents in familiar places, on the first syllable of "power," for example, or the second syllable of "enough." As with music, accents can be applied in many different ways, through loudness, duration, timbre, or other vocal inflections. It involves considerable nuance, but most of us learn as children to place accents naturally. Even at a remarkably young age, kids can string together complete sentences with intricate patterns of stressed and unstressed syllables.

There are no fixed rules that apply in all cases, but certain broad generalities exist. For instance, simple one-syllable function words, such as prepositions, articles, or conjunctions, are rarely accented. If you say the following sentence aloud—"Look on the counter for the car keys"—you will most likely place accents only on the verb and the nouns: "**Look** on the **count**er for the **car keys**."

In that particular sentence, there is no clear pattern of accent; it sounds like everyday speech because of its unpredictable rhythm. But if we make a small change—"**Look** on the **count**er and **check** for the **keys**"—it suddenly becomes almost musical, with a regular pattern of accent that sounds like a waltz: TUM ta ta / TUM ta ta / TUM ta ta / TUM. If we change the language to sound more stereotypically "poetic," these musical features become even more apparent: "**Leap** through the **win**dow and **soar** through the **night**."

In English metrical verse, lines have predictable numbers of accented syllables (the *total* number of syllables is often less predictable). If each line has two accented syllables, we call it dimeter. If three, trimeter. Four is tetrameter, five pentameter, and six hexameter. But the accented syllables in a line can also be paired with unaccented syllables in consistent, predictable groupings that poets refer to as metrical feet. These would include two-syllable groupings such as *iambs* (the weak / strong pattern we hear in Dickinson's "my **life** closed **twice** . . .") and *trochees*, such as the strong / weak pattern that we hear in Poe's "The Raven" ("**doubt**ing, **dream**ing . . ."). They would also include three-syllable groupings such as *anapests* (weak / weak / strong: "In the **mid**dle of **win**ter we **walked** in the **woods**") and *dactyls* (strong / weak / weak: "**Leap** through the **win**dow and **soar** through the **night**"). Other types of feet worthy of mention include *spondees* (two stressed syllables in a row), *pyrrhics* (two weak syllables in a row), and *amphibrachs* (weak / strong / weak), but the rest tend to be too exotic to be used pervasively in English verse—for example, the *bacchius, cretic,* or *molossus*—types that readers might wish to research further, but which are not a common basis for metrical poetry.

The Dickinson poem above alternates lines of "iambic tetrameter" with "iambic trimeter":

> My **life** closed **twice** be**fore** its **close** [tetrameter]
> It **yet** re**mains** to **see** [trimeter]

But just as musicians can play with metrical expectations and place accents in surprising places, so too can poets. Dickinson's poem ends, for instance, with a sudden change:

> **Par**ting is **all** we **know** of **heav**en
> And **all** we **need** of **hell.**

This ending retains the basic pattern of alternating four-stress lines with three-stress lines, but the word "parting," with its plosive attack and tragic implications, disrupts the poem's iambic regularity by placing a trochee (strong / weak) at the outset of the penultimate line.

These metric variations or substitutions are essential. Poetry would be plodding and tedious without variation, just as music would bore us if it stuck too strongly to predictable beats. Shakespeare is widely known for his masterful use of iambic pentameter, but he rarely adheres to a strict metrical pattern for a complete poem (ta-TUM, ta-TUM, ta-TUM, ta-TUM, ta-TUM). Such lines certainly occur, as in the second line of sonnet 5 — "The **love**ly **gaze** where **eve**ry **eye** doth **dwell**" — but more often, Shakespeare's lines have variations on the pattern, such as sonnet 77, which notes "**Time's thiev**ish **prog**ress to e**ter**nity."[6] In that line, the expected five stresses are present, but the iambic pattern is thoroughly disrupted with brilliant syncopations.[7] This distinction — the difference between the real accents of the language versus the expected, or virtual, accents of the metrical grid — is analogous to the distinctions I made above between syncopated, real accents in music versus the expected, virtual accents of a given meter. Songs often establish regular groupings of strong and weak beats, but the actual melodies, riffs, and rhythms of the song will vary in the degree to which they coordinate with an implied metrical pattern.

"Nonmetrical" Verse

Modern poetry often eschews predictable metrical patterns altogether. This is part of what it means to write free verse. Sylvia Plath's "Edge," for instance, begins with lines of unpredictable length:

> The woman is perfected.
> Her dead

> Body wears the smile of accomplishment,
> The illusion of a Greek necessity
>
> Flows in the scrolls of her toga.[8]

In some sense, this poem is nonmetrical, because it lacks predictable stress patterns throughout. No simple label can describe the complete poem, such as "iambic tetrameter" or "trochaic trimeter." But as with much free verse, we still might notice familiar patterns. "The il**lus**ion of a **Greek** ne**cess**ity" has three stressed syllables as does "**Flows** in the **scrolls** of her **to**ga." And the last line of the excerpt, with its string of *o*'s, is especially musical: TUM ta ta / TUM ta ta / TUM ta. This is what Eliot meant when he said "there is no escape from metre." Even in free verse, it operates like a ghost behind the scene, with various lines weaving their way in and out of familiar sounds and patterns.

I cited Frank O'Hara's "The Day Lady Died" as an example of an unmetered poem, and it is indeed self-consciously "free" in the way it begins by recounting a variety of mundane decisions that the speaker — presumably O'Hara himself — makes on the day Billie Holiday died (he describes "practically going to sleep with quandariness"). But there are certain lines that nevertheless begin to ring out with a sudden metrical familiarity. A lovely pentameter rhythm emerges, for instance, in a line that mixes iambs and anapests: "I **walk** up the **mug**gy **street** be**gin**ning to **sun**." That sound is then echoed at the poem's end, after the speaker learns of Holiday's death from a newspaper headline. He is suddenly seized with the memory of leaning against a bathroom door in the 5 Spot "**while** she **whisp**ered a **song** a**long** the **key**board." The poem never fully commits to a consistent pattern, but it pulses with metric vitality despite its free verse rhythms.

Meter in Song

The way language works in song is, of course, quite different from how it works in normal spoken poetry. In a poem our sense of beats, meter, and rhythm is entirely dependent on the organization of the words. With song, accompanying instruments often establish regular patterns of accent before the voice even enters. This means that the language can reinforce or resist those patterns and need not take full responsibility for defining the metrical patterns on its own. Indeed, in popular music it is common for musicians to sing with offbeat accents, in part because the beats themselves are so strongly accented by the other instruments. The voice can anticipate or delay a melodic arrival without really disrupting our overall sense of meter. In other vocal styles, such as Protestant hymns or nineteenth-century art songs, the accented syllables tend to fall much more predictably on strong beats in a measure.

In some cases, the words are written before the music, as happens when a composer sets a preexisting poem. With other songs, the melody precedes the words, as happens when a songwriter conceives a tune at the piano before matching it with lyrics. Sometimes words and music are conceived simultaneously. In all of these situations, the accent patterns of the music and the accent patterns of the language interact with varying degrees of conflict and correspondence.

To get a better sense of the possibilities, compare the four phrases in examples 2.4a–d. In example 2.4a, from the *Les Misérables* song "Master of the House," there is a strong alignment between three parameters: (1) *real* accents, (2) *virtual* accents, and (3) natural *linguistic* accents. (As a reminder, the dots above the music represent expected levels of accent. They are black if they coincide with an actual attack in the vocal line, gray if not.)

As this example makes clear, the second syllable in the word "compare" (1) is accented in the vocal line, (2) coincides with a place where we would *expect* an accent in the music (three dots above the score), and (3) is a syllable that we would accent when we speak the word "compare" naturally (Spotify playlist, track 29, 2:25). We might also notice that the *first* syllable of "compare"—which would not normally be accented in speech—is also unaccented in the music and happens on a weak beat. In other words, there is a consistent alignment among all three parameters for much of the song. Such correspondence is common, and though "Master of the House" is nothing like normal speech, the music and the words comfortably fit together.

In example 2.4b, a passage from Lamar Campbell & Spirit of Praise's "More Than Anything" (with words and music by Rick Robinson) something similar happens but with a bit more complexity (Spotify playlist, track 30, 0:20). The natural spoken accents in the phrase "I **lift** my **hands** in **to**tal **a**do**ra**tion **un**to **you**" coincide with accents in the vocal line, but the melody is syncopated. All seven accented syllables arrive "early," anticipating the subsequent strong beats that they "should" be aligned with. If you are able to tap your foot or nod your head along with the beat—something that you might try in the second verse (the 1:00 mark), when the percussion enters—you will notice that these syllables all occur when your body is in an "up" position (musicians refer to them as upbeats). Though such syncopations are mildly destabilizing, it is cru-

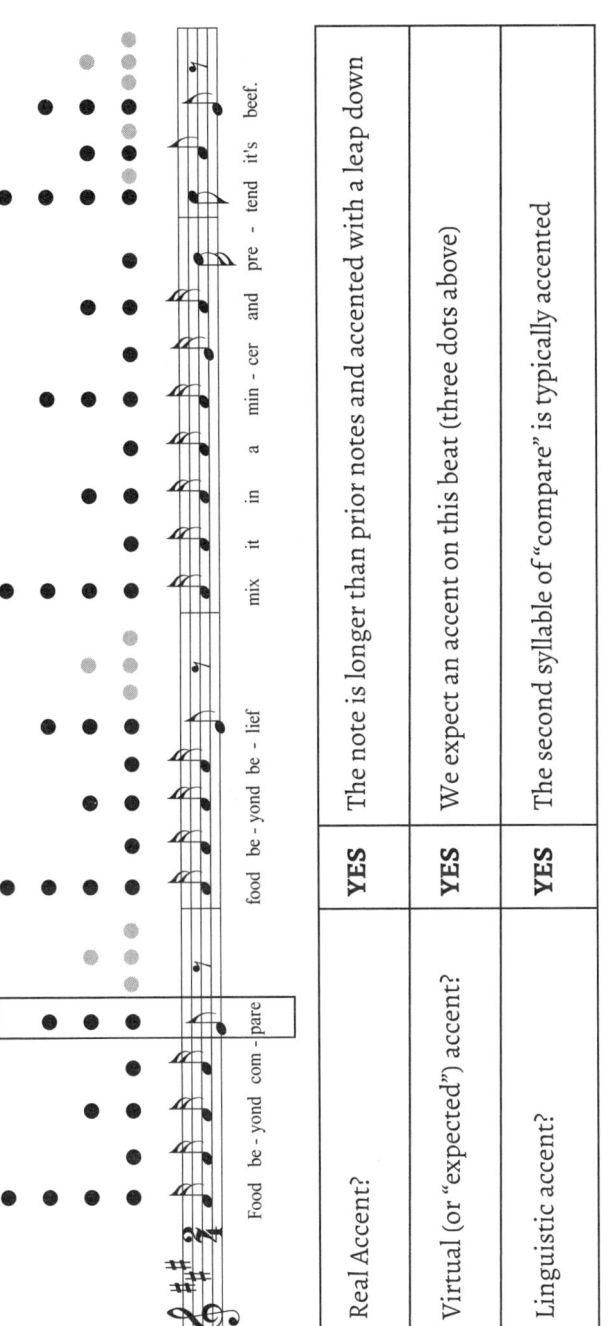

Example 2.4a. Alignments of accents in Claude-Michel Schönberg and Herbert Kretzmer, "Master of the House," from *Les Misérables*

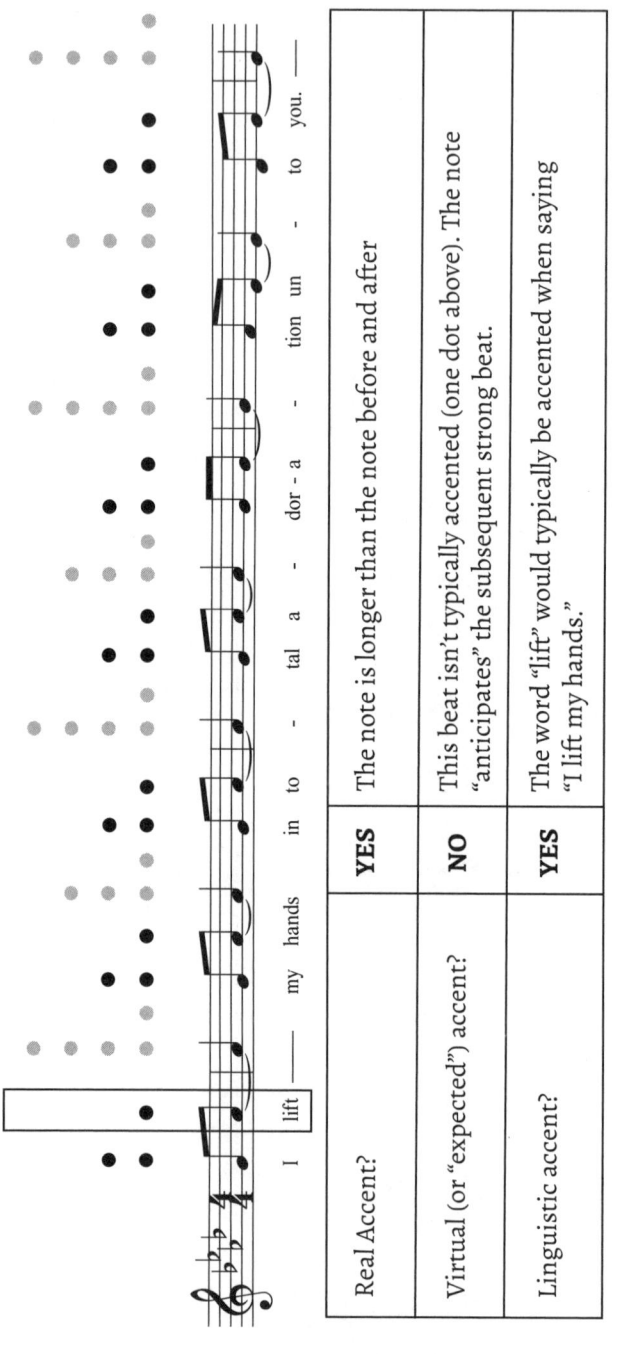

Example 2.4b. Syncopation in Lamar Campbell & Spirit of Praise, "More Than Anything"

cial to recognize how *common* syncopation is in popular music. Songs like this would undoubtedly sound much stranger (and much more "square") if all the vocal accents were predictably aligned with strong beats. In the gospel context of "More Than Anything," the emphasis on upbeats helps reinforce a sense of *uplift*, a rising upward in prayer.[9]

These examples from *Les Misérables* and Lamar Campbell are similar in that natural spoken accents are aligned with real musical accents, even if the latter are syncopated and the former are not. Occasionally, however, musicians do the reverse. In example 2.4c, Taylor Swift contradicts a natural linguistic accent by surprisingly emphasizing the *first* syllable of "again," which is aligned with both a real and virtual accent (Spotify playlist, track 31, 0:50). This makes a pleasing effect in that it creates a rhyme between "again" and "just in" that would not have existed otherwise. And although the pronunciation is not "natural," the eccentricity of the accent draws attention to the song's melodic properties; it draws attention, in other words, to what makes this *different* from normal speech—an effect which undoubtedly makes the melody even more catchy than it otherwise would be.

A slightly different version of this happens in example 2.4d, from the song "Whatever It Takes" by Imagine Dragons. The last syllable of "**dan**gerous" would not normally receive a strong accent, but it is held here longer than previous notes and is sung on a higher pitch (Spotify playlist, track 32, 0:14). More important, "dangerous" rhymes with "prepare for this" in the previous measure. The difference, however, is that we *expect* an accent on the word "this" when reading the phrase "pre**pare** for **this**" naturally. The accent on the last syllable of "dangerous" is far less natural, and it is perhaps more jarring because it is a syncopated note. Nevertheless, as with the Swift song, it enhances the musicality of the language and helps emphasize the rhymes.

These "misplaced" accents in "Wildest Dreams" and "Whatever It Takes" are effective—I doubt any listener of either song would be bothered by them—but such effects tend to be used sparingly by most composers and songwriters. There is good reason for that. If the accents in a melody vehemently contradict the natural accents of the language, certain problems can arise. For one thing, they can be difficult to sing. Many years ago, I gave students an assignment requiring them to set to music the Emily Dickinson poem cited above ("My life closed twice before its close"). I mistakenly assumed that students would easily recognize the inherent metrical patterns of the poem and write their musical accents accordingly. But several students mistakenly placed the poem's first syllable on beat one, which meant that they created melodic accent

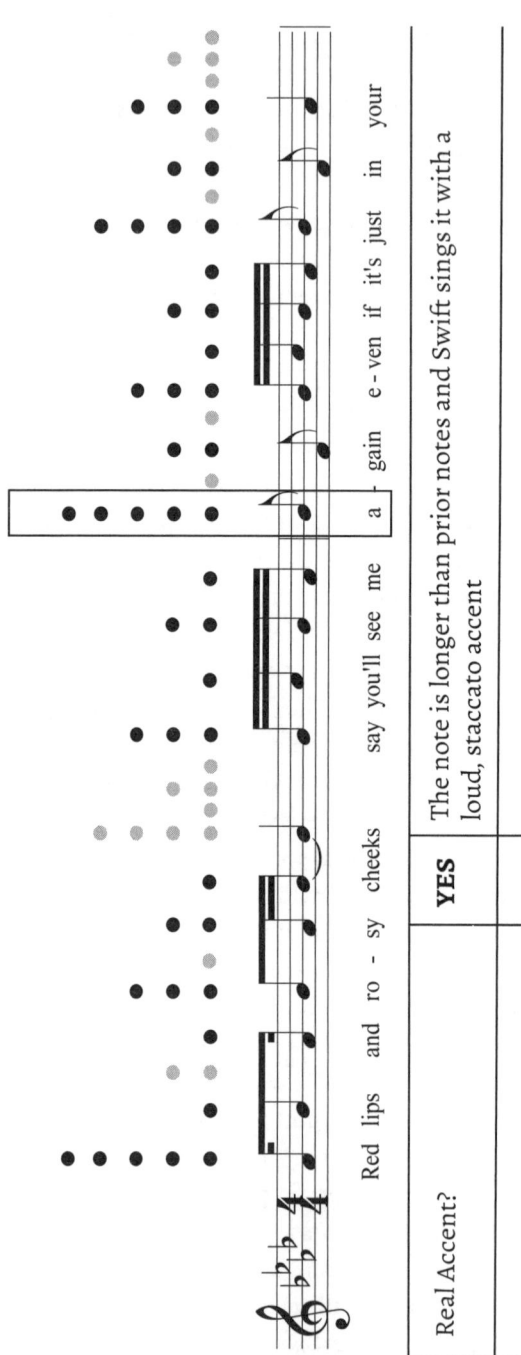

Example 2.4c. Real and virtual accents contradict linguistic accent in Taylor Swift, "Wildest Dreams"

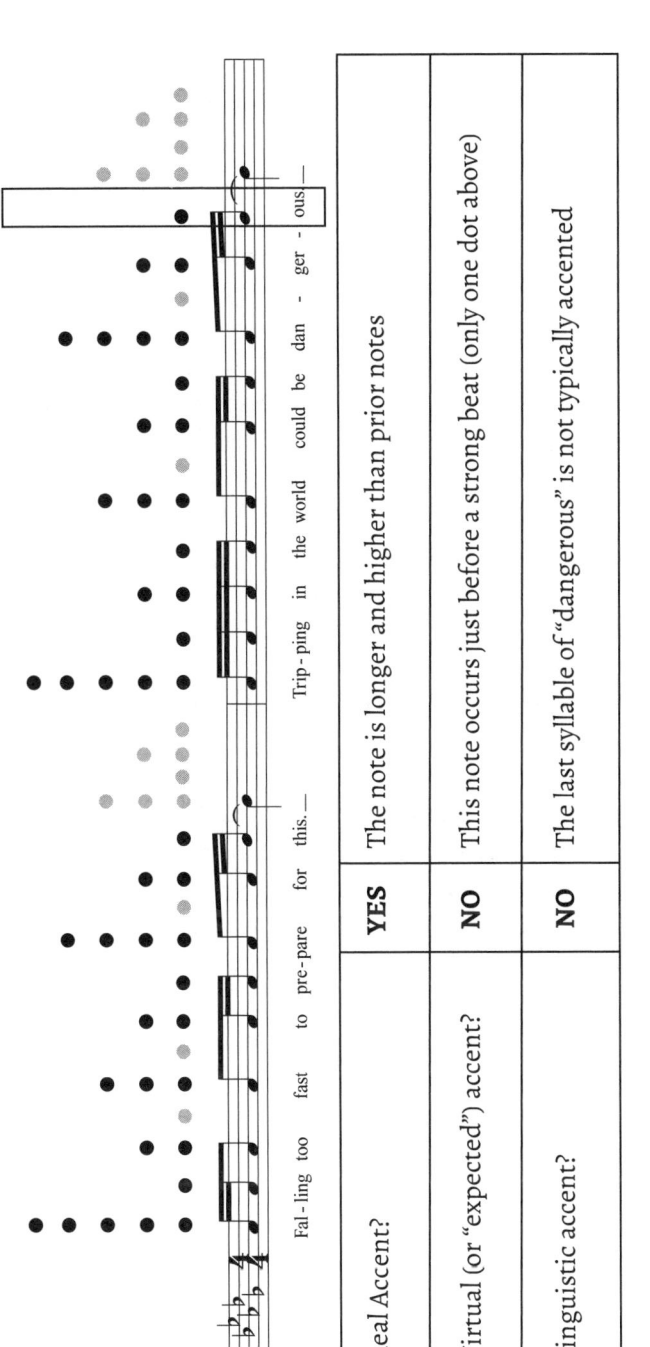

Example 2.4d. A real accent contradicts virtual and linguistic accents in Imagine Dragons, "Whatever It Takes"

patterns that were the exact opposite of a natural reading of the poem: "**My** life **closed** twice **before its** close." The melodies sounded bizarre, and when we attempted to sing them as a class, the singers—even those who were highly trained—struggled to articulate even the simplest melodic movement. What we experienced was a cognitive dissonance between what the melody was telling us to do and what the language was telling us to do.

As listeners, these conflicts can be disorienting and might even disrupt our understanding of a song's lyrics. Consider, for instance, "Blank Space," another hit song by Taylor Swift (Spotify playlist, track 33, 0:54). This song includes a line that frequently causes confusion: the phrase "got a long list of ex-lovers" is sometimes heard by listeners as "all the lonely Starbucks lovers" (the confusion is so common that it often appears on various lists of "most commonly misheard lyrics"). There are undoubtedly a great many factors that account for the misunderstanding, but I suspect that the main culprit is a single, unusual accent. In Swift's melody, the melodic accent pattern for the last six syllables goes "**long** list **of** ex-**lov**ers." That accented "of"—which coincides with both a real and virtual accent in the melody—is especially strange. We are not used to hearing prepositions accented so strongly. Here, then, is my best guess for what happens when people confuse the lyric: they assume, unconsciously, that "of" must not be the correct word, so they link it with the end of the word "list" to create the syllable "stuv," and then link *that* with "ex-lovers" to create "stuv-ex lovers"; and since they know that "stuv-ex" is not an English word, they imagine a likely replacement, and "Starbucks" is a pretty good guess. The rest of the confusion—"all the lonely" in place of "got a long list"—is most likely a retroactive way of making sense of the primary confusion, the odd presence of a group of "Starbucks lovers."

That such brief "misplaced" accents would occur in song should not be surprising. In a sense, songs are a form of heightened speech. And when people *speak* in an elevated fashion—rhetorically, emotionally, or both—they often put accents in unexpected places. If I wanted to tell you that I had just tasted the best coffee I'd ever had, I might accent the word "the" by pronouncing it "thee" and saying it louder than I otherwise would: "I just had THEE BEST coffee I've ever had." Similarly, a parent yelling at a child might emphasize words that are not normally accented: "I told you to use THIS pen, not the permanent marker."

To better understand how this might happen in song, let's return again to Emily Dickinson. Many American composers have set her poetry to music, and they often take radically different approaches. Ricky Ian Gordon's "Will There

Really Be a Morning?" (1983) offers an example of a song that sticks closely to the metric accents of the poem. Gordon's setting of the first verse can be heard on the Spotify playlist, track 34. Here are Dickinson's words, with the trochaic tetrameter marked in bold and the syllable count in parentheses:

> **Will** there **real**ly **be** a "**mor**ning"? (8)
> **Is** there **such** a **thing** as "**Day**"? (7)
> **Could** I **see** it **from** the **moun**tains (8)
> **If** I **were** as **tall** as **they**? (7)[10]

Gordon's setting is natural and intuitive; each syllable is sung to a note of equal length except for the last syllable of each line, which is extended to mark the end of the phrase. Moreover, each accented syllable appears *on* the beat while each unaccented syllable occurs *off* the beat. These strategies help reinforce the folksy, sentimental sound of the music as a whole. If Gordon had set the lines differently—with violent syncopations or complex accent patterns—the result would undoubtedly damage the musical aura of earnest expression and hopeful innocence (a sound that critics might find embarrassingly kitschy).

But even in such a straightforward setting, we find some surprises. Notice how Gordon emphasizes the second syllable of "morning" by leaping up to a high note and letting it ring out for several beats. He does this at the end of every eight-syllable line (that is, at both "morning" and "mountains"), and it creates a familiar type of phrasing, in which an initial phrase ends on a high pitch (the eight-syllable lines) and the subsequent phrases answer by ending on a lower pitch (as happens with the rhyming words, "day" and "they"). But no matter how conventional these melodic patterns might be, they still create an effect unlike any normal reading of the poem. The second syllable of "morning" is rather muted when we read it naturally. But in Gordon's melody, the accented syllable hits the beat on a low note and then ricochets upward, ringing out with a sustained "ee" for the second syllable's bell-like "ing" sound. What this suggests is that even the "simplest" settings of Dickinson will inevitably behave in ways that are unlike the sounds of the poems when read aloud. And if Gordon's setting can still be heard to transform the text in certain ways, what does a more disruptive setting sound like?

Consider George Perle's "The Loneliness One Dare Not Sound" (Spotify playlist, track 35). This is an atonal song in a mid-twentieth-century modernist style. The music amplifies the anxieties of the poem by pairing it with dissonant harmonies and fragmented melodies. But one of the more disorienting features—beyond the avant-garde sonorities—is the fact that Perle often puts

52   Meter

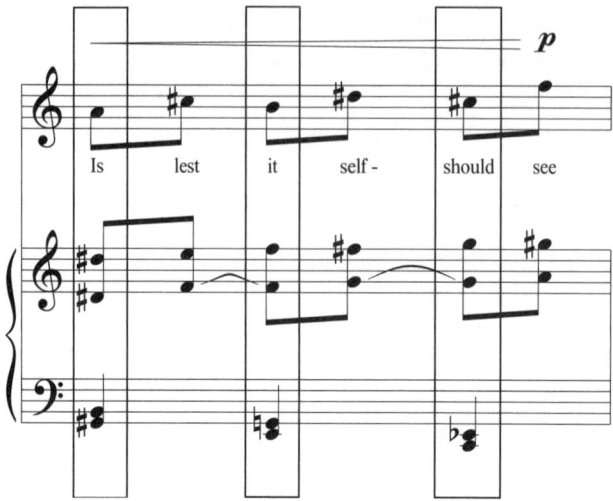

Example 2.5. Real accents contradict linguistic accents in George Perle, "The Loneliness One Dare Not Sound"

musical accents on unaccented syllables and vice versa. Moreover, this is not a minor, incidental effect such as we saw in the Taylor Swift songs. It is pervasive.

Example 2.5 isolates a passage from the second stanza (the 0:54 mark of the recording), which is in common meter (iambic tetrameter alternating with iambic trimeter):

> The **Loneliness** whose **worst alarm**
> Is **lest it**self should **see**—
> And **perish from** be**fore** it**self**
> For **just** a **scrutiny**—[11]

Notice that there are three beats in the measure, each accented by two notes played in the bass register. But Perle matches those beats with the *unaccented* syllables of the poem, essentially forcing a trochaic pattern onto an iambic pattern: "**Is** lest **it**self **should** see." This is similar to what happened when I assigned my students to set Dickinson's poetry to music and many got the accents wrong. The difference, however, is that my students wrote music that sounded like traditional church hymns and had no idea that they were accenting the wrong syllables; as a result, the misplaced accents were disorienting in a way that was more irritating than interesting (that is, they sounded wrong because they were inappropriate for the given musical style). With Perle's setting, it is clear that he is *trying* to produce an anxious, unsettling effect. He creates an intentional, destabilizing sound that helps amplify the shuddering prospect of self-revelation ("lest itself should see").[12]

Some listeners might hear this as an abomination, a willfully incorrect setting that fails to capture the "natural" sounds of the poem. But we should remember that *all* musical settings of poetry involve a radical transformation of the words (what the musicologist Lawrence Kramer, borrowing a neologism from Hart Crane, calls a "transmemberment").[13] And we might also remember that Dickinson's poems are still read today precisely because they continue to shock and surprise us. For that reason, the more "natural" settings by composers like Ricky Ian Gordon might strike some as almost *too* easy, a kind of musical wallpaper that comforts us without challenging us. For fans of George Perle, his music is an invitation to see something different, to view Dickinson's art in the funhouse mirror of avant-garde atonality, a place where the familiar is constantly in contact with the bizarre.

A Closer Look: Kendrick Lamar and Thomas Campion

Up until now, I have focused primarily on a simple binary: accented versus unaccented (or stressed versus unstressed). This distinction is at the heart of musical and poetic meter. But meter also involves a great deal of subtlety, including a wide variety of complex distinctions regarding duration, loudness, pitch, timbre, and much else. Anyone who has ever engaged in poetic scansion—the practice of identifying metric patterns in poetry—has probably recognized two common difficulties: different people often hear lines differently with regard to accents; and stress is often too nuanced to be analyzed from a simple binary perspective; syllable X might be more stressed than syllable Y, for instance, but less stressed than syllable Z. What matters most is that each individual moment—each articulated syllable—derives power and meaning from its place in a wider context. In this final section, then, I spotlight a few specific passages in which the metric properties of the language and the metric properties of the music interact in more complex ways than we have seen thus far.

Kendrick Lamar, "Element"

Most rap verses operate on a spectrum from more "speech-like" to more "song-like," in which the songlike moments involve structured rhythms and clearly identifiable pitches as opposed to the looser rhythms and irregular frequencies of normal speech. The song "Element," from Kendrick Lamar's 2017 Pulitzer Prize–winning album *DAMN.*, gradually eases into a structured flow. It begins with a few vocal samples and initial rhymes with a relatively loose, speech-like delivery. There is no percussion track for the first forty seconds, just synthesized keyboards and vocal samples. The passage that I am especially interested in—Spotify playlist, track 36, 0:39—starts to move the song in a more directed fashion, beginning with a sparse E-minor chord and several soft, percussive beats. (A simple synthesized kick drum hints at the more developed beats to come.) The lines that immediately precede this moment describe events in the past, but this section shifts to the present tense:

> Thirty millions later, know the feds watchin'
> Auntie on my telegram, like, "Be cautious!"
> I be hangin' out at Tam's, I be on Stockton
> I don't do it for the 'gram, I do it for Compton.

Each line is coordinated with a single four-beat measure, and the four lines as a whole help transition from the introductory material—the music without a percussion track—to the subsequent material, which, at the sustained second syllable of "Compton," launches into a complete drum and bass pattern.

As shown in examples 2.6a–d, each individual phrase is "end-accented"; they all begin *after* beat 1 of a given measure and they all arrive *on* beat 1 of the subsequent measure. In other words, each phrase is like an extended "upbeat" leading to a subsequent "downbeat."[14] But the entire four-measure group is also end-oriented in a different way: the arrival at the word "Compton" is

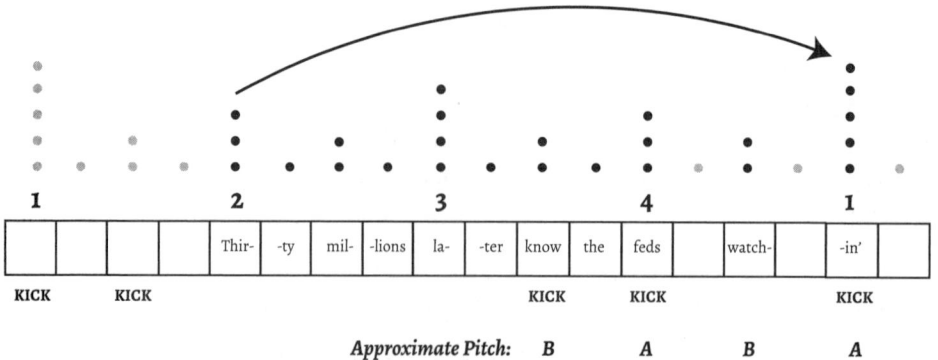

Example 2.6a. Kendrick Lamar, "Element," accent patterns in first measure of four-measure group

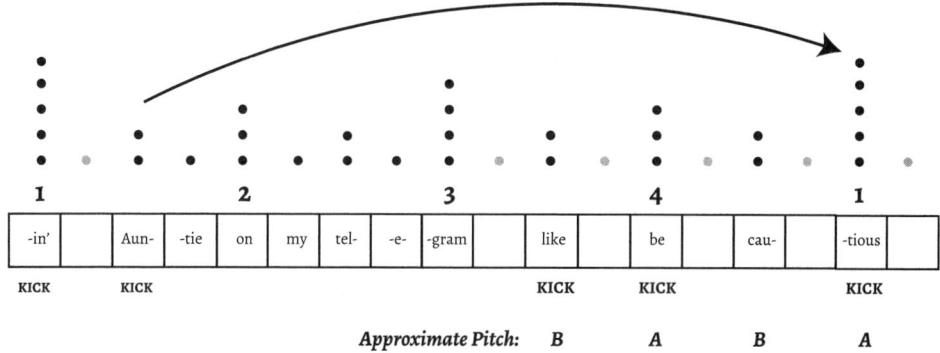

Example 2.6b. "Element," accent patterns in second measure

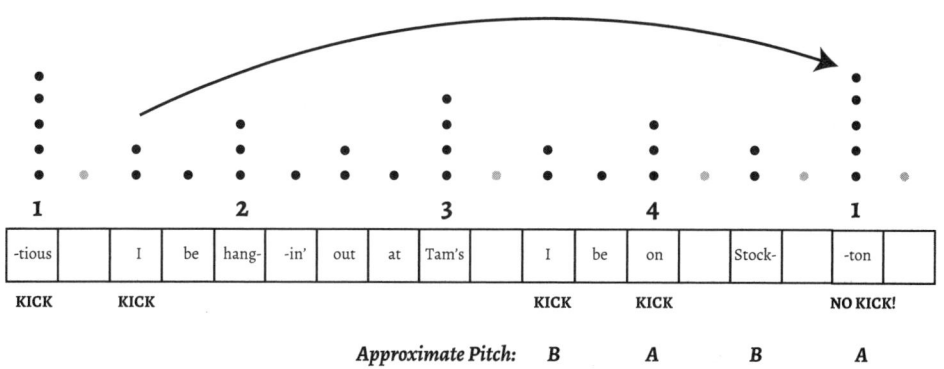

Example 2.6c. "Element," accent patterns in third measure

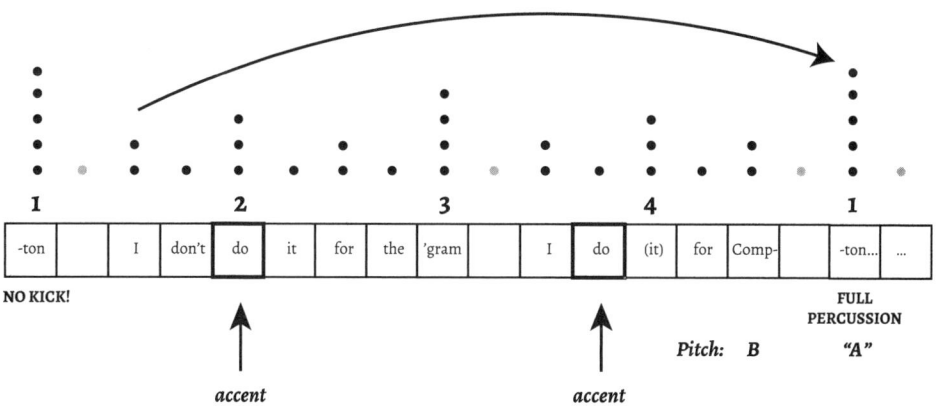

Example 2.6d. "Element," accent patterns in fourth measure

both a culmination of everything that happens in the passage up to that point and a launch pad for the rest of the song. One of the best ways to understand how that works is to think about this moment in terms of rhythm, meter, and accent.

Notice, for instance, that the first line in this group establishes a clear trochaic pattern with its first three words: "**Thir**ty **mill**ions **lat**er . . ." The dots above the phrases show the *expected* metrical stress for each part of a standard four-beat pattern (the virtual accents), and in the first measure, example 2.6a, all of the accented syllables at the beginning occur in places with at least two dots; unaccented syllables occur in the "weakest" part of the measure (represented by only one dot). As with the "Master of the House" example above, the virtual accents, real accents, and linguistic accents are aligned. But each phrase ends with a two-syllable word that would normally maintain the trochaic pattern that the verse had already established, with accents on the first syllable of "watchin'," "cautious," "Stockton," and "Compton." In each case, however, the *second* syllable lands squarely on the downbeat.

These "misplaced" accents are part of what makes this passage interesting. But consider some other features of the music. Each of the first three phrases begins with a rapid string of relatively speech-like syllables, followed by a slower group of syllables that are more songlike in the way they oscillate between clearly articulated pitches (B and A). The "pitch motive," appearing at the end of each line, sounds almost like a schoolyard taunt, possibly directed to the "feds" (which would suggest that the song's persona—presumably Lamar himself—may not be taking his aunt's advice to "be cautious"). More important, it suggests a kind of brash confidence, especially in the way the language stubbornly resists easy alignment between natural linguistic accents and musical accents. This is especially clear when we compare the phrase with an alternate version that sustains a trochaic pattern throughout by means of a string of end-directed sixteenth notes: "**Thir**ty **mill**ions **lat**er **know** the **feds** are **watch**in' **me**." This might have worked—assuming the subsequent rhymes were adjusted accordingly—but it would have been much less interesting. The actual line includes a surprising reversal—placing the first syllable of "watchin'" in a relatively weak metrical position compared to the second syllable, which lands on the downbeat. Each line of the first three measures, then, has two parts: a more "spoken" part, with accents in the expected places, and a more songlike, "taunting" part that warps the language by placing accents in unexpected places.

The "taunting" aspect of this delivery is significant, but the broader point of these four lines is not for Lamar to express resistance to the feds, or the concerns of his aunt, but to show that despite his current money and fame, he is still strongly rooted in his hometown. All four lines lead to the word "Compton," and there is a tension that builds up over the course of these lines in terms of how the "misplaced" accents of the first three lines might be resolved at the end. With that in mind, notice the effect of the simple word "do" in the last line. The first time we hear it—in the phrase "I don't *do* it for the 'gram"—it occurs on a relatively strong beat (beat 2), and Lamar puts special emphasis on the word, emphasizing its low vowel sound, which stands out in this passage.[15] The next time we hear the word "do," it appears at a metrically unaccented place in the measure (the last sixteenth note of beat 3). But Lamar emphasizes the word regardless, and it creates a syncopation that trips up the rhythm and displaces the taunting motive that would normally appear at this moment. For a microsecond, it sounds as if the line is suddenly unanchored, suspended for a brief moment in midair before the expected downbeat resolution.

This effect—creating a metric tension before a resolution—is extremely common in Western music. The fact that it happens here might lead us to expect that Lamar will neatly conclude the entire four-line group by articulating a single, stressed syllable on the downbeat (rather than landing on a "weak" syllable as he does with "watchin'," "cautious," and "Stockton"). What makes this moment remarkable, however, is that he instead doubles down on the tension in two ways: he stresses the second syllable of "Compton," sustaining it well into the next measure; and he lets his voice drift away from a clear, songlike pitch such that the word "Compton" still echoes the "taunting" motive from the previous lines, but with an extra stab of dissonance. It is like watching a gymnast land unconventionally but with the confidence and authority that make it work. And the addition of the full percussion clinches the effect. Notice that in the third measure (example 2.6c) the kick drum disappears at the end of the line (along with the accompanying chord), leaving the voice essentially unsupported. This provides an extra layer of suspense that is resolved when the full drum track comes in a measure later. Although the "taunting" motive is displaced at the end of that final line, all of its swagger gets rechanneled into the final culminating syllable.

Thomas Campion, "The Cypress Curtain of the Night"

In the history of English literature, we find few examples of great poets skillfully setting their own words to music. Thomas Campion's early-seventeenth-century lute songs provide a rare example. Campion was a physician by trade, but he also wrote treatises on both poetry and music. More important for our purposes, his songs, like those of John Dowland, are among the masterpieces of early English song. He was a poet who was deeply conscious of the nuances of metrical verse but also a composer capable of writing music with fascinating metrical and rhythmic complexity.[16]

Campion's poem "The Cypress Curtain of the Night" is presented below. While reading it, notice the strong iambic pentameter patterns but also the way the language occasionally resists those patterns as the poem progresses.

> The cypress curtain of the night is spread,
> And over all a silent dew is cast.
> The weaker cares by sleep are conquerèd.
> But I alone, with hideous grief aghast,
> In spite of Morpheus' charms, a watch do keep
> Over mine eyes, to banish careless sleep.
>
> Yet oft my trembling eyes through faintness close;
> And then the map of hell before me stands,
> Which ghosts do see, and I am one of those
> Ordained to pine in sorrow's endless bands,
> Since from my wretched soul all hopes are reft
> And now no cause of life to me is left.
>
> Grief, seize my soul, for that will still endure
> When my crazed body is consumed and gone,
> Bear it to thy black den, there keep it sure,
> Where thou ten thousand souls dost tire upon.
> Yet all do not afford such food to thee
> As this poor one, the worser part of me.[17]

A recording of Campion's song can be heard in the Spotify playlist, track 37. What makes the music especially striking is that it has a brilliant and near constant dissonance between groupings of twos and threes.[18] To understand how they work, look at examples 2.7a–b. In example 2.7a, we see the vocal line isolated and parsed into groups of two, with each accented syllable of the pentameter line accented in the music.

If you listen to the recording while focusing on this example, you will probably hear a duple grouping quite clearly. But Campion did not write the music

Meter 59

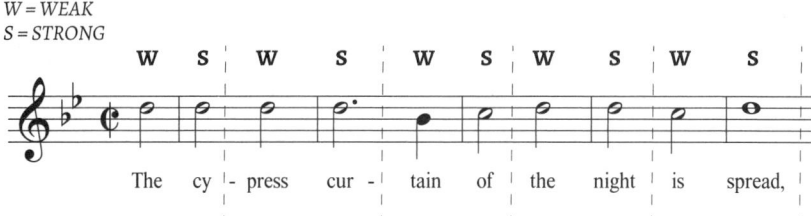

Example 2.7a. Thomas Campion, "The Cypress Curtain of the Night," opening melody parsed into groups of two (duple meter)

Example 2.7b. "The Cypress Curtain of the Night," notation of opening melody, parsed into groups of three (triple meter)

as shown in example 2.7a. He wrote it instead with triple groupings as shown in example 2.7b.

Notice how the lute accompaniment emphasizes groupings of three, with prominent arrival points on scale degrees 1 and 5 in the bass (the tonic and dominant notes in the key). This triple grouping is perceptible while listening to the recording, but it obviously contradicts the duple hearing of example 2.7a. What is happening, then, is a complex interaction between real musical accents (such as the bass notes in the lute) and the expected linguistic accents (the iambic pattern). Our awareness of virtual accents (duple or triple groupings) depends on which parameters we focus our attention on most. It is entirely possible for a listener to hear this tune as either duple or triple — and many are likely to hear one giving way to the other (most likely a triple grouping giving way to a duple grouping) — but it would be impossible to hear both groupings simultaneously. Our ears are essentially pulled in two different directions, with some layers of music saying, "Listen! This is duple meter!" while others say, "No! This is triple meter!" Most important is not that we definitively choose one over the other but that we recognize the sustained tension between the two.[19]

Part of what makes this metric conflict so compelling is that it has a distinct dramatic significance. The first stanza sets a fairly detailed scene in which night falls on the poetic speaker. He is in a state of "hideous grief" and tries to stay awake. In the second stanza, we learn why:

> Yet oft my trembling eyes through faintness close;
> And then the map of hell before me stands.

The speaker struggles to stay awake to avoid this horrifying premonition, and the grouping dissonance between twos and threes is indicative of that struggle. Something changes, however, in example 2.8, at the line "In spite of Morpheus' charms." The name "Morpheus" triggers the only moment in the song at which voice and lute combine to articulate an absolutely unambiguous grouping of three beats per measure. The god of sleep and dreams reorganizes our sense of time, and lulls the voice into triple beats (the 0:45 mark).

We have good reason, then, to hear a strong, symbolic association between triple meter and sleep. So the duple groupings in the voice—heard at the outset of the song—are a willful resistance to that.

As shown in example 2.9, these tensions culminate in the first stanza's final line. The music becomes especially syncopated and complex at the words "over mine eyes" (note especially the sustained second syllable of "over," which would not normally be accented). The music moves into a state of suspended time, disrupting any easy awareness of *either* duple *or* triple groupings. As with the Kendrick Lamar example, we have a passage that ends with a temporary rhythmic wavering that dramatizes the eventual moment when the singer "sticks the landing." That moment occurs, in this case, when a duple grouping is reacquired at the phrase "banish careless sleep." It works, to an extent, as a kind of victory, since the triple meter is temporarily "banished." But it is not a complete success. As the subsequent lines make clear, sleep can only be resisted for so long, and the song's speaker still has more to say.

The form of this song is strophic: each stanza of poetry is set to the same music. As a result, each metrical variation in the poem, from one stanza to another, will interact with a repeating vocal melody in different ways. In this song, the first two stanzas of poetry follow a traditional iambic pentameter

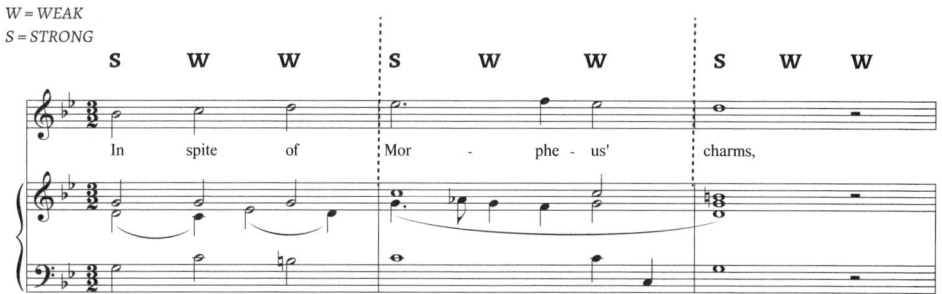

Example 2.8. "The Cypress Curtain of the Night," unambiguous triple groupings at "Morpheus' charms"

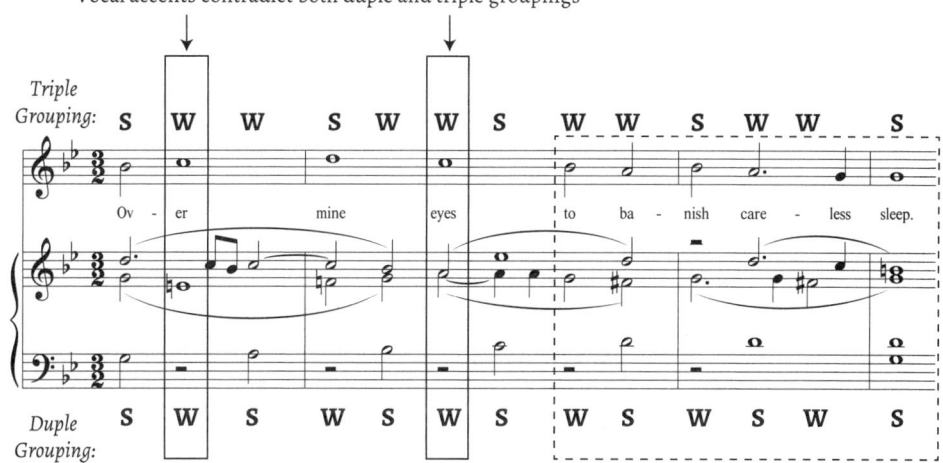

Example 2.9. "The Cypress Curtain of the Night," metric analysis of final phrase from the first strophe

pattern, strictly adhering to a recurring, predictable meter: ta-TUM, ta-TUM, ta-TUM, ta-TUM, ta-TUM. As a result, the shift from the first stanza to the second stanza does not create any complications.

With the third stanza, however, things change. The speaker imagines grief as an embodied, physical beast that gnaws on the souls of its victims. He addresses this monster directly:

> **Grief, seize** my **soul, for that** will **still** en**dure**
> When **my crazed bo**dy is con**sumed** and **gone,**
> **Bear** it to **thy black den,** there **keep** it **sure,**
> Where **thou** ten **thou**sand **souls** dost **tire** up**on.**

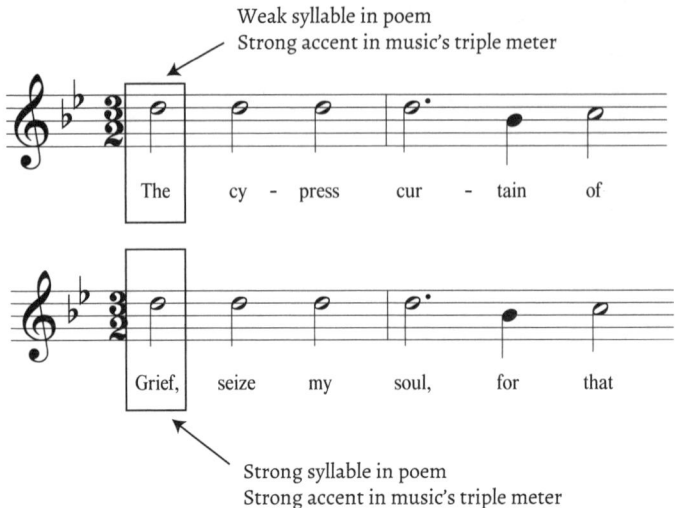

Example 2.10. "The Cypress Curtain of the Night," comparison of the openings of the first and third strophes

Notice how the masochistic turn in these lines is reinforced by several disruptions in poetic meter. Accents pile up on one another in phrases like "my crazed body" and "thy black den," a stunning change in rhythm and accent. And it might even be heard as a reflection of the speaker's failure to stay awake. Instead of addressing another person, as we might imagine happening in the opening stanzas, the speaker addresses grief directly. In other words, he not only envisions a nightmare scenario but speaks directly to the imagined beast, as someone might speak in a dream. Moreover, in doing so, he twice places accents at the beginning of a pentameter line: "**Grief, seize** my **soul**" and "**Bear** it to **thy black den.**" In doing so, he aligns the voice more strongly with the triple meter of the lute accompaniment (the "threes" of sleep).

As shown in example 2.10, which offers a comparison of the opening of the first stanza with the opening of the last stanza, there is a subtle shift toward a triple grouping in the voice with the emphasis on the word "Grief." More important, the irregular poetic accents throughout this section create a kind of ill-fitting melodic discomfort; the friction between words and melody intensifies the speaker's distress. The duple meter is again reestablished with the song's final phrase—"the worser part of me"—but the metric complexity throughout suggests a disoriented mind that wanders, often unwillingly, into deeply troubled places.

■ Both poetry and music rely on patterns of accent, and we often take pleasure in the way they might satisfy or thwart our expectations. But as we have seen throughout this chapter, the metrical properties of language are often transformed when they appear in song. Music can alter language, but language will often resist music. And the only way to truly appreciate the metric complexity of song is to develop a firm grasp of meter in *both* poetry and music.

In the examples above, the meter of the poems and songs often have an important relationship with rhyme. Rhymes are a way of drawing attention to the sounds of certain syllables, which is to say that rhyme is itself a form of accent. It is no surprise then, that rhyme often plays an important role in reinforcing our perception of metric patterns. But rhymes do far more than that. In the next chapter, I will consider the various functions and effects of rhyme in poetry and song, including how it engages with diction and meter, and how it begins to shape our perception of poetic lines.

CHAPTER THREE

Rhyme

A student sits down to write a song. She picks up a guitar, plucks a few chords, and starts humming a tune, something in a folksy, bluegrass style. Eventually, she settles on an opening line: "The day you walked away from me felt like sudden death." After singing this phrase several times, she decides to balance it with a rhyme. She tries out the following couplet:

> The day you walked away from me felt like sudden death.
> I dropped right down upon the ground and couldn't catch my
> > breath.

These lyrics fit the melody somewhat comfortably, but she's not happy with the words themselves. The rhyme of "death" and "breath" strikes her as too predictable. In fact, the whole couplet suddenly feels like an embarrassing cliché. Maybe, she thinks, there's a better rhyme for "death." She checks an online rhyming dictionary and finds only three realistic options: two of them are first names (Seth and Beth) and the other is a drug (meth). All other possibilities are too obscure. ("Heth," for instance, is a variant spelling of the eighth letter of the Hebrew alphabet—not an easy word to incorporate into a heartfelt break-up song.)

She could use a slant rhyme—a word that sounds similar but is not a conventional rhyme (for example, pairing "death" with "wrecked"), but she doesn't find that choice appealing either. Out of frustration, she considers rewriting her first line with a more "rhymable" word at the end, something like "die" instead of "death." But that might lead to a whole different set of clichés. When she considers words that rhyme with "die," she quickly conjures a tiresome wave of well-worn pop music pairings: "sky," "high," "fly," and "time passing by." At this point she begins to wonder whether she should abandon rhyme altogether. Is it really necessary? What does she lose if she writes a song without rhyme? What does she gain by embracing it?

Rhyme in Poetry, Rhyme in Music

It is impossible to use any language for an extended period of time without repeating the sounds of certain vowels and consonants. Of the forty-four phonemes commonly used in English, at least some will necessarily recur whenever we speak more than a few sentences. Most of the time we are unaware of these sonic similarities and differences. In this paragraph, for instance, I have done little to draw attention to how one word might sound similar to another. As with other didactic or functional uses of language, my emphasis is more on meaning than sound. If I had begun with the phrase "Here are four fun facts about forty-four phonemes," the sonic repetitions would be distracting; it would immediately suggest silly wordplay rather than sober academic discourse.

But drawing attention to similarities and differences need not always be silly. On the contrary, it is something that great writers have been doing for centuries. Poets and songwriters spend their lives artfully arranging words that brilliantly resonate with one another. Sometimes this involves dense clusters of similar sounds, as in the visionary poetry of Gerard Manley Hopkins:

> Glory be to God for dappled things—
>   For skies of couple-colour as a brinded cow;
>   For rose-moles all in stipple upon trout that swim;
>   Fresh-firecoal chestnut-falls; finches' wings.[1]

Sometimes it involves more subtle associations, as in the subdued opening of Matthew Arnold's "Dover Beach":

> The sea is calm tonight.
> The tide is full, the moon lies fair
> Upon the straits; on the French coast the light
> Gleams and is gone.[2]

An attentive listener to this poem will hear the rhyme of "tonight" and "light," as well as the alliteration in "full," "fair," and "French," or "gleams" and "gone," but Arnold does not foreground the similarities in the same way that Hopkins does. Nevertheless, in both cases, the arrangement of words draws our attention to their sound as well as meaning. There is a play of similarity and difference. Rhyme—in the broadest possible sense of the word—does this in a variety of ways.

Types of Rhyme

The most conventional rhymes involve words that begin with different sounds but end with the same sounds. The consonants at the beginning of "blue" and "you" are different, but the vowel sound at the end is identical. Rhymes with three phonemes, such as "red" and "bed," begin with different consonant sounds, but end with the same vowels *and* consonants. *The Princeton Encyclopedia of Poetry and Poetics* offers a useful rhyming taxonomy of single-syllable words with a "consonant-vowel-consonant" construction (CVC). As reproduced in table 3.1, this includes seven permutations, including the "standard rhyme"—number 6 on the chart—in which the opening consonant sounds are different but the other sounds are the same, as well as other familiar situations wherein, for instance, only the vowel sound is the same (assonance) or only the opening consonant is the same (alliteration). An eighth category, not shown in table 3.1, would be "zero rhyme," in which none of the phonemes are the same.

Needless to say, words can include many more than three phonemes, which means that the possibilities for similarity and difference can quickly proliferate in ways that cannot easily be captured in a single chart. Indeed, the concept of rhyme extends far beyond the simple identification of similar or different phonemes. Among other things, rhyme includes the *placement* of similar-sounding words in a poetic line or musical phrase (for example, end rhymes versus internal rhymes). There are *accents* in rhyme, which might occur in different places (such as "below" and "meadow"). We also find larger formal *arrangements* of rhyme, especially end rhymes, which can be represented with letters, as in *abba* or *abcb*. And this is to say nothing of broader issues of meaning, syntax, and morphology, all of which can play a role in distinguishing one type of rhyme from another.

For my purposes, rhyme, in a general sense, encompasses any of the various ways that one word might sound similar to another, but throughout this book I will mostly use conventional terminology: *standard* rhymes—what some authors refer to as "perfect" rhymes—include pairs like "run" and "sun" or "feather" and "weather." In these cases, the initial phonemes are different, but the final stressed vowel and all subsequent sounds are the same. *Slant* rhymes involve similar sounding words that do not rhyme perfectly, such as "little" and "middle" or "wall" and "bell." Under that broad category fall other, more specific types, such as *assonance*, which happens when we hear identical vowel sounds ("flows" and "sown"), and *consonance*, which matches closing consonants ("pill" and "call"). These technical terms are important to know, but

Table 3.1. Rhyming taxonomy of T. V. F. Brogan and S. Cushman, *The Princeton Encyclopedia of Poetry and Poetics*, 4th ed. (Princeton: Princeton University Press, 2012), 1185

1	<u>C</u>VC	alliteration (*bad* / *boy*)
2	C<u>V</u>C	assonance (*back* / *rack*)
3	CV<u>C</u>	consonance (*back* / *neck*)
4	<u>CV</u>C	reverse rhyme (*back* / *bat*)
5	<u>C</u>V<u>C</u>	[no standard term] frame rhyme (*back* / *buck*)
6	C<u>VC</u>	rhyme strictly speaking (*back* / *rack*)
7	<u>CVC</u>	rich rhyme, rime riche, or identical rhyme (*bat* [wooden cylinder] / *bat* [flying creature])

much more valuable is the ability to appreciate how authors distribute similar and different sounds into larger, more intricate patterns.

Networks of Similarity and Difference

Below is a passage from the "Burnt Norton" section of T. S. Eliot's *Four Quartets*. You can hear Eliot reading it aloud on the Spotify playlist, track 38, 7:50:

> Time and the bell have buried the day,
> The black cloud carries the sun away.
> Will the sunflower turn to us, will the clematis
> Stray down, bend to us; tendril and spray
> Clutch and cling?
>
>   Chill
> Fingers of yew be curled
> Down on us? After the kingfisher's wing
> Has answered light to light, and is silent, the light is still
> At the still point of the turning world.³

This is a remarkable tapestry of sounds. The first two lines are balanced with simple end rhymes ("day" and "away"), and those words also rhyme with "spray" at the end of line 4. But notice that line 4 is not at all like the opening lines. It is more syntactically open (it ends without punctuation), with the effect that we are unlikely to pause long at the word "spray" (as we would after "day" and "away"). Also, the word "stray" at the *beginning* of line 4 tells us that the placement of rhymes will not be as predictable as the opening lines might have suggested. Indeed, by line 3, the poem's syntax starts to move independently of the poetic lines, and with it the pacing of similar-sounding words shifts toward a palpable irregularity. There is the alliteration of "bell," "buried," and "black," which interacts with a different alliterative cluster: "cloud," "carries," "clematis," "clutch," and "cling." And interwoven with those groups is a resonant collection of three-word phrases: "turn to us," "bend to us," and "down on us." The various tonal clusters culminate in the extraordinary repetitions at the end of the passage, with identical words being repeated ("light" and "still") as well as continued networks of similar phonemes ("fingers," "king," "wing," and "turning," or "will," "tendril," "chill," and "still").

These similarities also subtly emphasize the words that do *not* rhyme in any obvious way. For instance, the word "point" in the final line strikes me as having a special significance in that it sounds nothing like any of the surrounding words. It shares the same closing *t* sound as "light" and "silent," but the plosive *p* does not occur anywhere else in the passage, and it sounds especially forceful compared with the liquid *l*'s and sibilant *s*'s that resonate nearby. The effect reinforces the meaning. An anxious, dizzying movement permeates these lines, but they conclude with the reassuring image of a comforting light, fixed in place, at the "still *point* of the turning world." Amid all the intricate webs of similar sounds, the simple word "point" cuts through and establishes itself as a singular event, a sound that the other rhymes encircle but do not directly engage. (Readers familiar with the *Four Quartets* will recognize that the idea of the "still point" is a crucial, recurring theme throughout the entire work.)

The Russian composer Sofia Gubaidulina set this passage to music in her *Hommage à T. S. Eliot* (1987). It occurs as an isolated soprano solo within a larger piece for voice and chamber ensemble, and it gives us occasion to briefly consider how musical settings can either reinforce or deemphasize poetic rhymes. Listen to the beginning of Gubaidulina's setting (Spotify playlist, track 39) and follow along with the annotated score (example 3.1). Notice how the rhymes of "day," "away," "stray," and "spray" are *musically* reinforced, because at each word the soprano sings the same three-note motive (featuring an ascending major third). But notice also how that motive recurs in four other places as well, at the nonrhyming words "buried," "sun," "blend," and "us." The melody, in other words, features several repeating musical ideas—a strictly musical kind of "rhyming"—but these do not always align with the poetic rhymes in a predictable or systematic way. Both the language and the music involve complex networks of similarity and difference, which sometimes reinforce each other and sometimes do not.

The kinds of musical rhymes that we find in Gubaidulina's music—the re-

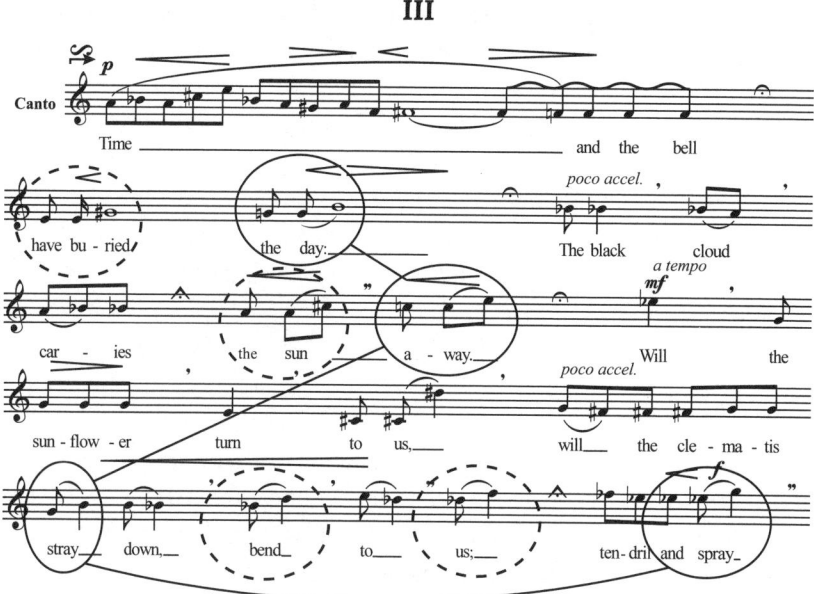

Example 3.1. Sofia Gubaidulina, *Hommage à T. S. Eliot*, third movement, annotated opening

peated pitch and rhythmic configurations—are not restricted to the "high art" classical tradition. Listen, for instance, to the opening verse of the song "Jane Says" from the 1988 album by Jane's Addiction, *Nothing's Shocking* (Spotify playlist, track 40). This is a somewhat unusual song in that the lyrics scrupulously avoid rhyme in favor of colloquial speech:

> Jane says, "I'm done with Sergio.
> He treats me like a ragdoll."
> She hides the television.
> Says, "I don't owe him nothin'."

The song is not structured by regular, predictable rhymes, but there are, nevertheless, a variety of ways in which the vocal melody makes sonic connections between words. Perhaps the most obvious is the descending leap at the words "Jane says," "ragdoll," and "she hides" (a minor third, from A to F#). None of these words rhyme, but the repeated melodic interval draws them together and transforms the prose-like language into something patterned and familiar. And there is a subtle rhyme in the way both "television" and "nothin'" end with the same "n" sound. The lead singer, Perry Farrell, draws attention to that by letting his voice slide down to a relatively low point (a D) at the end of both words. On the page, the lyrics offer a rather unvarnished account of a woman's dismal circumstances, but the music aestheticizes and transforms the unrhymed prose into lyrics that frequently chime with structured repetitions. The diction is simple, with relatively little beyond declarative sentences and quoted dialogue, and the music, with its jangling major chords and steel drum melody, seems oddly distant from everything being described. Listeners might hear these sounds as either callously uncaring or warmly sympathetic, but in either case, they transform the language into networks of similar sounds that are impossible in regular speech.

The Pros and Cons of Rhyme

Songs like "Jane Says" are no doubt an inspiration to aspiring songwriters who feel oppressed by the pressure to rhyme. In the song "Stressed Out" by Twenty One Pilots, the singer expresses a common frustration: "I wish I didn't have to rhyme every time I sang" (a line that he delivers while self-consciously disrupting a rhyming pattern). But why would this pressure be so acute in the first place? What makes rhyme so effective that it has been used in songs for centuries? Here are a few tentative answers:

- Rhymes make language more *memorable*, which is why they are often used for advertisements, political slogans, and various mnemonic devices. For songwriters, having listeners remember the lyrics is often critical for success.
- Rhymes create *expectations*. We begin to anticipate how one word might be matched with another and it is often pleasurable when our expectations are fulfilled. It can also be pleasurable when our expectations are denied in surprising ways.
- Rhymes in English can be *challenging*. They restrict options, and it can be exciting when artists rise to that challenge. The appeal of freestyle rap is largely based on this.
- Rhymes help provide *structure*. In poetry, they interact with other elements, especially meter, to segment words into lines, stanzas, and larger forms such as sonnets. In song, they help segment the music into phrases, subphrases, and larger sections, such as verses and choruses.
- Rhymes make language more *musical* by drawing attention to sound, and if they are used well, we enjoy listening to them; a song like "Jane Says" transforms colloquial speech into music, but rhymed lyrics are *already* a form of "musical" language.

- Rhymes shape language into something that is *different* from conventional, everyday prose. Using rhyme is one of the most obvious ways to mark language as "poetic," even if it is tired or silly.

This brief list helps account for the enduring popularity of rhyme, but there are also good reasons for artists to worry about using it. Three hundred years ago, in his "Essay on Criticism," the poet Alexander Pope satirized the overuse of certain rhymes:

> Where-e'er you find "the cooling Western breeze,"
> In the next line, it "whispers through the trees."[4]

This is an amusing critique of poetic clichés, but for many young aspiring writers, it could be genuinely alarming. After all, if certain rhymes were already considered embarrassingly trite in the early eighteenth century, how can writers expect to breathe new life into them now? Different genres, perhaps, can reanimate old rhymes, but the problems of overuse will always be an issue. Pope's criticism, for instance, has been echoed in the twentieth century by many songwriters who lament clichéd rhymes such as "moon" and "June" (a rhyme that was especially overused in the Tin Pan Alley tradition). And Adam Bradley describes "overdetermined" rhymes in hip hop, which "the MC or poet chooses not out of conscious design but out of desperate necessity or lackadaisical passivity.... They signal the loss of poetic control."[5] This might then lead to an unnerving question: Is it possible that *all* rhymes could eventually become overdetermined? After all, the English language has only so many rhymable words. How much novelty can be sustained after more than five hundred years of English verse?

This is an understandable concern, but good counterarguments can easily be found. The English language is not a fixed entity with a finite vocabulary and no potential for changes in pronunciation. If it were, the potential for rhyme would indeed be limited. But language evolves and changes, and the language of poets and songwriters changes with it. This is especially clear in the music of hip hop, which, more than any other current genre, draws heavily upon regional dialects, slang, pop culture, and other rapidly changing aspects of contemporary life. Rappers, moreover, are not afraid to bend and twist language into sounds that suit their needs. Consider what happens in Kanye West's verse from Rick Ross's "Sanctified" (Spotify playlist, track 41, 1:34):

> So you can go'n and make them lies
> But I'm so sanctified

> I don't sweat it
> Wipe my forehead with a handkerchief.

As performed by West, the phrase "make them lies" rhymes with both "sanctified" and—more surprisingly—"handkerchief." Like many other modern rappers, West takes words that do not rhyme and *makes* them rhyme ("handkerchief" is pronounced more like "handker-*chive*," with West extending the final syllable and sliding up in pitch).[6] The lesson is clear: language progresses, and performers are free to manipulate sounds as they see fit. For an optimist, the possibilities for rhyme are endless.[7]

But we must also recognize that rhymes are neither good nor bad *in and of themselves*. Using a common pair of rhymed words need not be a problem, as is often assumed when songwriters warn about the dangers of rhyming "moon" with "June." The idea is that those two words paired together are automatically doomed to failure. But this significantly misrepresents the issue. As Alexander Pope's quote makes clear, the individual rhyming words themselves are not the cause of the trouble; rather, familiar rhymes are often paired with familiar images and sentiments, such that every aspect of a lyric, not just the rhyme, feels like a cliché. When a lyricist rhymes "high" with "sky," it is not necessarily hopeless—there are undoubtedly many ways to rhyme those words in extraordinary, surprising, or elegant ways. But if the rhyme compels familiar images and metaphors ("I want to fly so high / I can touch the sky") it will fail to do anything exciting or original.

Even when a songwriter does match a clichéd sentiment with a clichéd rhyme, the song may not be a failure. As with meter and diction, the success of rhyme depends on how it interacts with everything else. Compare, for instance, two rock songs that use rhyme with very different results in terms of critical and commercial success. First, listen to "It's All Over Now, Baby Blue" by Bob Dylan, a song that has received a great deal of critical acclaim since its debut in 1965 (Spotify playlist, track 42). Here are some sample lyrics from the 1:57 mark:

> Your lover who just walked out the door
> Has taken all his blankets from the floor
> The carpet, too, is moving under you
> And it's all over now, Baby Blue

Now compare those lines with lyrics from a significantly less successful song: "Road of a Thousand Dreams" by the early-nineties rock band Trixter (Spotify playlist, track 43, 0:31):

> Some live the life, the lap of luxury
> Where everything goes right.
> But some live so painfully
> Another day, another fight.

It might be hard to imagine many people preferring Trixter's lyrics to Dylan's, but it would be impossible to evaluate one over the other based solely on end rhymes. Dylan's pairings of "door" / "floor" and "you" / "blue" are hardly original. Indeed, in isolation, one might even argue that Trixter's rhyme of "luxury" and "painfully" is more impressive: it rhymes three-syllable words and draws attention to the opposing connotations of each. The problem with Trixter's lyrics is not that their rhymes are clichéd but that *everything* is clichéd: the music is clichéd, the contrast of rich versus poor is clichéd, and almost every phrase in these few lines is based on a clichéd idiom ("live the life," "lap of luxury," and "another day, another dollar").

The best line in the Dylan passage is also based on a familiar idiom ("having the rug pulled out from under you"), but Dylan transforms it into something far more appealing than anything in the Trixter lyrics: "the carpet, too, is moving under you." This is a charming iambic pentameter line that matches the meter of the line that precedes it ("has **ta**ken **all** the **blan**kets **from** the **floor**"). Moreover, the vowel sounds of "too" and "moving" and "you" nicely resonate with all the other "ooh" sounds throughout the song (especially "baby blue"). All these verbal effects are important, but the lines are effective for reasons that have to do with far more than the poetic language, including the flow of the melody, the rhythmic syncopations, the harmonies, and the unique timbre of Dylan's voice. The rhymes are effective — what would these lyrics be without them? — but they cannot be evaluated in isolation. Rhymes can be entirely predictable or shockingly original, but a single rhyme on its own cannot guarantee that we will find a given passage moving. It cannot, by itself, transform a song or a poem into a work that we want to experience again and again.

Musical Functions of Rhyme

Poets often refer to the musical properties of rhyme. To an extent, this is intuitive. Rhyme draws attention to sounds and patterns and makes language into a kind of music. But this is a rather loose metaphor, and we might want to think more precisely about how rhyme functions in ways that are analogous to *specific* features of music rather than just being broadly "musical." This is especially important in song, in which the linguistic functions of rhyme may or may not align with certain musical devices. Here are three important comparisons.

End Rhymes Are Like Cadences

In music, cadences are generic musical formulas that signal a point of arrival (usually a point of "rest"). They can vary in their degrees of stability. Some cadences, especially those that we hear at the ends of classical pieces, are remarkably stable. The music has no need to go elsewhere. It arrives on what musicians refer to as the tonic chord, which is often compared to an arrival at home (the tonic would be C major if the piece is in the key of C major, D minor if the piece is in D minor). At other times, cadences involve an arrival on a non-tonic chord—a chord that might sound relatively stable in the moment, but is not as stable as the tonic; such cadences suggest that the point of rest is only temporary, and that the music will eventually move on.

Example 3.2 is a popular old English tune called "Rogero," which was based, most likely, on a mid-sixteenth-century Italian tune known by a similar name. (You can hear an embellished lute version on the Spotify playlist, track 44; it does not have the same notes as example 3.2, but they are similar.) As shown in the annotations above the score, there are two strong cadences: one at the beginning of measure 4 and one at the beginning of measure 8.

The first cadence, which pauses on scale degree 2 (suggesting a dominant chord), is less stable than the final cadence, which arrives on the tonic (scale degree 1). This type of phrasing is extraordinarily common in Western music, and scholars often make a grammatical analogy when explaining it: the first cadence is like a comma (a syntactic break, but not full closure), and the second cadence is like a period (full stop). In fact, musicians often refer to these phrase pairings as "periods," making the grammatical analogy explicit. "Rogero" was often performed on the lute as a purely instrumental melody, but it was also frequently matched with words in the English ballad tradition. In such cases, the cadences were reinforced with rhymes. This can be seen in the example, where the two phrases of "Rogero" are matched to a rhyme in common meter:

> All such as lead a jealous life,
> as bad as pains of hell,
> Bend down attentive ears to this
> which I shall briefly tell.[8]

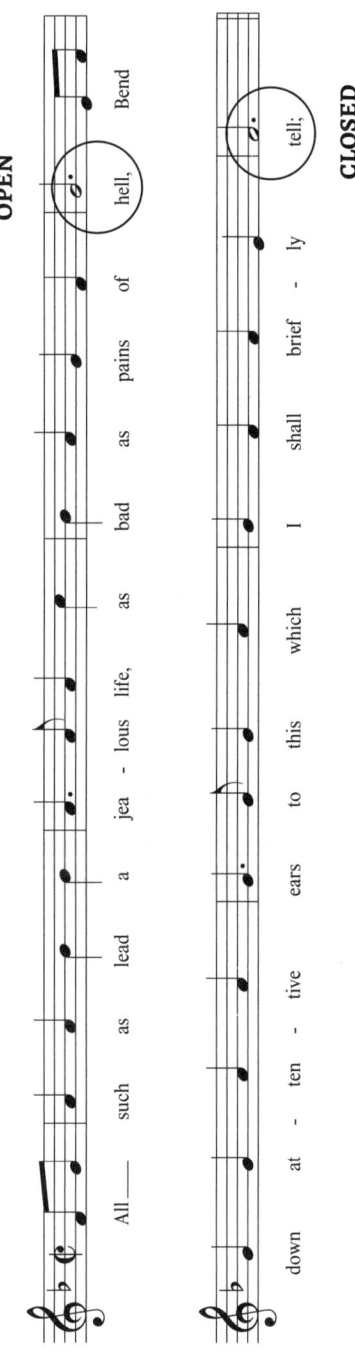

Example 3.2. "Rogero," cadences aligned with end rhymes

As should be clear, the cadences and rhymes reinforce one another because they share similar functions: they indicate a pause in their respective phrases (whether musical or poetic); and—if we are familiar with the conventions of their respective genres (baroque dance and Elizabethan verse)—they set up a situation in which we expect that the first cadence/rhyme will be answered by something like the second. An experienced listener who hears only the first four measures of the instrumental tune might not know *exactly* how the tune will end but will be likely to expect that the first cadence will be answered by the second (the pause on scale degree 2 will be answered by a pause on scale degree 1). Similarly, a person familiar with English poetry, when hearing the first line of the above couplet, will expect "hell" to be rhymed with a word like "tell."

When poets use end rhymes, they are creating something similar to musical cadences; when composers write balanced cadences, they are creating something similar to poetic end rhymes. It is no surprise, then, that songwriters have been fusing cadences and rhymes for centuries. The two have strikingly similar functions.

Small Rhymed Units Are Like Sub-Phrases

Example 3.3 is another popular English dance tune from the seventeenth century known as "The Merry, Merry Milkmaids," a recording of which can be heard on the Spotify playlist, track 45. Notice how the music pauses in three places: measure 2, measure 4, and measure 8. Each of those pauses comes at the end of a two-measure motive, which occurs in different guises in measures 1–2, 3–4, and 7–8. Measures 5 and 6 are different: they are rhythmically identical to each other, but they move in different directions (measure 5 goes up, measure 6 down). The result is that the entire eight-measure phrase can be subdivided into smaller groups: 2 + 2 + 1 + 1 + 2. When British balladeers matched this tune with words in the seventeenth century, they used a familiar form of light verse that we now know as the limerick (though the term was not coined until the end of the nineteenth century):

> I married a wife of late,
> The more's my unhappy fate;
> I took her for love,
> As fancy did me move,
> And not for her worldly state.[9]

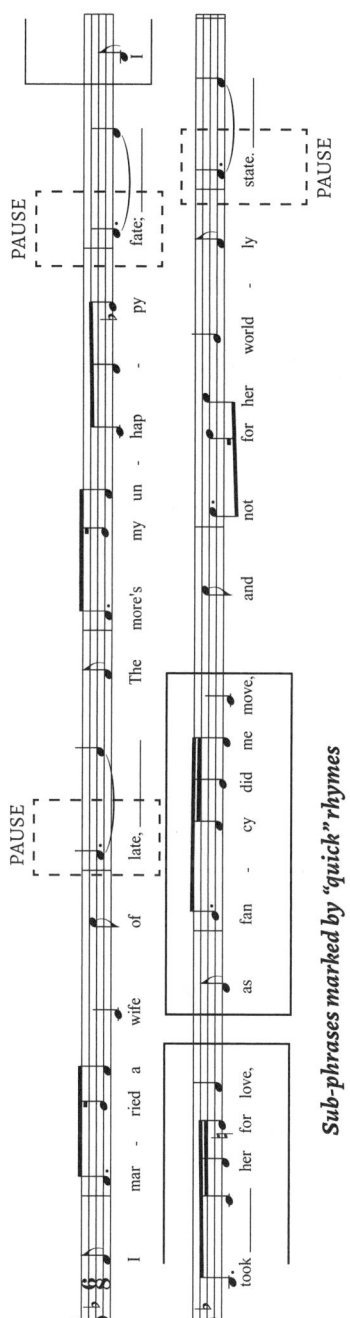

Example 3.3. "The Merry, Merry Milkmaids," parsed with internal rhymes

Notice how the rhymes match the segmentation of the music exactly. "Late," "fate," and "state" mark the pauses at the ends of every two-measure group in the music. And the "quick" rhymes of "love" and "move" create a different subgrouping that matches the accelerated 1 + 1 musical rhyme in measures 5–6. In the music, the complete tune is a single phrase, but it contains several subphrases, which are segmented by various kinds of repetition. In the limerick, the entire five-line group is a complete unit, but it involves metrical subdivisions that are each capped with a rhyme.

This musical structure is not unique. Like the period form, it is a theme type that has been popular in Western music for centuries. The composer Arnold Schoenberg, who first identified this phrase design in the 1920s, called it a "Satz" and translated it into English using the term "sentence." Composers paired these sentence forms in music with limerick-like poetry frequently throughout the seventeenth century, and it is a practice that continues well into the present. As the music scholar Michael Callahan has pointed out, these "sentential limericks" are a regular feature of the tunes in the Great American Songbook.[10] Here, for instance, is the opening of Andrew Sterling's 1904 "Meet Me in St. Louis, Louis," made famous when Judy Garland sang it in the 1944 film *Meet Me in St. Louis* (Spotify playlist, track 46):

> When Louis came home to the flat
> He hung up his coat and his hat.
> > He gazed all around,
> > But no wifey he found,
> So he said, "Where can Flossy be at?"

Similar patterns can be heard in rock music. Tom Petty's "Breakdown," from 1977, is representative (Spotify playlist, track 47, 0:31):

> It's all right if you love me
> It's all right if you don't
> > I'm not afraid
> > Of you runnin' away
> Honey, I get the feelin' you won't.

And the same patterns also frequently emerge in modern rap. Here, for instance, is an example from J. Cole's 2010 hit "Who Dat?" (see near the 1:00 mark of any available recording; not currently on Spotify):

> So if you're sellin' crack
> Or if you're sellin' rap

> Make sure it's mean
> So them fiends
> Keep on comin' back.

These patterns reflect a broader principle: rhymes not only help to mark cadential boundaries in music, they also help create subphrases by segmenting passages into smaller metrical groups. And their effect on tempo and pacing is crucial. In each of the above cases, the quick rhyme of the limerick (the rhyme that occurs in lines 3–4) creates an acceleration—it builds tension as the phrase makes its way toward the final rhyme (the closing cadence).

This same effect can be achieved without limerick-like poetry, as can be heard in the opening of Bob Dylan's "Like a Rolling Stone" (Spotify playlist, track 48). The song begins with two parallel phrases, which climb upward by placing harmonies on each step of an ascending scale, ultimately reaching a plateau on scale degree 5 (the dominant). The rising chords are each two beats long and the dominant chord—the arrival harmony—is held for eight beats (sixteen beats total). Table 3.2 shows what happens if we match the language with the chords.

Each segment of the phrase—each rung of the harmonic ladder—is matched with a rhyming syllable. The top of the ladder ("didn't you?") does not rhyme with the previous segments, but it does rhyme with the peak of the subsequent phrase:

> C major (2 beats): People called
> D minor (2 beats): Said, "Beware doll
> E minor (2 beats): You're bound to fall"
> F major (2 beats): You thought they were all
> G major (8 beats): Kiddin' you.

The primary structuring rhyme of this phrase is "didn't you?" and "kiddin' you," both of which are cadential arrivals (plateaus on the dominant chord). But the internal rhymes help segment the passage into smaller units. In this case, they help create tension: the music builds pressure simply by rising upward, but the rhymes also create a kind of tension. We know that the options for rhyming words are limited, and this means that every additional rhyme is like a circus performer adding to a set of spinning plates—it can only go on for so long before it all collapses.

Table 3.2. Bob Dylan, "Like A Rolling Stone," rhymes and chord changes aligned

Once upon a *time* C MAJOR	you dressed so *fine* D MINOR	threw the bums a *dime* E MINOR	in your *prime* F MAJOR	didn't you? G MAJOR
2 BEATS	2 BEATS	2 BEATS	2 BEATS	8 BEATS

Internal Rhymes Are Like Syncopations (Sometimes)

The opening of "Like a Rolling Stone" features a series of quick rhymes that help segment the melody into small, two-beat units. But listen closely to the recorded version and you'll notice that Dylan doesn't sing each of those rhyming syllables in the same places (table 3.3).

In fact, they each appear in a different part of their respective two-beat units: "time" appears in the middle of the second beat; "fine" appears at the end of the first beat; "dime" appears exactly on the second beat; and "prime" appears earliest—in the middle of the first beat. The word "dime" is the only rhyming word that is actually *on a beat*. The other rhymes are all syncopated.

Dylan's syncopations mostly result from his performance choices rather than from intrinsic properties of the language. It would be easy (albeit severely damaging) to rearrange the melody such that the rhyming words were all aligned exactly on beat 2. But with metrically regular verse, poets often use internal rhymes to disrupt familiar patterns and create something akin to musical syncopations. Consider these lines from "God's Grandeur," another poem by Hopkins:

> Generations have trod, have trod, have trod;
>   And all is seared with trade; bleared, smeared with toil;
>   And wears man's smudge and shares man's smell: the soil
> Is bare now, nor can foot feel, being shod.[11]

Table 3.3. "Like A Rolling Stone," irregular placement of rhymes in two-beat units

BEAT 1				BEAT 2			
Once		u-	pon		a	**TIME**	you
dressed		so	**FINE**				
threw	the	bums	a	**DIME**			in
	your	**PRIME**					

These lines are in iambic pentameter, and the iambic rhythm is clear in certain segments ("have **trod**, have **trod**, have **trod**"). But the internal rhymes in the second line create accents that disrupt the regular iambic patterns:

And **all** is *seared* with **trade;** *bleared, smeared* with **toil.**

The word "bleared" occurs at a place where we would expect an unaccented syllable. And although the pattern could have been disrupted with any other accented word ("blurred" would also have been disruptive), the rhyme draws special attention to the sense of syncopation. It ensures heavy emphasis on several successive syllables.

Rappers have been using rhymes in similar ways for decades. Public Enemy's "Louder Than a Bomb" from the 1988 album *It Takes a Nation of Millions to Hold Us Back* illustrates the point (Spotify playlist, track 49, 0:54). The first verse ends with the following four lines (slashes indicate the beginning of a four-beat unit):

/ Although I live the life that of a resident,
/ But I be knowin' the schemes that of the president.
/ Tappin' my phone whose crews abused
I stand ac/cused of doing harm . . . 'cause I'm louder than a / bomb.

Notice that the first two lines are fairly straightforward, with the rhymes of "resident" and "president" occurring on beat 4 of their respective measures. There is a strong sense of balance in this couplet, with relatively little metric disruption. But the next two lines close out the verse by piling up a series of five rhyming "ooh" sounds: "whose," "crews," "abused," "accused," and "do." As shown in example 3.4, these syllables create a number of offbeat accents. They trip up and disrupt the song's earlier balance. And the tension is resolved when the whispered word "bomb" falls directly on the downbeat of the song's chorus (making a slant rhyme with "harm").

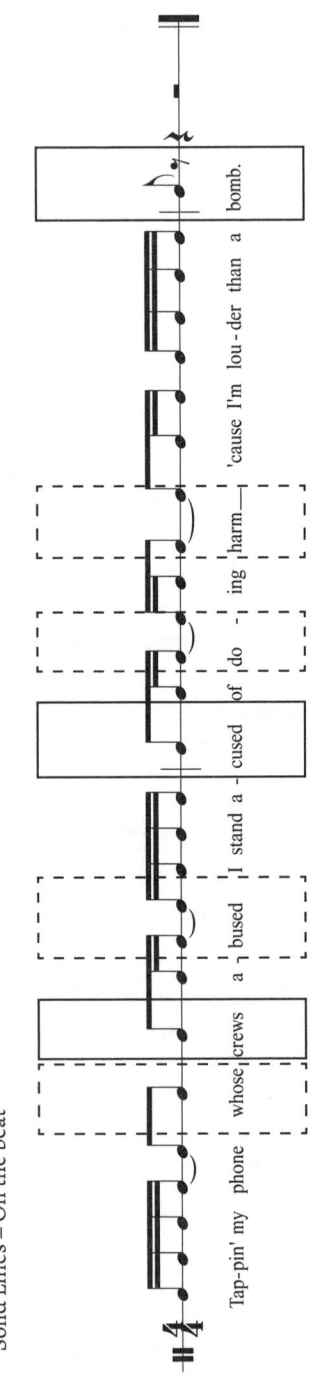

Example 3.4. Public Enemy, "Louder Than a Bomb," rhyme and syncopation

At this point, it might be useful to make a clear distinction between these last two categories: rhymes that create balanced subphrases and rhymes that create syncopation. In both cases, the rhymes segment the poems or songs into smaller units. The difference has to do with expectation and regularity. In Samuel Taylor Coleridge's "Rime of the Ancient Mariner," for example, we often hear internal rhymes that neatly divide a line into two equal halves. And as the poem progresses, these patterns become more and more predictable:

> And through the drifts the snowy clifts
> Did send a dismal sheen:
> Nor shapes of men, nor beast we ken—
> The ice was all between.[12]

In these lines, the rhymes parse the language into small subphrases of equal length: the first line has four iambic feet, and the rhymes divide it into two groups of two. Compare that with the following rhymes from Big Boi's "Shutterbug," in which the segmentation is far less regular and far less predictable (Spotify playlist, track 50, 0:39):

> I'm Sergeant / Slaughter, I keep my shit cooked to order in order
> To /satisfy my people in Georgia and 'cross the water.

The words "slaughter," "order," "Georgia," and "water" combine to create a radically destabilizing network of sounds. They break the phrases into irregular, asymmetrical chunks that keep the listener off balance, never sure where or when another rhyme might occur.

Broader Uses of Rhyme

Rhymes in music help delineate cadences, subphrases, and syncopations by segmenting the language into smaller groups, whether regular, in the case of balanced phrases and subphrases, or irregular, in the case of syncopations. The segmentation, moreover, is based on accent: rhymes draw attention to certain syllables and phonemes because of their similar sounds, a form of accent that differs from the various metric accents discussed in chapter 2. As the poet Kenneth Koch observes, "Rhyme is more obvious than meter. It's louder. It draws attention to itself and can be heard right away."[13]

But how do rhymes assert themselves over larger spans of music? How might rhymes change over the course of a song? The following case studies offer examples of how music can interact with rhyme in a long, unfolding dramatic trajectory. The first example is from late-1960s classic rock, the second from a nineteenth-century art song.

"And then you fall...": The Ecstasy of "Madame George"

Van Morrison's "Madame George" is often thought of as a rock & roll classic for rock & roll critics. Casual fans are likely to know "Brown Eyed Girl," "Wild Nights," and "Into the Mystic," but not "Madame George." It is the centerpiece of Morrison's landmark 1968 album *Astral Weeks*, but it is not radio friendly. In nearly ten minutes of music, it never once wavers from a looping, hypnotic, three-chord vamp (Spotify playlist, track 51). The lyrics, moreover, are somewhat mystifying. They are evocative, but also fragmentary in the way they loosely describe the various goings-on in a drag queen's Dublin apartment. For some, the result is aimless and interminable. For others, it represents Morrison's greatest masterpiece.

Among the song's champions, the most notorious is Lester Bangs. In a 1979 essay, he argues that "Madame George" is "possibly one of the most compassionate pieces of music ever made": "It asks us, no, *arranges* that we see the plight of what I'll be brutal and call a lovelorn drag queen with such intense empathy that when the singer hurts him, we do too.... The beauty, sensitivity, *holiness* of the song is that there's nothing at all sensationalist, exploitative, or tawdry about it." Bangs, it seems to me, sometimes reads more into these lyrics than the words actually supply—I see no evidence, for instance, that Madame George is "lovelorn," nor am I sure what Bangs means when he says that "the singer hurts him"—but he is especially convincing when writing about Morrison's uncanny ability to wring as much expressivity as possible from simple words and phrases. As Bangs eloquently puts it, "Van Morrison is interested, *obsessed* with how much musical or verbal information he can compress into a small space, and, almost conversely, how far he can spread one note, word, sound, or picture."[14] In "Madame George," this approach—this obsessiveness—is inextricably linked with a compulsive need to rearticulate certain sounds. The song is obsessed, in other words, with rhyme.

The lyrics begin by describing a vaudevillian landscape of sights, sounds, and smells:

Down on Cyprus Avenue	A
With a childlike vision leaping into view	A

Clicking, clacking of the high-heeled shoe	A
Ford and Fitzroy and Madame George	B
Marching with a soldier boy behind	C
He's much older now with hat on drinking wine	C
And that smell of sweet perfume comes drifting through	A
The cool night air like Shalimar.	D

The lyrics arrange this scene into groups of simple, balanced phrases. Each of the lines ends with a rhyming word except for the final lines of each four-line group, where the punctuating words—"George" and "Shalimar"—conspicuously avoid the sealed closure of a terminal rhyme. The line lengths and end rhymes are not entirely predictable, but the passage nevertheless offers a rather sturdy lyrical architecture, with primarily stable, symmetrical proportions (a sense of balance that will be repeated in several later sections of the song).

What I am most interested in, however, is the way these balanced frameworks eventually dissolve. This, in many ways, is the song's defining feature. Morrison paints a vivid scene—he even begins to initiate a story of sorts—but then abruptly says good-bye to Madame George by allowing the entire lyrical edifice to unravel in an ecstasy of repeated words and phrases. This becomes especially obvious at the end of the song, but there are already hints of it at the 1:38 mark when Morrison gets stuck on the phrase "that's when you fall." Structurally, these words belong to another four-line group, which is similar to the opening with its *aaab* rhyme scheme:

> That's when you fall into a trance
> Sitting on a sofa playing games of chance
> With your folded arms and history books you glance
> Into the eyes of Madame George.

These words occur at the song's 2:03 mark. But at 1:38, Morrison isolates the phrase "that's when you fall" and repeats it three times, such that "fall," "fall," and "fall" becomes its own small, three-rhyme group, preceding the eventual triple rhyme of "trance," "chance," and "glance."

This is significant. To begin with, it is the first time that the second-person narrative voice is made clear. "You" is established as a character in the scene. As will be discussed in chapter 5, Morrison's commitment to a second-person voice here is highly unusual. The pronoun "you" is ubiquitous in popular music, but it is usually matched with a first-person "I." In this song, "you" could certainly be heard as a *substitute* for "I," but we could also hear these lyrics as a true second-person address, with Morrison inhabiting a disembodied voice that narrates everything that happens to "you." We might even interpret "you" as referring to us (the listeners). By using this less common form of address—by potentially situating the listener in the context of the song—Morrison almost seems to take on the role of a singer-hypnotist. In a sense, the moment "when you fall" is the point at which he attempts to send "you" (the listener) into a trance.

But how might something like that be achieved? The art of hypnosis is strongly linked with the art of repetition ("That's when you fall ... that's when you fall ..."). It is the vehicle by which Morrison conjures a meditative, dreamlike state. Perhaps most important, it is the first hint of the way the song itself will eventually fall apart—how all those early, well-built lyrical structures will dissolve into repetitive fragments. This does not happen immediately—the song continues, after this initial hypnotic event, with more familiar *aaab* patterns—but the moment nevertheless reveals that the song can and will get stuck in obsessive loops of repetition and rhyme.

The crucial turning point, at which things truly begin to "fall," occurs at about the three-minute mark when Madame George hears what she assumes to be the police:

> And then from outside the frosty window raps
> She jumps up and says, "Lord, have mercy I think it's the cops"
> And immediately drops everything she gots
> Down into the street below
>
> And you know you gotta go
> On that train from Dublin up to Sandy Row
> Throwing pennies at the bridges down below
> And the rain, hail, sleet, and snow

The first four-line group repeats the familiar *aaab* pattern, but does so with palpably slang-oriented slant rhymes: "raps," "cops," and "gots." This is a subtle but meaningful change in diction—it gives voice, in a way, to Madame George—and it triggers a disruption in the rhyming patterns. The last line ends with "below," which then becomes the basis for the end rhymes of the entire subsequent group. The sense of leave-taking here, the retreat away from Dublin, is echoed in the disintegration of the previous pattern. It is a decisive moment, at which the lyrics begin to get lost in repetitive rhyme ("below," "go," "row," "below," "snow").

What we hear next are lines that will continually recur throughout the remainder of the song:

> Say goodbye to Madame George
> Dry your eye for Madame George
> Wonder why for Madame George

For Greil Marcus, this repetition resists the implication of the words. The lines tell us that it's time to leave, but the song won't let go. Familiar sounds recur again and again: "bye," "dry," "eye," "why," and especially "Madame George." The singer is "commanding himself," according to Marcus, to say good-bye, but he "has to keep saying it, and in that way ... the song doesn't end."[15] By this point, Morrison has begun to fully initiate the process by which the song will finally unravel into repetitive loops. But before that, one last bit of text wraps up the song proper (the 4:28 mark). These are the last words we hear before the song fixates entirely on repetition:

> And as you leave, the room is filled with music
> Laughing, music, dancing, music all around the room
> And all the little boys come around, walking away from it all, so cold
> And as you're about to leave she jumps up and says, "Hey love, you forgot your glove."

For the first time in the song, Morrison sings lines without end rhymes. There is repetition, of course, but it is no longer structured with balanced rhymes. The sense of lineation begins to break down. What I find most fascinating, however, is that this long, dizzying passage, which has *lost* end rhyme as a structuring device, nevertheless concludes by bluntly articulating a rhyme of almost childlike simplicity. Indeed, it is arguably the silliest, most "forced" rhyme of the entire song: "hey love, you forgot your glove." The music will go on for several minutes, but these are the last real lyrics of the song. All else is just repetition, echoes, and minor exhortations ("get on the train"). And given that people experience this song with such extreme profundity, it is truly remarkable that the last full line — the last words spoken by Madame George — would be so absurd.

"Love," of course, is ubiquitous in poetry and song, but it is not an easy word to rhyme. In the Elizabethan period, it was common to pair it with words that are spelled similarly but do not share the same vowel sound in modern pronunciation (for example, "love" would be rhymed with "move" and "prove"). In more contemporary settings, the common options would be "dove," "glove," and "above" ("shove" is also available but less likely). Of these possibilities, the "glove" / "love" pairing might be the hardest to work with, especially if the writer wants to avoid clichés about how a person's love "fits like a glove." Morrison's rhyme—"hey love, you forgot your glove"—has a certain playfulness to it, but it also sounds remarkably self-conscious, a rhyme for rhyme's sake. And that, perhaps, is the point. It is the definitive moment when the song begins to embrace the repetition of certain sounds *as an end in itself*.

But notice that, in addition, these are the only words in the song that are spoken directly by Madame George to "you." Up until this point, rhyme and repetition had been established as the primary vehicle by which Morrison, playing the role of singer-hypnotist, conjured ecstatic, trancelike states. But here it is the voice of Madame George that triggers the hypnotic event. And it has an immediate effect, sending Morrison spinning at the 5:10 mark with a repetitive whirlwind that almost sounds as if he's begun speaking in tongues: "the love that loves the love that loves the love that loves the love" etc.

For Bangs, Morrison is on a quest here for nothing short of "illumination." When he is at his best, Bangs argues, "The most mundane overused phrases are transformed," and Bangs zeroes in on this repetition of "love" in particular.[16] It is the quintessential case of an unpoetic statement ("hey love, you forgot your glove") being transformed into an extraordinary musical moment. Morrison lets the words ring out again and again, with a repetition that quickly becomes enveloped in the loose, improvisatory undulations of the studio musicians (especially the acclaimed bass playing of Richard Davis). For much of the song, rhyme plays an essential role in holding the lyrical architecture in balance, but it is also the agent of the song's undoing, the device that allows a transformation from vivid imagery to hypnotic trance. For several minutes after Madame George speaks, the song simply dissolves in repetition and rhyme.

Edward Elgar's "Where Corals Lie": Rhyme, Balance, and Closure

Rhymes might indeed be "loud" in poetry, but composers can choose to soften them, alter them, or amplify them in a variety of ways. To get a better sense of how they might do so, let us look, first, to the end rhymes of a poem by Richard Garnett called "Where Corals Lie" (1859):

The deeps have music soft and low
When winds awake the airy spry,
It lures me, lures me on to go
And see the land where corals lie.

By mount and mead, by lawn and rill,
When night is deep, and moon is high,
That music seeks and finds me still,
And tells me where the corals lie.

Yes, press my eyelids close, 'tis well,
But far the rapid fancies fly
To rolling worlds of wave and shell,
And all the land where corals lie.

Thy lips are like a sunset glow,
Thy smile is like a morning sky,
Yet leave me, leave me, let me go
And see the land where corals lie.[17]

This is a tightly structured poem. The four stanzas of iambic tetrameter display a rigorous pattern of end rhymes: *abab / cbcb / dbdb / abab*. There is also a great deal of repetition here. Besides the continuously thumping iambic pattern (ta-TUM ta-TUM . . .), we see the repeating refrain ("And see the land where corals lie"), as well as a constant recurrence of the long *i* sound at the end of every even-numbered line, and the circular return to the *abab* rhyme scheme in the final stanza.

If we were to hear this poem read aloud, we would almost certainly notice that end rhymes mark the conclusion of each four-beat line: "spry . . . lie . . . high . . . lie." The rhymes are among the most salient aspects of the poem. A composer, however, need not adhere to the rhyming accents in a slavish, predictable way.

Edward Elgar's setting of this poem can be heard on the Spotify playlist, track 52. It is the fourth song from his *Sea Pictures*, op. 37. The rhymes are noticeable, but we do not experience them the same way when listening to the song as we do when listening to a reading of the poem. Most obviously, the song takes more time; each stanza is stretched out over nearly forty seconds, much longer than it would take to read the words aloud. But we can find other differences as well. The rhythm and pacing of the language are more erratic in the song. Some of the rhymes can be heard clearly, but others are far less salient than they would be in a spoken version.

As shown in example 3.5, Elgar sets the first two lines with balanced two-measure phrases in which the final words in each line—"low" and "spry"—are accented in at least three ways: they occur on a downbeat, arrive at a melodic peak, and are accompanied by a stable harmony (B minor).

The subsequent rhymes, however—"go" and "lie"—are less marked in the music. To begin with, they are noticeably set apart from the previous lines by an "unnecessary" measure that occurs between the second and third phrases. But more important, the rhymes occur on "weaker" beats (beat 4 instead of beat 1), and they are accompanied by unstable harmonies. They are also compressed in time. The first two lines were spread out over two measures apiece, but the next two lines are condensed into a single measure. The accelerated pace might suggest the "lure" of the ocean deeps, but notice that Elgar calls for an expressive *allargando* (slowing of the tempo) here, which creates an odd effect: the music speeds up in one sense, but the performers *resist* the acceleration by slowing down. This compression creates temporal and harmonic effects that work against the language of the poem. In the text, the end rhymes create a sense of closure and balance. But in the song, the words "go" and "lie" are *unbalanced* and *unstable* in comparison with "low" and "spry." They create neither closure in the music, nor a sense of equilibrium. Indeed, the music is so open ended after the last line of the stanza that Elgar needs to repeat it, though with an adjustment: he places the end rhyme ("lie") on a downbeat and accompanies it with a stable chord. This "corrected" version of the line offers a resolution of the earlier tensions, but the final word "lie" nevertheless feels removed from its rhyming word "spry" seven measures earlier. In the poem, the rhyming words are tightly bound. In the music, the poetic balance is reshaped into a more complex, dramatic unfolding.

If the end of the first phrase achieves a certain degree of stability, it is only partial. The vocal melody at the phrase "where corals lie" in measures 13–15 suggests that the voice will settle into a relatively positive major key (D major, to be specific). But the piano undercuts that conclusion by arriving on a B-minor chord rather than the expected D major (musicians sometimes refer to such progressions as deceptive; see the annotations at the final cadence in example 3.5). The disjunction between piano and voice creates a sense of unease, and thus the refrain—"And see the land where corals lie"—further undermines the poem's relative stability. The music, unlike the poem, projects an unsettling duality right from the start. It does this by combining folklike melodic

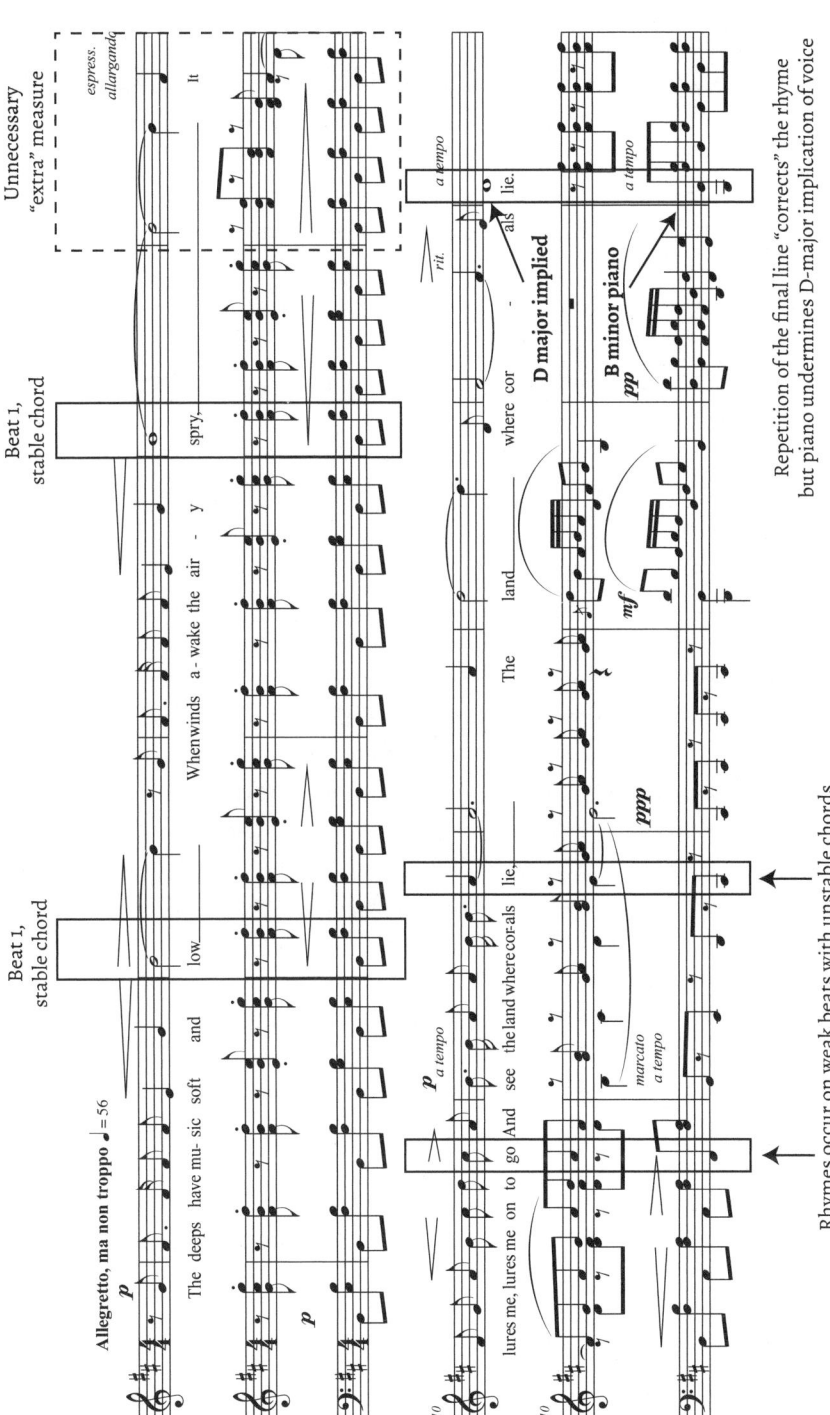

Example 3.5. Edward Elgar, "Where Corals Lie," from *Sea Pictures*, first stanza

fragments that suggest a major key (D major, mm. 9–10) with the darker shadows and offbeat rhythms of a minor key (B minor, mm. 1–4). And it does this without ever allowing a final balance between the two. One could argue that the poem also projects an uneasy duality—contrasting life and afterlife, "lawn and rill" versus ocean "deeps"—but that abstract, conceptual difference gradually arises over the course of the whole poem. The music is more palpably agitated from the start.

This uneasiness continues in the second stanza, which repeats the same music as the first, with the same complications and the same lack of closure. But the third stanza is different (example 3.6). It begins with an alarming imperative—"Yes, press my eyelids close"—which not only suggests, for the first time, a direct address to a specific individual, but also implies that the speaker might be dying or possibly dead already; the word "yes" contributes to the unsettled mood by disrupting the iambic pattern.

As we will see in chapter 5, lyrics that move toward an explicit direct address often trigger an accompanying change in the music. In this case, we hear a radical restructuring of the earlier phrase organization. To begin with, Elgar repeats the *first* line of the stanza rather than the last line. This sets the section off on a strikingly different course from the earlier music, but it also shares similarities with it. As shown in the score, the word "well" occurs on a downbeat at both statements of the stanza's opening line. The first suggests B minor while the second suggests D major. The previous harmonic duality, in other words, is still in effect. There is also another compressed acceleration in this stanza, but whereas the first and second stanzas compressed lines 3 and 4 into a single two-measure unit, here the compression occurs at lines 2 and 3. The effect, however, is the same. The words "fly" and "shell" flutter past in a hurried vocal line that "softens" those words in comparison to their louder rhyming partners ("well" and "lie"). The last line slows things down and achieves a notable sense of closure—it is the first phrase in the song to end with a stable, conclusive cadence—but it comes in the key of B minor, briefly confirming the darker, more ominous key.

The final stanza returns to the earlier music, but it readjusts the final vocal cadence so that it concludes not with a deceptive cadence but with full closure in D major, with both piano and voice arriving at the same place (example 3.7).[18]

In a sense, this offers a positive conclusion—the bright comfort of D major rather than the bleak darkness of B minor. And it seems to finally offer a punctuated musical closure that arguably matches the closure of the poetic rhymes. But even here the musical duality persists. The accompaniment extends for

Example 3.6. "Where Corals Lie," third stanza

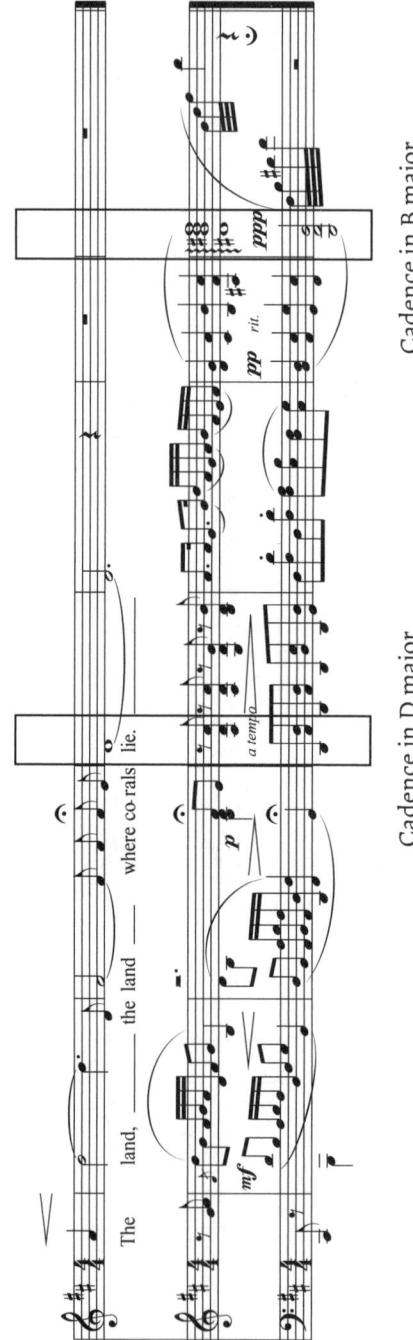

Example 3.7. "Where Corals Lie," ending

one last passage beyond the vocal cadence, and returns to the key of B, only now offering a brightening B *major* rather than the pervasive hints of B minor that we had heard earlier. The song continues to undo and revise all previous attempts at closure, even after the voice has stopped singing. And the changes in harmony and key, the continual vacillation between opposite moods creates a dramatic trajectory that not only *differs* from that of the poem; it alters and undercuts some of the poem's balance, which is based primarily on repetition and rhyme.

▆ When we think about aspiring songwriters, such as the hypothetical student from the beginning of this chapter, it is not hard to sympathize with their potential frustrations. Rhymes, like almost every other element of music and poetry, can easily lead to lifeless banality. This is also true of harmonic patterns, rhythmic groupings, formal designs, and much else. Great art often involves familiar devices ingeniously rearranged, but beginners frequently produce art that is just plain familiar, and tiresomely so.

When we study rhymes in great poems and songs, then, we may wonder why they work as well as they do. Rhymes can create a wide variety of effects, often productively interacting with the other attributes of a poem or song.

One of the most significant of these interactions is the relationship between rhyme and lineation. In chapter 2, we saw that lines of verse are often defined by regular patterns of accent, whether the common meter of a Dickinson poem or the iambic pentameter of a Shakespeare sonnet. But rhyme can also play a vital role in articulating a poetic line—it often tells us, more clearly than any other poetic feature, that a line ends *here* as opposed to *there*. Nevertheless, much else shapes how we perceive lines beyond meter and rhyme. In the next chapter I tackle this issue with a special focus on the relationship between lines and syntax.

CHAPTER FOUR

Lines and Syntax

A student sits down to write a poem. He is aware that modern poets constantly seek new ways to express their ideas, sometimes arranging words into pictures, tweets, or heavy blocks of prose, but he prefers to write in *lines*. He enjoys the way lines can seize and steer the readers' attention, affect tempo and pacing, draw them toward beats and rhymes, patterns established and patterns broken.

The student knows that lineation is one of the most powerful tools that he has at his disposal, but he finds the options overwhelming. He first considers a traditional approach, a poem in iambic pentameter. But even then questions arise: Should his lines be "end-stopped" (concluding with punctuation) like the rhymed verse of Alexander Pope?

> Is there no bright reversion in the sky,
> For those who greatly think, or bravely die?[1]

Or would that be too neat and tidy? Too balanced and predictable? Should he dispense with rhyme, perhaps, and let his sentences flow with surprising *enjambments*—line endings that offer no natural break in the syntax—as appears throughout the blank verse (unrhymed iambic pentameter) of Milton's *Paradise Lost*?

> And now their mightiest quelled, the battle swerved
> With many an inroad gored. Deformèd rout
> Entered and foul disorder. All the ground
> With shivered armor strewn and on a heap...[2]

The student marvels at Milton's coiled tensions, the way a fixed pattern of pulsing pentameter is counterpoised against a free-wheeling syntax. The syntax propels readers forward, telling them to move through the line endings and quickly shift their eyes back to the left and let the prose-like pace guide their reading, but the lines hold them back, asking them to pause and relish the last word in each neat iambic row.

This push and pull is appealing. But the student wonders if he should dispense with metric regularity altogether and allow an even greater freedom and flexibility into his lines. They could be short, like some of his favorite poems by William Carlos Williams:

> The stroke begins again—
>   regularly
> automatic
>   contrapuntal to
> the flogging
> like the beat of famous lines
> in the few excellent poems
>   woven to make you
>   gracious.³

Or they might be long and flowing, extending outward like the irrepressible verse of Walt Whitman:

> O you singer solitary, singing by yourself, projecting me,
> O solitary me listening, never more shall I cease perpetuating you.⁴

Perhaps he should blend these styles together, letting each project itself in sharp relief against the others.

He considers the options but decides not to choose—not just yet. First come up with some interesting sounds, he thinks, then see where they lead.

Lineation in Poetry

When we see lines on a page, we immediately think, "This must be poetry." Lineation transforms language into something that readers instinctively perceive as "art," even in instances when they recognize it as *bad* art. The effect is not unlike taking an everyday object and placing it on a pedestal in a museum. Here, for instance, is the first sentence of this paragraph, rewritten in "verse" lines:

> When we see
> lines on a page,
>
> we immediately
> think, "This

> must be
> poetry."

This is not poetry, of course. But it *looks* like it. Poetry, after all, involves extraordinary uses of language, and the act of organizing sentences into discrete lines is *not ordinary*. The very presence of the lines tells us that something unusual is happening.

Is lineation, then, a mere gimmick? A cheap way to elevate everyday language into an artistic statement? In the hands of bad poets, the answer is certainly yes. But any poem worthy of our attention is likely to use lineation in subtle and sophisticated ways, often creating complex interactions with the other elements of the poem, including meter, rhyme, syntax, and diction.

Lineation evolved in poetry for specific reasons. As discussed in chapter 2, poetic lines often create recurring patterns of accent: trimeters, tetrameters, pentameters, and so on. And lines can be punctuated by rhyming words to create a sense of structure. These effects are crucial, but lineation can do much more. In this chapter I focus especially on the relationship between lines and syntax, a relationship that might seem rather dry in the abstract, but that provides vital energy to many of the greatest poems and songs.

In the opening of Robert Frost's "To Earthward," something jarring happens as the poem moves from the first stanza to the second:

> Love at the lips was touch
> As sweet as I could bear;
> And once that seemed too much;
> I lived on air
>
> That crossed me from sweet things,
> The flow of—was it musk
> From hidden grapevine springs
> Downhill at dusk?[5]

What do we do when reading the word "air"? Frost clearly prepares the moment as a possible endpoint for the stanza. It seals off an *abab* rhyme scheme, a closing gesture that reinforces the stanza division. In addition, each of the first three lines has three accented syllables, but the fourth line has only two, leaving an empty space—a missing pulse—that might be heard as a kind of punctuation. Relatedly, the end of the first stanza *might* have been the conclusion of a complete grammatical sentence; indeed, it will probably sound that way to a first-time reader of the poem ("I lived on air"). All these devices cre-

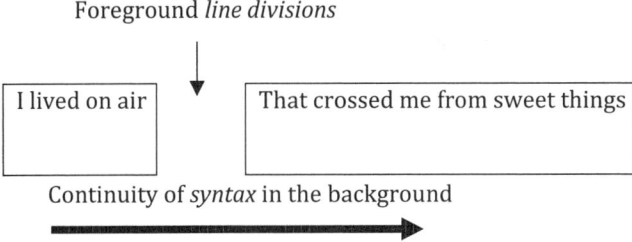

Example 4.1. A line-oriented reading of Robert Frost's "To Earthward"

ate the overwhelming feeling that the word "air" marks a point of closure. The poem, however, remains stubbornly open: there is no literal punctuation after "air," and the syntax continues with a surprising enjambment, which spans the chasm between the two stanzas: "I lived on air / that crossed me from sweet things." How, then, should we read this poem aloud?

Two possibilities might be employed. Option 1, a *line-oriented* reading, exaggerates the poem's meter and rhyme scheme and allows for a significant pause after the word "air":

> **Love** at the **lips** was **TOUCH** [short pause]
> As **sweet** as **I** could **BEAR;** [short pause]
> And **once** that **seemed** too **MUCH;** [short pause]
> I **lived** on **AIR** [long pause]
>
> That **crossed** me **from** sweet **THINGS**

With this option, we clearly hear the stanza's pattern of stressed syllables (3 + 3 + 3 + 2) and the simple *abab* end rhymes. But the syntax is violently fractured at the end of the first stanza. What happens is that we foreground certain *predictable, consistent* patterns in the lines, thereby disrupting the more *irregular* syntactic flow, which we only hear in the "background," so to speak (example 4.1).

In option 2, a *syntax-oriented* reading, each syntactic unit is read as naturally as possible, almost as if the poem moves into a kind of irregular free verse:

> Love at the lips was touch
> As sweet as I could bear;
> And once that seemed too much;
> I lived on air that crossed me from sweet things,
> The flow of—
> was it musk from hidden grapevine springs downhill at dusk?

100 Lines and Syntax

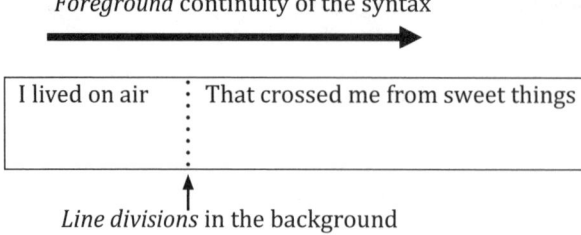

Example 4.2. A syntax-oriented reading of "To Earthward"

With this reading, the first stanza elides directly into the second without any pause whatsoever. And the same strategy applies to the question at the end of the second stanza, which is read continuously without interruption. A reader who chooses this option will foreground the *irregular* syntactic flow and hear it against the *predictable, consistent* patterns of the line divisions in the background (example 4.2).

Needless to say, we need not choose between these extreme possibilities; many readers will prefer to find a balance between the two options by subtly emphasizing the meter and rhyme scheme but also allowing for a clear, flowing movement as the syntax stretches across the stanza's boundaries. Indeed, hearing the counterpoint between line and syntax can be one of the greatest pleasures of reading verse.[6] And though we might think of the enjambments in Frost's poem as a "problem"—something that frustrates our ability to read the poem with ease—it would be better to think of them as exquisite, irresolvable tensions. Developing a keen ear for such tensions is part of what it means to become an adept reader of poetry. How, then, might such tensions be translated into song?

Lineation in Popular Music

Composers arrange the words of every song into various chunks. Because singers need to breathe at regular intervals, most songs have perceptible rests between phrases. These phrases often comprise a complete syntactic unit, and they often end with a rhyme. This is what happens, for instance, in the chorus of Whitney Houston's "How Will I Know?" (Spotify playlist, track 53, 1:29):

> How will I know if he really loves me?
> I say a prayer with every heartbeat.

When we hear melodic phrases like this, which are both clearly bracketed off from other material and conclude with a rhyme and an implied punctuation mark, it makes sense to think of them as lines, even if the lyrics were never written down on paper. Indeed, we talk about lines in pop songs all the time, and for good reason. Many song lyrics have been published in the form of written poetry, and when handwritten lyrics from great songwriters are preserved, they frequently show that the lyrics were conceived in lines and stanzas, much like a poem. For that reason, we still talk about musicians *writing* lyrics, because the act of putting pen to paper still feels like a vital aspect of the enterprise, even if some musicians now create songs entirely in studios without ever writing anything down.

Not all songs, however, are parsed as neatly as the Houston lyric above. What if the pauses in the vocal line were not aligned with rhymes or complete syntactical units? What if the phrases were deployed with irregular, unpredictable lengths? How can we know what constitutes a line, especially if we do not know what the songwriter might have had in mind? In the appendix ("Transcribing Lyrics"), I go into considerable detail addressing these questions, especially in relation to a lyric by Cole Porter. But for now, I simply want to acknowledge a basic fact: "lines" in pop songs are not especially stable entities. When faced, for instance, with a song like Björk's "Triumph of a Heart" (Spotify playlist, track 54) — a song that avoids clear end rhymes and predictable melodic phrases — five different listeners might transcribe the lyrics in five different ways (just as listeners at a reading of free verse poetry might struggle to recognize where lines begin or end). Given this uncertainty, how can we speak of a tension between lines and syntax? How can we identify enjambments if we cannot first identify a line?

These questions expose a very real problem, but one that is rarely unmanageable. Most songs offer clear signals about what might qualify as a line. Indeed, the reason we can speak of enjambments and other syntactic tensions in pop music is that the songs often *teach* us how the lines work. They do this by establishing patterns against which we hear later deviations. This is not unlike the Frost poem, which established regular metrical and rhyming patterns that eventually came into conflict with the poem's syntax.

Consider Johnny Cash's "I Walk the Line" (Spotify playlist, track 55):

> I keep a close watch on this heart of mine.
> I keep my eyes wide open all the time.
> I keep the ends out for the tie that binds.
> Because you're mine, I walk the line.

Each of the first three phrases is a complete sentence ending with a rhyming word. The rhymes occur within the space of eight equally spaced beats in the music, and clear pauses punctuate the ends of each phrase. Once we have heard this opening, we can reasonably make a basic assumption: the "lines" in this song are eight beats long and end with a rhyme. As a result, when Cash sings the culminating phrase—"Because you're mine, I walk the line"—we are likely to hear it as a single "line," despite the caesura and the internal rhyme. We do so because the song has *taught us* exactly how long we should expect lines to be (eight beats). It would be irrelevant, in that sense, whether Cash or anyone else transcribed this song differently, perhaps breaking the final line into two separate lines: "Because you're mine / I walk the line." Such visual differences are not entirely insignificant, but they are not decisive either—the musical organization is far more meaningful than any written arrangement. The song creates patterns and deviations, and it encourages a basic awareness of lineation even if we do not see the lines on the page.

Enjambments in Rap: Line Versus Syntax

Our two options for reading the Frost poem involved a conflict between predictable, consistent patterns and irregular syntactic groups. Which do we emphasize in the foreground? Which do we push into the background? In some rap music, especially in the genre's early years, this conflict does not arise. Rhyming couplets typically occur within four-beat measures, and they are often complete syntactic units. The following lines from Run DMC's "King of Rock" (1984) are representative (Spotify playlist, track 56, 1:37—the bolded syllables are stressed by the performers, but they are also supported by audible percussive beats):

> It's / **not** a trick or **treat** and it's **not** a April **fool**
> It's / **all** brand **new** never **ever** old **school.**

As with the Cash example, the song lets us hear quite clearly that each line is tethered to a predictable group of beats. And, similarly, there is no tension between the syntax and the lines.

In the late eighties, however, rappers started experimenting more frequently with different types of rhythmic flow, often resisting predictable patterns. This was especially prominent in the music of rappers like Big Daddy Kane and Rakim in the late 1980s, and it frequently occurs in modern rap as well. Listen, for instance, to a passage from Eminem's "Lose Yourself" (Spotify playlist, track 57, 3:25). These rhymes appear in the song's third verse, the longest and most virtuosic of the three:

/ All the pain inside amplified by the
/ Fact that I can't get by with my nine-to-
/ Five and I can't provide the right type of
/ Life for my family.

If you tap your foot or clap along to the beat, you will quickly notice that each of these lines occurs within a regular pattern—four beats, each punctuated by end rhymes on the fourth beat: "by the," "nine-to" (pronounced "nine-tuh"), and "type of" (pronounced "type uh"). You will also notice a distinct pause at the end of each line, which palpably interrupts the syntactic flow; the pause in the middle of the phrase "nine-to-five" is probably the most conspicuous. What happens, then, is similar to the "line-oriented" reading of the Frost poem: Eminem foregrounds the *predictable, consistent* patterns of the "line" (the four-beat pattern), which disrupts the *irregular*, backgrounded flow of the syntax. This creates a vital tension in the music, one that perhaps reinforces our sense of syntactic continuity precisely because it so vigorously disturbs it; the surprising disruption in the language draws attention to the fact that it "should" be continuous.

But listen now to a different kind of tension in the opening of Outkast's "Da Art of Storytellin' (Part 2)" (Spotify playlist, track 58):

/ Baby did you hear that? Yeah, baby I heard it too
Look / out the window, golly, the sky is electric blue
/ Mama earth is dyin' and cryin' because of you
Rainin' / cats and jackals all shackles disintegrate to resi-/due.

Here, the first three lines end with a rhyme on the fourth beat of a four-beat pattern: "too," "blue," and "you." The moment I am most interested in, however—a moment that might require several hearings to fully process—comes in the fourth line, where the last syllable of "residue" spills past the four-beat grouping and into the next measure. As with the Eminem example and the Frost poem, we have a case in which the syntax pushes past a boundary point. But this is different from the Eminem passage because there is no decisive pause or rhyme at the end of the fourth line. Instead, the flow simply spills past the four-beat boundary so that the rhyming syllable appears exactly one beat later than expected. This is an obvious case of music reflecting meaning: the "shackles" of the line seem to "disintegrate," leaving a "residual" rhyme after the expected beat.

This Outkast example, then, is analogous to the "syntax-oriented" reading of the Frost poem: a way of foregrounding the *irregular* syntax against the *predictable, consistent* patterns of the four-beat measure. This type of tension is crucial in rap and is memorably explained by Jay Z in his *Decoded* (2010): "When a rapper jumps on a beat, he adds his own rhythm. Sometimes you stay in the pocket of the beat and just let the rhymes land on the square so that the beat and the flow become one. But [other times,] the flow chops up the beat, breaks the beat into small units, forces in multiple syllables and repeated sounds and internal rhymes, or hangs a drunken leg over the last *bap* and keeps going, sneaks out of that bitch."[7] The word "enjambment" is derived from the French word for leg (*jambe*) and Jay Z references its etymology with his evocative metaphor of a "drunken leg" hanging over the last beat in a four-beat pattern. This is not unlike a similar metaphor that the poet Robert Pinsky uses in *The Sounds of Poetry*, in which he describes enjambment as a moment when "the syntax throws its leg over the hedge or low wall of the line."[8] With both authors, the metaphor suggests a transgression of boundaries, an encroachment beyond a point of closure.

Similar Tensions in Art Songs and Pop

Rap musicians write original lyrics that may or may not create tension with the accompanying musical beat. But composers of art songs face a different challenge: How might the inbuilt tensions of a poem be translated into song? Theodore Roethke's poem "The Waking," for instance, was set to music by Ned Rorem in 1961. Each line in the poem's opening tercet is a complete sentence, all in clear iambic pentameter.[9] Line, syntax, and meter are fully in sync:

> I wake to sleep, and take my waking slow.
> I feel my fate in what I cannot fear.
> I learn by going where I have to go.[10]

As the poem proceeds, the syntax changes somewhat, with lines frequently divided into smaller sentences or clauses (for example, "God bless the Ground! I shall walk softly there."). But the regular procession of end-stopped lines makes the mild enjambment in the fifth tercet especially surprising by comparison, perhaps even a bit unsettling:

> Great Nature has another thing to do
> To you and me. So take the lively air.

A sensitive reader will recognize a distinct tension, when reading these lines naturally, between the organization of the lines, with their regular stress patterns and end rhymes, and the flow of the syntax, which stretches here beyond the end of the line ("to do / To you and me").

In Western art songs, composers frequently set poems in which each line is a distinct syntactic unit. More often than not, they transform these lines into discrete melodic phrases. This is what happens at the beginning of Rorem's setting of "The Waking" (Spotify playlist, track 59). Each syllable is matched with an almost mechanical regularity to a simple, recurring pulse, and all accented syllables are placed on accented beats (example 4.3).

What happens, then, when Rorem sets the enjambment in the fifth tercet? As you can hear at the 1:41 mark of the audio recording, the voice maintains *exactly the same* rhythms of the previous phrases. Indeed, these phrases are direct repetitions of vocal melodies from earlier in the song, except they were used for unenjambed lines. What Rorem is doing, then, is choosing a "line-oriented" grouping—he is foregrounding the pentameter lines and thereby disrupting the syntactic continuity (example 4.4).

Someone who was unfamiliar with Rorem's poetic sensitivity might wonder whether he simply failed to recognize the enjambment in the poem. Why else would he break the syntax so sharply? But the piano accompaniment makes clear that he was well aware of the syntactic flow. Try listening to this passage again (the 1:41 mark), this time focusing specifically on the piano, and compare it to the song's opening. You will immediately recognize how active the piano becomes at this moment. It bridges the gap between vocal phrases by rising up to a dissonant clash in the highest register of the piece and then dissolving into loose contrapuntal tissue immediately thereafter. The vocal melody ignores the enjambment, but the piano does not.

Ultimately, the piano line reinforces the tension in the vocal part by drawing attention to its odd regularity, a regularity that interrupts the continuous flow of the syntax. The song's persona eerily repeats the same mechanical rhythms of the poetic lines, as if caught in a hypnotic, somnambulistic state. As with the Eminem example from "Lose Yourself," this approach arguably *accentuates* the syntactic continuity precisely because the vocal groups so strongly disrupt it.

Similar tensions can appear in popular music as well, as exemplified by "Little Talks," a hit song by the Icelandic group Of Monsters and Men (Spotify playlist, track 60, 0:45). The passage shown in example 4.5 is crucial. It occurs

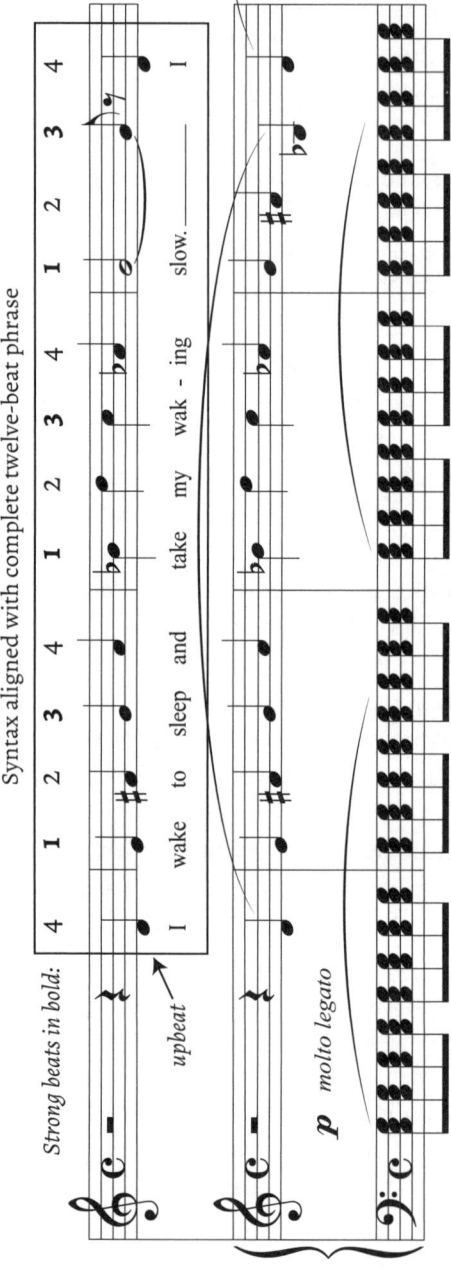

Example 4.3. Ned Rorem, "The Waking," mm. 1–4

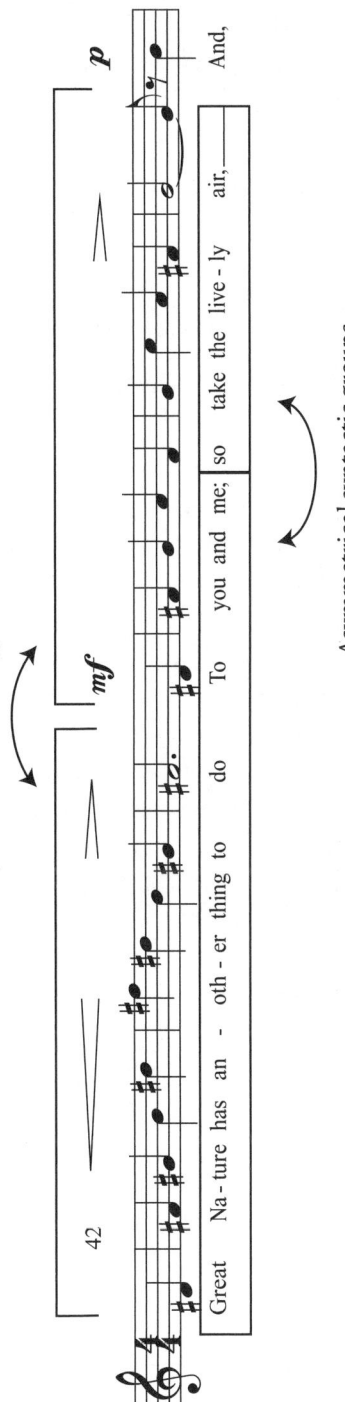

Example 4.4. "The Waking," a line-oriented enjambment

at the end of each chorus and eventually concludes the entire song. The melody parses the language in a way that strongly disrupts the continuity of the syntax, similar to my earlier line-oriented examples. A syntactically aligned grouping, however, might look like this:

> 'Cause though the truth may vary
> this ship will carry
> our bodies safe to shore

Yet as we see in the example, the melodic grouping parses the words like this:

> 'Cause though the truth may vary this
> ship will carry our
> bodies safe to shore.

Over the course of the phrase, the melody gradually relaxes into a secure, stable resting point. The musical enjambments—the way the language is jarringly interrupted at simple function words ("this" and "our")—create a sense of anticipation, a need for syntactic closure. This places the passage within a long tradition in Western music in which cadences—moments of arrival on a stable chord or note—are often preceded by some type of rhythmic or harmonic uncertainty, something tense and disruptive to make the cadence sound more stable and secure by contrast (similar to what we saw in the Kendrick Lamar and Thomas Campion songs in chapter 2). Here it produces a clear case of what is known as word painting, as the phrase eventually settles into the protected harbor of a stable major chord, bringing the melody "safe to shore."

It also has a more specific effect on the vocal melody. The similarity of "vary" and "carry" comes across clearly, but the rhyme is nicely inflected by the subsequent words ("vary this" versus "carry our"). In addition, the syllable "our" is transformed into "ore" at the cadence. This arrangement results in a string of descending vowel sounds at the end of each unit, matching the descent of the melody: "this," "our," "ore."[11] The disruptions in the syntax, in other words, allow us to hear a variety of sonic associations that would disappear if the enjambments were removed or altered.

The Rorem and Of Monsters and Men examples relate to the line-oriented reading of the Frost poem, because in both the music disrupts the syntactic flow in order to reinforce certain regular predictable groupings. But what about syntax-oriented phrases—passages like the Outkast example—in which a foregrounded syntactic flow actually fights *against* regular groupings in the music?

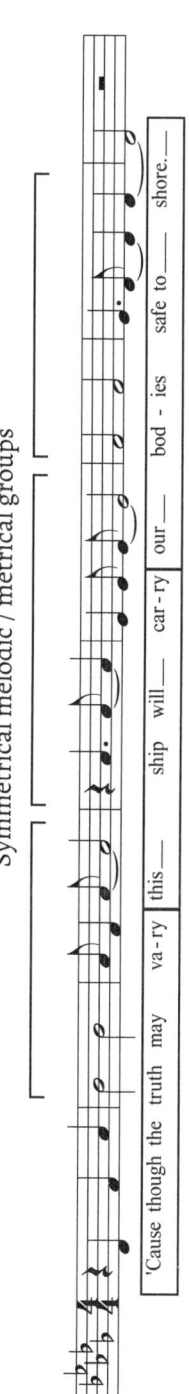

Example 4.5. Of Monsters and Men, "Little Talks," tension between melodic groupings and syntactic groupings

One of the best examples of this comes from the eminent song composer Hugo Wolf, in a phrase that is both clear enough and beautiful enough to warrant a brief detour into the complexity of late-nineteenth-century German lieder. Wolf's "Auf eine Christblume I" sets a poem by Eduard Mörike that has twenty-eight lines, twenty-five of which are end-stopped. The first enjambment comes in the poem's fifth stanza. Up to that point, Wolf has contained each of the poem's iambic pentameter lines within regular phrase groupings. Listen, for instance, to the 0:41 mark of Spotify playlist, track 61, a short passage from the song's second section (example 4.6).

This is a simple rhyming couplet with each poetic line separated into two clearly balanced musical phrases (the rhyming words are "blühtest" and "hütest"; a rough translation is "Whose hand helped you bloom here, / I do not know, nor whose grave you guard"). The poem's fifth stanza, however, begins with an enjambment:

> In deines Busens goldner Fülle gründet
> ein Wohlgeruch, der sich nur kaum verkündet;
>
> Deep within the golden abundance of your bosom lies
> a fragrance, which barely makes itself known. (Translation mine.)

Readers unfamiliar with German will understandably struggle with this language, but I call attention to a simple, crucial feature: there is no distinct syntactic break after the word "gründet." A natural, syntax-oriented reading of the poem would flow past the endpoint of the line: "gründet / ein Wohlgeruch." Wolf sets these lines against the backdrop of simple balanced phrases, but he lets the words "goldner Fülle gründet" luxuriate beyond the rigid confines of the previous musical groupings (see the 2:33 mark of the Spotify recording; example 4.7).

The first pentameter line casually meanders into the space of the second. It oversteps the expected boundary, creating a tension between the vocal melody and the recurring two-measure units (the piano continues to articulate predictable groups). This is analogous to the tensions that would occur with a syntax-oriented reading of the poem. But in the poem the syntax stretches beyond the end of the line and we can emphasize that by reading it aloud with a continuous flow, whereas in the Wolf song, the *line itself* stretches past a musical boundary (a boundary erected by metric groupings in the music that can persist independent of the poetic lines). This is an entirely different way of drawing attention to syntactic continuity.

Example 4.6. Hugo Wolf, "Auf eine Christblume I," pentameter lines in two-measure groups

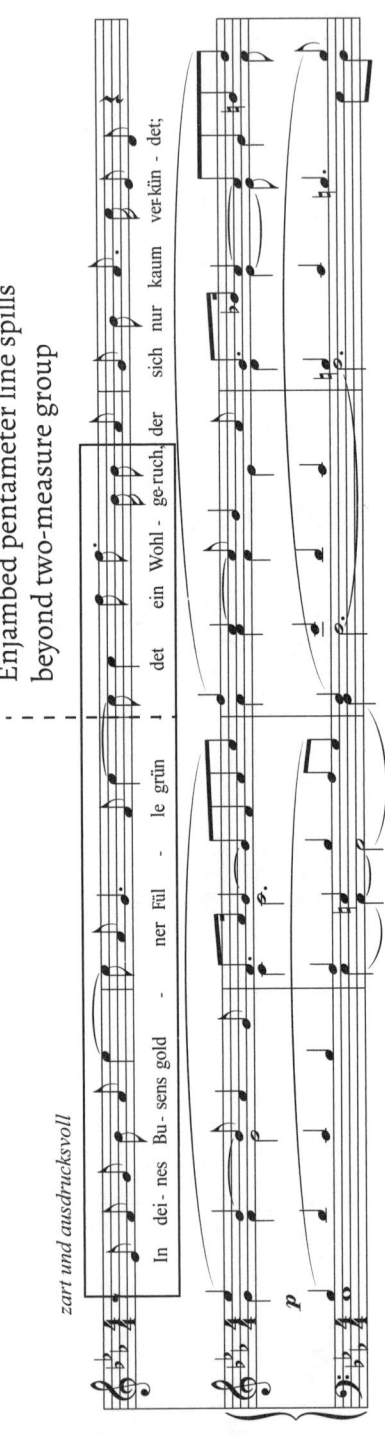

Example 4.7. "Auf eine Christblume I," a syntax-oriented enjambment

We should recognize, however, that Wolf's decision to set this particular poem to music was unusual. Most composers and songwriters avoid setting texts that feature complex enjambments. Giuseppe Verdi was explicit about this issue while working on his operas. He sometimes recommended that his librettists rephrase their lyrics so the line endings would correspond more closely with syntactic closure. Here he is, for instance, explaining why he would have to alter a particular passage in a poem by Goffredo Mameli for the patriotic hymn "Suona la tromba": "It will be necessary to have the question in the fourth line of the second verse eliminated *and to make the sense end with the line* [my italics]. I could set the lines as they are, but then the music would become difficult, thus less popular."[12] The implication is clear—unbalanced poetry leads to unbalanced phrases, and unbalanced phrases do not always appeal to the masses. As we saw above, enjambments do appear in popular music, but Verdi's concerns are understandable nonetheless.

Songs That Obscure Poetic Tensions

Thus far, we have looked at two primary types of tension among lines, phrases, and syntax. These often arise when composers set poems that involve complicated syntax and lineation. But composers sometimes obscure poetic tensions by downplaying the regular attributes of the poetic line in metrical verse. As a representative example, consider the "Sonnet" from Benjamin Britten's *Serenade for Tenor, Horn and Strings*, op. 31. This music sets the poem "To Sleep" by John Keats, which we looked at briefly in chapter 1. It begins with a single, eight-line sentence:

> O soft embalmer of the still midnight,
> Shutting, with careful fingers and benign,
> Our gloom-pleas'd eyes, embower'd from the light,
> Enshaded in forgetfulness divine:
> O soothest Sleep! if so it please thee, close
> In midst of this thine hymn my willing eyes,
> Or wait the "Amen," ere thy poppy throws
> Around my bed its lulling charities.[13]

The poem evokes the traditions of Greek prayer. It begins with an incantation, a calling forth, to the deity of sleep, who, like other deities, must be carefully named, described, and praised. But the extended "naming" of Greek prayer is typically followed by a command: for example, "come forth," "protect me," or "avenge me." The command in Keats's poem is withheld until the end of the fifth line: "close / In midst of this thine hymn my willing eyes."

This is a forceful enjambment because it introduces the main verb of the sentence (the lines boil down to a single imperative: "close ... my eyes"). But it is also jarring because it occurs after four lines that end with punctuation marks. Any composer setting the poem must make a choice about how to handle this passage in the vocal melody. For Britten, the solution was to foreground the syntax rather than the line, cleaving off the word "close" from the end of the poem's fifth line and using it to launch the sixth (Spotify playlist, track 62, 1:05; example 4.8).

This passage projects an effortless, idyllic beauty. It has none of the tension we found in the previous examples. The syntax is not in conflict with the vocal groupings (the line-oriented option), nor are these melodic phrases in conflict with any previously recurring musical groups (the syntax-oriented option). The entire song moves so slowly—forty beats per minute—and aligns the melody and syntax so thoroughly, that we never feel a strong sense that the phrasing disrupts our expectations. Other types of tension occur, of course—such as the unnerving dissonance between the strings' harmony and the voice at "O soothest Sleep!"—but the song lacks significant conflict between phrasing and syntax.

There is, however, one tension that we might still perceive: a tension between the song and the poem. I imagine that many listeners, especially modern listeners, might not recognize the rhyme scheme and pentameter lines of Keats's sonnet. Britten diffuses the language so thoroughly into flexible, slow-moving syntactic groups that it nearly transforms the poem into a kind of free verse. But listeners who are familiar with Keats's poem, or with sonnets generally speaking, might be able to hear the poem *through* the music. We might hear those pentameter lines pulsing in the background, despite the fact that Britten frequently separates them into smaller syntactical units. And we might still hear the end rhymes, even though the rhyming words do not always appear at the end of a given phrase. To hear this as a genuine tension requires sensitivity to the poem. But such tensions offer their own pleasures. And since many art songs, especially in the twentieth century, shape the music according to the poetic syntax rather than the line, it is a tension that appears frequently, even if it is imperceptible to many listeners.[14]

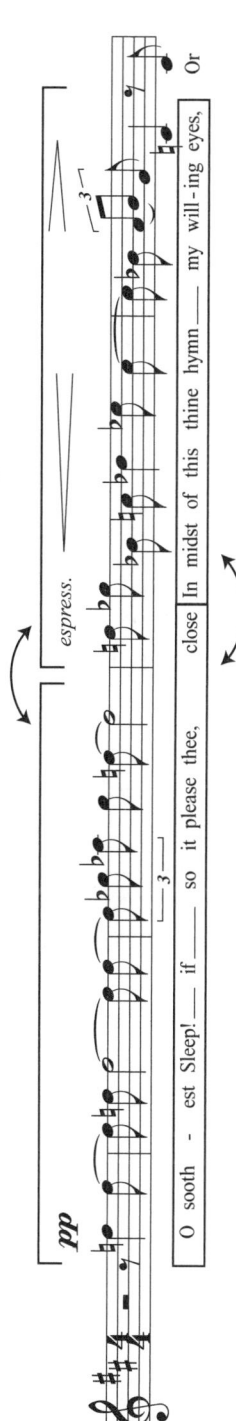

Example 4.8. An enjambment in Benjamin Britten's "Sonnet," from *Serenade for Tenor, Horn, and Strings*

The Rhythms of Syntax

The examples thus far have focused primarily on enjambment. But there are many other ways to think about poetic syntax. A reader might trace the rhythm of sentences and clauses in relation to one another; the idiosyncratic deployment of subjects, objects, and verbs; or the syntactical interruptions and complications that are sometimes contrasted with sudden, dazzling simplicity. All these can be relevant to song, and although the possibilities are too numerous to cover here in any comprehensive way, a few specific examples will be useful.

Outkast and Anne Sexton's "The Truth the Dead Know"

Anne Sexton's poem "The Truth the Dead Know" begins:

> Gone, I say and walk from church,
> refusing the stiff procession to the grave,
> letting the dead ride alone in the hearse.
> It is June. I am tired of being brave.[15]

Sexton reads this poem on the Spotify playlist, track 63. The first three lines are a single sentence, but she parses them into four-beat groups that subtly change as they go. The first line is rigidly trochaic, and Sexton marks the heavy stresses with a marching rhythm: "**Gone,** I **say** and **walk** from **church.**" It is assertive and direct, a clear, fixed, duple pattern: ONE and TWO and THREE and FOUR. By line 3, however, the poetic rhythm moves much more fluidly, and we can hear a sense of acceleration as Sexton produces a wave of light, dactylic triplets: "**letting** the **dead** ride a**lone** in the **hearse.**" The "stiff procession" of the first line is disrupted (or "refused") in the second line and completely transformed into a waltz by the third line: ONE-and-uh-TWO-and-uh-THREE-and-uh-FOUR. But the real power of this quatrain comes at the end, when the long unspooling sentence of the first three lines is contrasted with two, shorter sentences that slam on the brakes: "It is June. I am tired of being brave." This is a disruptive shift, and it fittingly rejects the dreariness of the opening, funeral-march rhythm. The midline caesura in particular stops short the flowing triplets of the previous line. Sexton's reading, with her matter-of-fact pronunciation of "June" and "tired," drives home the point. The whole stanza enacts a subtle rebellion against the "stiffness" of the opening line.[16]

None of the lines in this stanza is enjambed. They all end with punctuation. But the rhythm and pacing of the syntax plays a crucial role in generating tension and drama. Such tension can be vital in song as well. Just because a melodic phrase ends with syntactic closure does not mean that it will not have any interesting attributes regarding syntax generally speaking. Let us return, for instance, to Outkast's "Da Art of Storytellin' (Part 2)." In the earlier discussion, I focused on the way the rapper's flow in the fourth line of the song charges past the expected four-beat grouping:

> Rainin' / cats and jackals all shackles disintegrate to resi-/due.

But notice that there are also *internal* syntactic tensions in the three preceding lines:

> / Baby did you hear that? Yeah, baby I heard it too
> Look / out the window, golly, the sky is electric blue
> / Mama earth is dyin' and cryin' because of you

All these lines end with strong syntactic closure, and each is punctuated by an end rhyme on beat 4 of the measure. They also have the same consistent vocal rhythm: each syllable is articulated as a string of equally spaced pulses (four per beat). If we mark off each *beat* with double lines, the grouping of the first line would look like this: "|| ba-by-did-you || hear-that-yeah-ba-||-by-I-heard-it || too." The language pours forth in an unchecked flow, even though the syntax is remarkably varied. Line 1 features dialogue, which, if read naturally, might sound like this:

PERSON ONE: Baby (pause), did you hear that? (pause)
PERSON TWO: Yeah, baby (pause), I heard it too (pause)

But this is not natural speech, and André 3000, the rapper on this track, delivers the line with an unbroken, machine-gun precision. There is a wonderful tension, in other words, between the symmetrical string of equally spaced syllables and the asymmetrical grouping of the syntax. The same thing happens in the next line, but now the syntactical groups are slightly varied, though still presumably in dialogue (PERSON ONE: "Look out the window"; PERSON TWO: "Golly, the sky is electric blue"). The third line, however, consists of a continuous syntactic flow issued by a unitary voice ("Mama Earth is dyin' and cryin' because of you"). And the momentum from that unbroken syntax arguably generates the necessary energy to catapult the next line beyond its four-beat boundary (as happens when it "disintegrates to residue"). Internal rhymes play a significant role in these effects. The first two lines have no obvious internal rhymes. The third line, where the syntax begins to flow more steadily, speeds up with a short, simple internal rhyme ("dyin' and cryin'") and the fourth line, where things fall apart, careens ahead with a much more complex mouthful of rhymes ("cats and jackals all shackles").[17] In some ways, this acceleration is the opposite of what happens in the Sexton poem: there the lines featured a continuous syntactic flow at the beginning leading to small broken sentences at the end; here the passage begins with small syntactic units that become longer and more continuous at the end. These two examples have many other differences as well, of course (among other things, the former involves irregular speech rhythms while the latter is tethered to a metronomic grid), but in both cases the syntactical groupings create powerful tensions even when they do not involve enjambments.

"Closer" by the Chainsmokers

In 2016, the Chainsmokers, a duo of American DJs, released the song "Closer," which became a massive pop hit with its especially catchy chorus (Spotify playlist, track 64, 0:49):[18]

> So / baby pull me closer
> in the / backseat of your Rover
>
> that I / know you can't afford.
> Bite that / tattoo on your shoulder.
>
> Pull the / sheets right off the corner
> of the / mattress that you stole
>
> from your / roommate back in Boulder.
> We ain't / ever gettin' older.

This sounds nothing like the Outkast example, but the words are articulated with a similar equally spaced regularity. There are exactly two syllables per beat for the entire chorus with only two exceptions (a brief pause after the words "afford" and "stole").

I have transcribed the lines into four groups of two because the repeating chord loop is two lines long (eight beats total). But notice that this chord-based grouping—2 + 2 + 2 + 2—is only one way to parse these lines. The first complete grammatical sentence is three lines long, followed by a one-line sentence. That pattern then repeats, which yields a grammatical grouping of 3 + 1 + 3 + 1.[19]

> So / baby pull me closer
> in the / backseat of your Rover
> that I / know you can't afford.
>
> Bite that / tattoo on your shoulder.
>
> Pull the / sheets right off the corner
> of the / mattress that you stole
> from your / roommate back in Boulder.
>
> We ain't / ever gettin' older.

Notice also that the rhyme scheme draws our attention to a very *different* grouping. Three lines end with perfect rhymes ("shoulder," "Boulder," and "older") and three lines end with related slant rhymes ("closer," "Rover," and "corner"). The only pauses in the melody occur after the lines that end *without* rhyme — "I know you can't afford" and "mattress that you stole" — lines that draw attention to negative attributes. If we group the chorus according to rhyming lines versus nonrhyming lines (making no distinction, for the moment, between slant rhymes and perfect rhymes), we get the following grouping: 2 + 1 + 2 + 1 + 2.

> So / baby pull me *closer*
> in the / backseat of your *Rover*
>
> that I / know you can't afford.
>
> Bite that / tattoo on your *shoulder.*
> Pull the / sheets right off the *corner*
>
> of the / mattress that you stole
>
> from your / roommate back in *Boulder.*
> We ain't / ever gettin' *older.*

There is a palpable tension, then, between at least three different grouping mechanisms: the chord loops, the grammatical sentences, and the rhyme scheme. An underlying complexity persists despite the fact that, in many ways, this is an extraordinarily simple chorus. The melody focuses obsessively on just three notes, and it is supported by a straightforward, highly formulaic three-chord loop. If the lyrics had been written with more predictable syntax and rhymes, this simplicity might have been fatal to the song's success. But as it stands, the tensions between symmetrical and asymmetrical patterns infuse the track with an energy that no doubt contributes to its widespread appeal. None of these lines features especially strong enjambments, but we can still trace syntactic rhythms that operate in tension with other musical and linguistic groups.

"Alexander Hamilton"

The opening number of Lin-Manuel Miranda's *Hamilton* has been justifiably celebrated for its wordplay and elaborate rhyme schemes, but it is also remarkable in the way its syntactic rhythms unfold. The text of the first four measures, including the anacrusis (Spotify playlist, track 65), reads:

> How does a / bastard, orphan, son of a whore and a
> / Scotsman, dropped in the middle of a forgotten
> / Spot in the Caribbean by Providence, impoverished, in / squalor,
> Grow up to be a hero and a scholar?[20]

This is a dense, complicated sentence, and its complexity starts with the word "bastard." That might have been the only descriptive word applied to Hamilton, in which case the sentence would have been quite simple and short: "How does a bastard grow up to be a hero and a scholar?" Instead, "bastard" is the first of several modifiers that allow the sentence to branch off into vivid descriptors of unequal length. It starts with three nouns: "bastard," "orphan," and "son." But the word "son" triggers a prepositional phrase that stretches the sentence out farther: "son of a whore and a Scotsman." After that there is a shift toward adjectives—"dropped," "impoverished," and "in squalor"—but "dropped" is modified by a string of prepositional phrases that sends the sentence careening even farther outward: "dropped (in the middle) (of a forgotten spot) (in the Caribbean) (by Providence)." It then returns to shorter units with "impoverished" and "in squalor." If we represent the word "bastard" and its modifications in separate lines, it looks like this:

- Bastard
- Orphan
- Son of a whore and a Scotsman
- Dropped in the middle of a forgotten spot in the Caribbean by Providence
- Impoverished
- In squalor

We can easily see that the units expand and contract irregularly, and also how they push against the boundaries of the four-beat measures. It is almost as if the sentence itself enacts the improbability of what it describes. Hamilton's unlikely path from the humble to the heroic is mirrored in the twisting, maze-like path of the syntax, which takes several complex turns before reaching a conclusion.

But equally important, sentences such as these contrast with sentences of differing length and complexity. The initial verses of this opening number, sung by the character Aaron Burr and others, tend to be long, like the excerpt above. But the complexity of those opening sentences puts a spotlight on Hamilton's signature entrance (1:18):

> Alexander Hamilton.
> My name is Alexander Hamilton.

The simplicity of this—the meekness and humility of the moment—is bolstered by its contrast with the earlier linguistic complexity. If the musical had opened with these lines, if would have been far less effective. And the contrast does not end there. The character Eliza brings back a layered, syntactical intricacy—"When he was ten his father split, full of it, debt ridden . . ."—but the entire set piece ends with a climax of short, direct sentences from a variety of characters (3:31):

> Me? I died for him.
> Me? I trusted him.
> Me? I loved him.
> And me? I'm the damn fool that shot him.

The brevity of the sentences creates a series of punctuated conclusions. And the difference from the earlier grammatical complexity is essential.

This is a musical number full of contrasts—contrasting characters, contrasting styles of singing, contrasting musical textures—and one could easily see how variations in linguistic syntax might not be the first thing a listener would attend to. But the language of *Hamilton* is one its greatest sources of pleasure, and the rhythm of the music is fully intertwined with the rhythm of the syntax.[21]

"Under Pressure"

As a final example, let's consider an exceptional moment at the end of Queen's 1982 hit "Under Pressure," a duet between Freddie Mercury and David Bowie. The song peaks with a stadium rock climax about two and a half minutes into the song when Mercury belts out a repeated question: "Why can't we give love one more chance?" Bowie then responds with a single, extended, run-on sentence, remarkable for its sheer extravagance (backslashes indicate the beginning of measures; lines are organized according to four-measure phrases; Spotify playlist, track 66, 2:52):

> 'Cause / love's such an / old-fashioned
> / word and love / dares you to / care for the / people on the
> / edge of the / night and love / dares you to / change our way of
> / caring a-/ bout ourselves.

Most of the sentences in this song are short, sometimes reduced to simple fragments (for example, "people on streets" or "no man ask for"). But this is something entirely different: a run-on sentence that not only stitches together several subphrases but also radically—and ungrammatically—shifts pronouns from "you" to "our." As transcribed above, the sentence features the same kind of enjambments that I have discussed throughout this chapter, fitting itself uneasily against a grid of four-measure groups. But it also stands out for its linguistic oddity. Bowie's voice cannot match the virtuosity of Freddie Mercury's, but he offers instead a soulful counterpoint to Mercury's vocal pyrotechnics. And the moment is exquisitely staged. It represents an apotheosis of sorts, a culminating gesture in which the sprawling syntax heightens a variety of complex musical tensions.

Three attributes, in particular, stand out. First, we see a metrical tension that arises when the melody begins grouping pulses into asymmetrical units of 3 + 3 + 2 (example 4.9). This is not an uncommon rhythm in popular music—it is ubiquitous in the blues/rock tradition, and it also appears in the music of many other cultures, probably originating in West African drumming—but Queen's use of it here is especially suggestive in the way it creates a sense of struggle, an almost limping gait. The tension is particularly poignant when paired with a second tension, namely, the wedge-like contrary motion between the voice, which goes up, and the bass, which goes down (table 4.1).

The bass features a continually looping descent of four notes, D, C#, B,

1	2	3	1	2	3	1	2	3	1	2	3	1	2
Love's			such			an			old-			fash-			ioned	

| Eight pulses, divided asymmetrically as 3 + 3 + 2 | Eight pulses, divided asymmetrically as 3 + 3 + 2 |

Example 4.9. Asymmetrical groupings in Queen, "Under Pressure"

and A (only part of which is represented in table 4.1), and the voice struggles upward against that descending energy. After Mercury's high-pitched climax, Bowie rises up with an almost oracular pronouncement, sometimes clashing with the bass notes by continually fighting upward. When he reaches "word" (see the table), we hear an especially dissonant interval (a major seventh); the melody is seeking the note D, but it does not reach it on the downbeat and only resolves on the next beat at "and."

These two tensions—the staggering, asymmetrical rhythm and the clashing, contrary motion—account for much of the expressiveness of this moment. But a third tension, this one syntactical, is also relevant. Much like the melody itself, Bowie's syntax keeps pressing ahead, using the word "love" as a recurring launch pad: "love's such … love dares … love dares …" What starts with an almost accusatory "you" transforms into a communal "our": "love dares *you* to change *our* way of caring." Moreover, when Bowie takes a breath, this too creates a tension with the syntax, but in a way that differs from the other aspects of musical phrasing (such as the four-measure phrases). You can hear audible inhalations, for instance, at the following moments: "'Cause love's such an old-fashioned word (breath) and love dares you (breath) to care for (breath) the people on the (breath) edge of the night (breath)."[22] Little of this is predictable, and it clearly cuts against the syntactic groupings, almost like the labored breath of a person who tries to speak after climbing a flight of stairs. The entire passage, then, unfolds as a physical achievement, gradually rising upward despite palpable obstacles.

Yet the heroic aspects of the passage are potentially undercut by the pessimistic implications of Bowie's lyric. His words seem to suggest that we *won't* give love another chance, not only because it is "old-fashioned," but also because it asks us to do too much; the final lines of the song are "This is our last dance / This is ourselves under pressure." I suspect, however, that many

Table 4.1. Contrary motion between voice and bass in Queen, "Under Pressure"

F♯						
E						love
D						and
C♯					ioned word	
B				fash-		
A			an old-			
G		such				
F♯	love's					

BASS NOTES DESCENDING:

B → A   D → C♯

listeners hear a positive message at this point in the song. Much of that can be explained by its musical features, especially the upward surge of Bowie's melody, but the effect is also bolstered by the syntactic extravagance, the continual spilling forth of the language beyond repressive musical boundaries. It suggests an optimistic assertion that people *will* change, even if the lyrics refuse to say so. The enjambments are especially relevant here, but so too is the simple sense of *difference*, the way these words work against so much else in the song."[23]

Poets have long recognized the powerful tensions that can arise between lines and syntax. They are just as vital in the Elizabethan poems of Shakespeare as they are in the modern poetry of Marianne Moore. Music scholars tend to be less sensitive to these issues, but, as I have shown throughout this chapter, tensions among lines, phrases, and syntax can have a dramatic impact on songs in a variety of styles and genres. Such tensions will not always be relevant to the analysis of a given song (nor will syntax necessarily be an important feature of a given poem), but when they are relevant, we should think carefully about what roles they might play within the larger context of a complete song.[24] Even relatively local effects can have far-reaching implications, often interacting with other crucial poetic devices. Some of these devices include pronoun shifts and changes in narrative voice—as we saw in the Queen and Outkast examples—which raises an essential question that will be addressed in the next chapter: Who is singing to whom?

CHAPTER FIVE ||||||||||||||||||||||||||||||||||||||||||||||||||||||||||||

Address

That's another way of writing a song, of course. Just talking to somebody that ain't there. That's the best way. That's the truest way.
—Bob Dylan

Who speaks to whom in a poem? Who sings to whom in a song? In some ways, these are odd—perhaps even absurd—questions to ask. Songs and lyric poems are not like operas, novels, or films. In most cases, they are too brief to relay extensive information about whatever fictional characters might inhabit their strange, imaginative worlds. Nevertheless, as we will see throughout this chapter, poems and songs often foreground certain shifts in tone and address that make the question "Who speaks to whom?" especially pressing, even if it remains unanswerable.

Consider the poem "Old Couple" by Charles Simic. The first three stanzas paint a stark picture of an elderly couple anticipating a painful death.

> They're waiting to be murdered,
> Or evicted. Soon
> They expect to have nothing to eat.
> In the meantime, they sit.
>
> A violent pain is coming, they think.
> It will start in the heart
> And climb into the mouth.
> They'll be carried off in stretchers, howling.
>
> Tonight they watch the window
> Without exchanging a word.
> It has rained, and now it looks
> Like it's going to snow a little.

In the fourth and final stanza, something changes—an "I" appears:

> I see him get up to lower the shades.
> If their window stays dark,
> I know his hand has reached hers
> Just as she was about to turn on the lights.[1]

This is a radical shift. Most first-time readers will probably assume that the opening stanzas are spoken by an omniscient third-person narrator, someone who not only sees the old couple but has access to their thoughts: "a violent pain is coming, they think." The ending, however, disrupts that assumption. The appearance of the "I" raises immediate questions. Is this "I" a character in the same general environment as the old couple, someone who watches them, perhaps from an opposite window in an apartment or house? Or is the "I" Charles Simic, the author of the poem, who enters the text in order to narrate his own creative act, saying, in effect, "I am imagining this old man, and as I do so . . . I see him get up to lower the shades"? Both possibilities seem plausible, but the "I" could also be imagined and understood in many other ways. How could we settle the issue with any certainty?

The simple truth is that we cannot. Lyric poems rarely give us enough information to respond to the question "Who speaks to whom?" with a clear, definitive answer. This does not mean that we should not ask the question, but it does suggest that we might usefully modify it by breaking it down into several more pointed questions, such as, How does the lyric present certain kinds of communicative acts? What are the expressive effects of the enacted discourse? and How would the poem be different if the modes of address were changed or altered?

In Simic's "Old Couple," we know very little about the "I" of the poem, but we do know that the *appearance* of the "I" has a forceful effect. Most important, it activates a web of complexity regarding positions of distance and intimacy. The poem concludes by suggesting a private, physical gesture: the old man touching his wife's hand behind a closed shade in the dark.[2] And yet this intimacy—the way the poem "zooms in" on those hands—is presented simultaneously with our sudden knowledge that although the "I" is somehow in close proximity to the couple, he or she is apparently outside of their living quarters, with a voyeuristic gaze now obscured by the closed shade.

The poem begins with specters of death, starvation, and eviction. In the third stanza, it presents a quiet description of the weather. At the end, it offers an imagined gesture of tender intimacy. But this "softening" trajectory might have been achieved with different pronouns and different modes of address.

What if the poem had begun with the couple themselves as the speakers ("*We're* waiting to be murdered")? What if it had ended not with the entrance of an "I" but with the entrance of a "you" ("*You* see me get up to lower the shades")? Its effect would be dramatically different in both cases. As it stands, the poem moves from a somewhat chilled description of horrifying scenarios to a quiet tenderness at the end, but it also moves from a position of apparent omniscience to a point of limited—perhaps even dubious—speculation. This effect would be lost if the couple narrated their own thoughts and actions. We would lose that crucial movement toward a limited, not fully reliable narrator. And if the poem introduced a "you" instead of an "I" at the end, it would redirect the poem's camera *outward* toward us (the readers) rather than *inward*, where the lonely "I" looks across at a couple who cannot really be seen at all.

Poems, Prayers, and Pink Floyd

The poet Robert Hass writes that "the impulse of prayer seems to be very near the origin of the lyric."[3] Many of our oldest poems are prayers, and they are often based on a simple structure, which Hass summarizes succinctly as "praise, then ask." We see this in ancient Greek prayers to gods like Apollo and Athena, and we see it in a great many Christian prayers (such as "Our Father" and "Hail Mary"). We also see it in Romantic poetry, such as Keats's sonnet "To Sleep," discussed in chapter 4. These addresses to a god involve statements of meditation and devotion that can easily be transferred from the sacred to the sexual by replacing the divine with the beloved.

The link between lyric and prayer is important because it helps explain the importance of the "I" and the "you." Many modern lyrics, like ancient prayers, involve an effusive address to a loved one. As the poet Rosanna Warren explains, "After [the] early Greeks, the lyric cry rolls down the centuries, inflected differently in different eras and languages, but usually saying or pleading or insisting 'I want' and 'I hurt.'"[4] When we read poems and listen to songs, we often enjoy a pleasurable catharsis by adopting the role of the song's "I," sometimes imagining the outpouring of emotion as our own. For this reason, no doubt, most modern songs—art songs and popular songs both—involve a first-person narrator, usually addressing a specific "you."

This also helps explain the *unpopularity* of songs that tell stories with a consistent third-person narrative (such as songs in the tradition of historical ballads). To paraphrase Warren, we prefer to hear "I want" and "I hurt," rather than "she wants" or "he hurts." Many popular songs do involve third-person stories, but the third person is rarely maintained for an entire song. Paul McCartney's Beatles songs, for instance, sometimes involve colorful tales about fictional characters, but the impulse toward a personal outpouring of emotion almost always arises at some point in the song. "Eleanor Rigby," for instance, has verses in the third person, but the chorus shifts to an imperative direct address: "Ah, look at all the lonely people." Other songwriters will maintain third-person narratives throughout but include quoted dialogue that allows for a more personalized effusive outburst. Bon Jovi's "Livin' on a Prayer," for instance, begins from a position of third-person distance—"Gina works the diner all day"—but it then moves toward quoted dialogue ("She says, 'We've gotta hold on to what we've got'"). By the time we reach the chorus, we may have forgotten entirely that the lyrics are still the quoted speech of a fictional character ("'Take my hand, we'll make it I swear'").

All of this suggests that voice and address are inextricably tied to expressions of intimacy and distance. And it goes without saying that these are linguistic features that can be powerfully amplified by music. Pink Floyd's "Wish You Were Here" (1975) echoes, in some ways, the paradoxes of Simic's "Old Couple." Like the poem, the song arrives at its most intimate point at the end, but its intimacy also acknowledges a strong sense of distance. Here is the concluding verse (Spotify playlist, track 67, 3:14):

> How I wish, how I wish you were here.
> We're just two lost souls swimming in a fish bowl,
> Year after year.
> Runnin' over the same old ground
> What have we found?
> The same old fears.
> Wish you were here.

This is the second of two vocal sections in the song, and though the music is largely the same as that of the first section, it features an unmistakable surge in texture, dynamics, and melodic expression. It is the song's emotional core. But it is also the pinnacle of a larger musical and lyrical trajectory, which begins with an early movement from distance to intimacy that happens entirely in the sonic dimension.

The first thing we hear in the album version, before the song proper begins, is the crackling of an AM radio, the sound of someone switching between stations (talk radio, Tchaikovsky). Soon after, the song locks in on the jangling chords of a twelve-string guitar (the 0:16 mark). But this guitar is filtered to sound like another radio transmission, music arriving from far away, faintly and imperfectly. After about forty seconds, the distant guitar begins to repeat its chord progression in a loop, but now we hear the entrance of an acoustic guitar soloing above (0:57). Most important, the new guitar is in the forefront of the mix; it sounds *present*. Soon after this, the "distant" guitar disappears, replaced entirely by the strumming of the "nearer" guitar. We then hear the song's first words, ushered in by the warmth of a C-major chord: "So, so you think you can tell..." The entire introduction leads from a point of detached distance to a state of direct intimacy.

The first verse continually emphasizes the pronoun "you," but with the notable absence of an "I" (the 1:33 mark). The lyrics come across as accusatory, with questions that seem to probe for weakness and personal failing ("Did they get you to trade your heroes for ghosts?"). But David Gilmour's voice is not unsympathetic. And there is a sense of desperation in the expanding litany of questions, repeatedly calling out to a specific "you" but giving the ominous impression that this "you" is not available to respond.

After an instrumental interlude, the song arrives at the effusive climax ("How I wish you were here"). It is the first moment in the song in which it becomes clear that the "you" is not physically present, and yet, paradoxically, it is the most intimate moment. One of the things that makes it immediately expressive is that we finally hear the pronoun "I." The accusatory tone of the opening is fully dispensed with, so much so that we might imagine this as an entirely different voice, or perhaps a different side of the same persona. And after the "I" appears, it quickly leads to a "we"—"we're just two lost souls"— a gesture that draws the "I" and the "you" closer together, despite what appears to be an unbridgeable distance. Notice also that the final line of the song (as well as its title) is the most colloquial phrase we hear. In a song that often uses high-minded poetic imagery ("two lost souls swimming in a fish bowl"), it stands out as a simple, heartfelt expression, something that real people might actually say to one another: "wish you were here."

Paths Toward Intimacy in Song

Intimate confession and direct address have been fundamental to Western lyric poetry at least since the time of Sappho (sixth–seventh century BCE). It is no surprise, then, that songs that begin from a position of distant reflection will ultimately turn toward a more intimate mode of address. In popular music, shifts of address often happen within the context of verse-chorus forms (or the tripartite variant: verse-prechorus-chorus). The chorus typically involves a heightening of energy and emotional intensity, and a shift in tone, diction, or address can amplify the effect. Here are a few examples from rock music:

- The Rolling Stones, "Ruby Tuesday" (1967), Spotify playlist, track 68
- Verse, third person (0:00): "She would never say where she came from"
- Chorus, direct address (0:36): "Goodbye, Ruby Tuesday..."

- The Police, "Don't Stand So Close to Me" (1980), Spotify playlist, track 69
- Verse, third person (0:36): "Young teacher, the subject of schoolgirl fantasy"
- Chorus, direct address (1:03): "Don't stand so close to me"

- Paul Simon, "You Can Call Me Al" (1986), Spotify playlist, track 70
- Verse, third person (0:14): "A man walks down the street..."
- Chorus, direct address (0:43): "If you'll be my bodyguard, I can be your long-lost pal"

We could also find many examples in which a shift occurs as the song moves from one verse to another, as in "Wish you were here," often reserving a climactic change of address for the final verse. In such cases there is usually no significant structural change in the music, which would necessarily result in a different section (such as a bridge). Rather, musical changes, if they happen at all, are relegated to variations in the vocal melody, timbral changes, or changes in dynamics and texture. Think, for instance, of the moment in U2's "Pride (In the Name of Love)" when the song's persona addresses Martin Luther King directly: "Free at last they took your life, but they could not take your pride." Or the moment in Andrew Lloyd Webber's "Memory" from *Cats* at which the final verse shifts into an extravagant direct address: "Touch me, it's so easy to leave me.... If you touch me, you'll understand what happiness is." In both songs, the earlier verses avoid direct address, reserving it for an explosive culminating moment.

In rap songs, changes of voice and address often take place with whiplash frequency, but they also sometimes occur in clearly structured ways. In chapter 4, we saw how Eminem creates tensions between lines and syntax in the third verse of "Lose Yourself." But notice also how the song moves through Eminem's origin story from the past to the present with pronoun shifts that amplify the song's rising anger and disillusionment (Spotify playlist, track 57). The first verse is in the third person ("his palms are sweaty"), but in the second verse we hear a brief first-person intrusion ("this world is mine"). The third verse fully adopts the first-person perspective ("I'm 'a change what you call rage") but also includes a brief moment of direct address ("Mom, I love you"). And all of this is interspersed with the direct-address imperative of the chorus ("lose yourself..."). The song, in other words, tracks a clear path from a position of distance (third-person storytelling) to a position of intimate first-person confession and direct address. These changes ultimately amplify the song's rising anger, with the third verse, the longest of the three, providing the most virtuosic rhythmic and metrical complexity to match the intensity of the expression.

Composers of art songs often choose to set poems that feature similar movement toward more intimate language. Ruth Crawford's "White Moon," a setting of the poem "Baby Face" by Carl Sandburg, presents an example in which the music changes dramatically along with a shift in poetic address (Spotify playlist, track 71). The poem begins with descriptive imagery: "White Moon comes in on a baby face / The shafts across her bed are flimmering." There is a sense of cinematic distance here—we are told about *a* baby, not *my* baby or *your* baby. But the poem ends with a turn toward intimacy, a direct prayer to the moon as if issued by a loving parent:

> Keep a little of your beauty
> And some of your flimmering silver
> For her by the window to-night
> Where you come in, White Moon.[5]

The piano part throughout the song projects sonic imagery that most listeners are likely to identify with the poem's "flimmering" moonlight (example 5.1), but the turn toward direct address silences the piano. The singer's enchanting entreaty, with its wide leaps and angular contours, leaves the moon stunned in rapt attention. Time stops for a moment. Only after several beats of unaccompanied address does the moonlight begin again its "flimmering" movement (refer to the 1:06 mark of the recording; example 5.2).

A similar turn toward direct address happens in Igor Stravinsky's "In Memoriam Dylan Thomas." In 1954, shortly after Thomas died, Stravinsky decided to set to music his most famous poem, "Do not go gentle into that good night" (Spotify playlist, track 72). Like Sandburg's "Baby Face," the poem concludes with an entreaty, but the child-parent relationship is reversed. After five tercets seemingly addressed to a broad audience, the poem makes a sudden "turn" and reveals itself as a poignant, intimate prayer, a son's supplication to

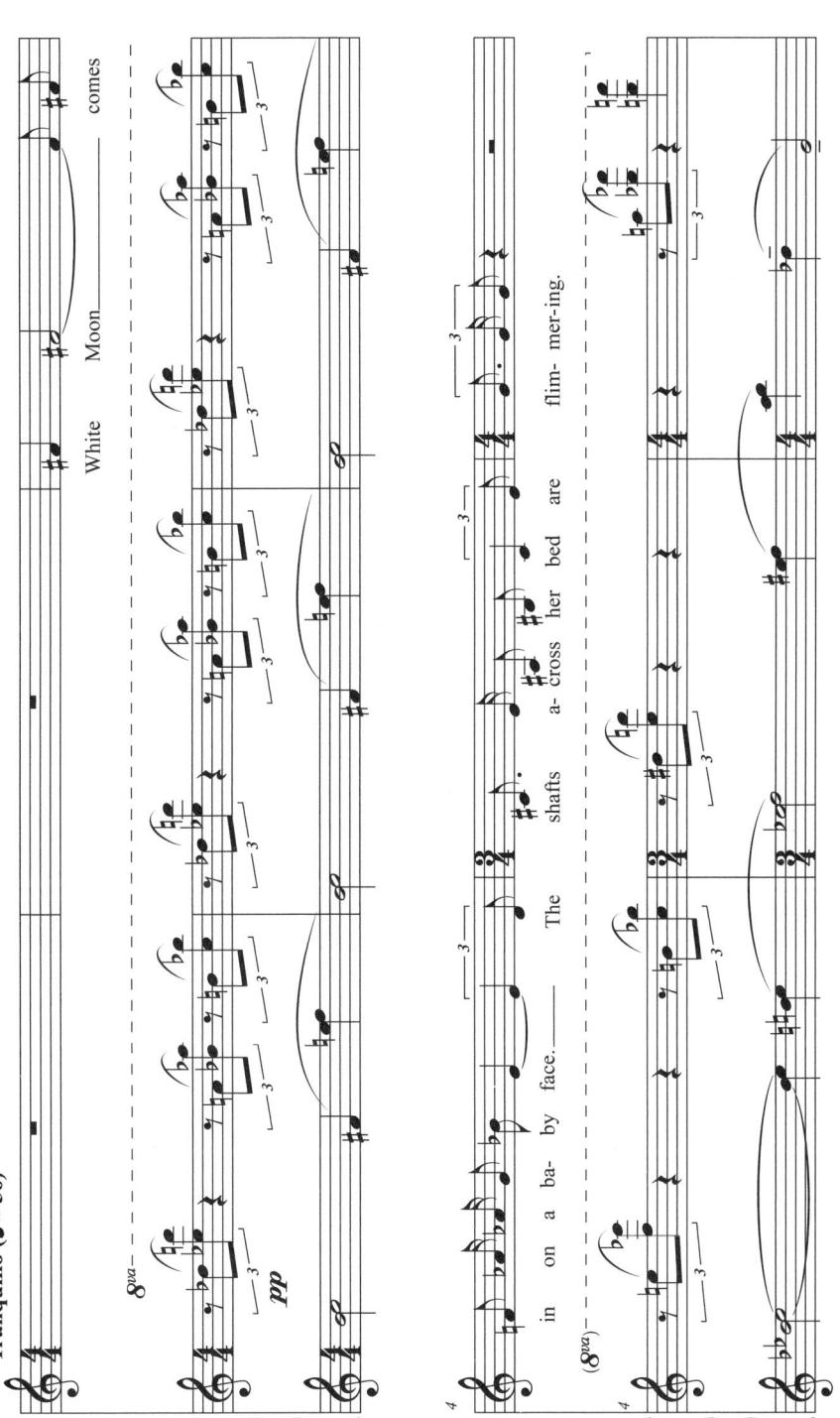

Example 5.1. Ruth Crawford, "White Moon," mm. 1–6

Example 5.2. "White Moon," mm. 18–29

his dying father: "And you, my father, there on the sad height, / Curse, bless, me now with your fierce tears, I pray."[6]

The poem opens with an imperative—"Do not go gentle into that good night"—but the target of the address is ambiguous. And the second line ("Old age should burn and rave at close of day") suggests a broad, general philosophy rather than an urgent message for an individual. The subsequent tercets, moreover, describe, from a third-person perspective, how "wise men," "good men," "wild men," and "grave men" approach their deaths. These men are viewed from a point of omniscient distance with a panoramic lens that captures the "sun," the "bay," "lightning," and "meteors." But they set up the emotional climax. Even readers familiar with the ending will appreciate the shock of sudden intimacy when the poem's voice desperately turns toward the dying parent ("And you, my father ...").

When listening to Stravinsky's setting, however, we might find the relatively subdued expression at this moment somewhat unnerving (see the 3:18 mark). Very little seems to happen. Any sensitive analyst of the piece will notice a crucial shift in the form and pitch organization of the song. But there is no dramatic outcry, no painful sonic lamentation. There is, however, one detail worth attending to—the placement of the vocal part (example 5.3). The first five tercets of the poem are preceded by a mournful refrain in the string section (for example, at 0:00 to 0:07). As this music recurs throughout the song, it begins to take on qualities somewhat similar to a Greek chorus, quietly grieving when the voice is silent. But the poem concludes with a *quatrain*, adding an additional line beyond the previous tercets.[7] This is the poem's "turn." And Stravinsky places that crucial extra line—"And you, my father ..."—within the space of the mournful refrain. The voice, in other words, joins the strings for the first and only time in their expression of quiet resignation.

For casual listeners, the moment is unlikely to stand out; the voice essentially follows a familiar, restrained melodic path that maintains the mood and overall atmosphere of the previous sections. There is nothing *musically* that matches the power and surprise of the sudden direct address in the poem. And yet the subdued prayer to the father makes the poetic turn much more expressive. The fact that the voice joins the melancholy refrain of the strings suggests an almost hopeless despair, which renders the famous, final exhortation—"Rage, rage against the dying of the light"—impotent, despite its recurring forcefulness in the music. Stravinsky's solemn, grief-stricken turn toward the father suggests that any possibility of a fight against death has long since passed.

136   Address

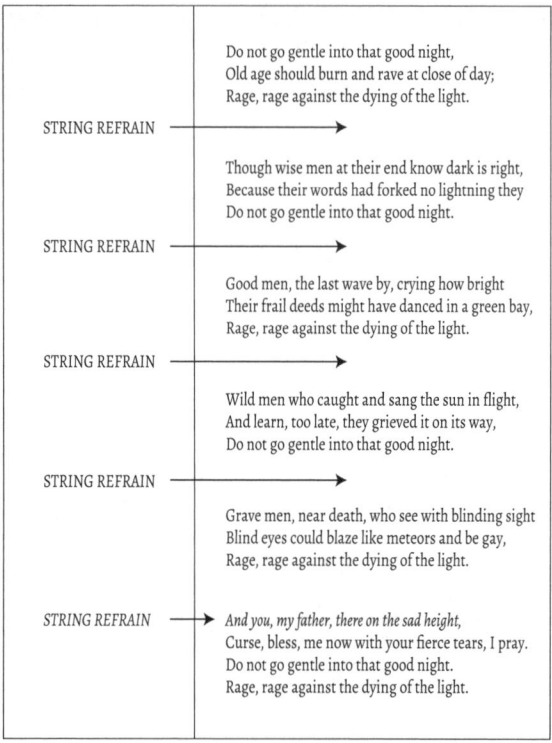

Example 5.3. Igor Stravinksy, "In Memoriam Dylan Thomas," form diagram of song

The "Covert" Second-Person Narrator

In both the Stravinsky and the Crawford songs, a shift toward direct address occurs that makes the poetry more intimate and less "distant." When shifts like this happen, we usually imagine that the speaker is attempting a direct line of communication, even if the addressee is absent or out of reach (for example, the child and the father in the Dylan Thomas poem or the speaker and the moon in the Carl Sandburg poem). There is another form of second-person address, however, that can create a strong sense of intimacy, but in a stranger, much less common way. This involves a second-person narrator who is both covert and omniscient. In other words, the speaker addresses a "you" directly, but essentially does so by entering "your" mental space and narrating everything that happens to "you" from a distant, disembodied position.

We saw an example of this in Van Morrison's "Madame George." That song begins with what seems like third-person description of a particular scene: "Down on Cypress Avenue / With a childlike vision leaping into view." But a crucial change takes place at the line "That's when you fall." The "you" is clearly part of the scene—someone who inhabits the same space as Madame George and her acquaintances—but the speaker seems to exist only as a narrative voice inside the head of this "you." On the one hand, it creates a special sense of intimacy: this is a voice *inside* "your" head—it knows your thoughts, and even explains them to you as they happen (for example, "you know you gotta go / On that train from Dublin up to Sandy Row"). On the other hand, it feels weirdly distant, because it speaks not as an interlocutor but as a narrator.

Notice that the song could have been sung with a more conventional first-person narrative. It could have been "that's when *I* fall" instead of "that's when *you* fall." Indeed, it is natural for people to imagine that the "you" is a surrogate for an "I." Lester Bangs makes that same assumption when he claims that "the singer hurts [Madame George]." He conflates the singer with a person *in the scene*. This is understandable, perhaps, because people often do this when they recount stories about themselves. They change the "I" to a "you." We hear this frequently when athletes talk to reporters after a game:

Question: "What was going through your mind when you caught the game-winning touchdown?"
Answer: "Well, when you see the ball coming, you just have to focus on fundamentals and not let yourself get distracted."

Responses such as these simultaneously *distance* the athletes from their actions—they are not something "I" did; they are something "you" do—and also create a sense of *intimacy* with listeners, because the audience is now placed in the position of the "you." The athletes are inviting "you," the listener, to imagine what it is like to be them.

Van Morrison's song arguably does the same thing: it creates intimacy by inviting listeners into the fictional universe he has created. It describes the scene, explaining what "you" see and what "you" feel. We sense an unmistakable intimacy even though the voice inhabits a narrative position displaced from the areas and events being described.

Such second-person narration is not particularly common in either poetry or popular song, but it is worth recognizing its effect when present. Some genres of song seem to utilize it more than others. Heavy Metal songwriters, in particular, seem to enjoy writing songs with a narrator who describes an unfolding nightmare scenario that happens to "you." We see this in songs like

"Keeper of the Seven Keys" by Helloween: "You can feel cold sweat / Running down your neck / And the dwarves of falseness / Throw mud at your back." When shifting toward this form of address, songs often create a sense of intimacy—someone inhabits your mind—but they do so by simultaneously creating a sense of distance: the narrator is strangely disconnected from the narrative events.

Movement Toward Distance

The examples above show that there can be a great deal of ambiguity in the way certain songs fall on the "distant/intimate" spectrum. The discourse can be quite complicated. But the general movement toward intimacy is nevertheless noticeably common to almost all genres of song. And yet, though it is rare, some songs move in the opposite direction: from a position of intimacy to a position of distance.

Simon and Garfunkel's "The Boxer" begins with a first-person story: "I am just a poor boy / Though my story's seldom told …" This intimate, confessional narrative, however, is supplanted in the final verse (Spotify playlist, track 73, 2:51) by a shift to the third-person: "In the clearing stands a boxer, and a fighter by his trade …" This is a change in discourse that casts an elegiac shadow over the song as a whole, leading, eventually, to a melancholy conclusion: "he cried out / in his anger and his shame / 'I am leaving, I am leaving' / but the fighter still remains." The singer at the outset *embodies* the boxer, and tells his story with a poignant "I." But at the end, the singer *disengages* and describes the scene from a distance, putting the listener behind the lens of a camera rather than inside the boxer's mind.

We see a similar effect in the song "When I Was Your Man" by Bruno Mars. Each verse-prechorus-chorus cycle features direct address right up until the end. As can be heard in Spotify playlist, track 74, 0:50, the chorus begins with the phrase "I should have bought you flowers" but ends with the lines "Now my baby's dancing, but she's dancing with another man." The movement away from direct address—the loss of the "you"—reinforces the overall tone of melancholy regret, an effect underscored musically with the wistfully formulaic minor chord at the word "dancing" in the phrase "but she's dancing with another man."

Such distancing effects appear in some of our most beloved poems. Whitman's famous "O Captain! My Captain" begins with an address to Lincoln after his assassination:

Example 5.4. Franz Schubert, "Erlkönig," final measures

> O Captain! My Captain! Our fearful trip is done;
> The ship has weather'd every rack, the prize we sought is won.

Several changes of address follow, but the most significant occurs at the opening of the third stanza, when a third-person description reflects the tone of pained resignation:

> My Captain does not answer, his lips are pale and still;
> My father does not feel my arm, he has no pulse nor will.[8]

Readers familiar with the German lieder of the nineteenth century will perhaps see in this a similar strategy to the one in Goethe's "Erlkönig," set to music by Franz Schubert in 1815. Goethe's poem is unlike any of the lyrics discussed thus far. It is a dramatic scene with four different speaking roles: a narrator, a father, his son, and the Erlking (a supernatural being, who in this poem preys on children). The first stanza of the poem sets the scene and is spoken by the narrator. It introduces us to the situation: a father riding through the night with his son. The next six stanzas feature alternating dialogue, with the Erlking trying to lure the boy away, the panicked boy calling out to his father, and the father—who cannot hear the Erlking—trying to calm the boy. Schubert's setting expertly moves through a range of keys and vocal patterns to depict each of the different voices in the poem. The last stanza returns to the narrator of the poem's opening, a person "outside" the dramatic scene who announces the boy's death from a distance. This provides an obvious sense of balance—the narrator begins and ends the song—but it need not have happened that way; the poem could have ended with the father grappling with the boy's death in his own voice. The effect of the narrator's return is expressive in its move to a more distant position, and Schubert emphasizes this by letting the song's galloping rhythms unwind into empty narrative declamation followed by an abrupt and almost chillingly formulaic cadence (Spotify playlist, track 75, 3:29, example 5.4). We move from a position of intense pathos to ironic detachment, a sharp turn away from the "I" and the "you."

Copland and Dickinson: A Complicated Case

When doing a close analysis of any given song, we will want to give careful thought to the deployment of pronouns such as "I," "you," "we," "her," and "him." What do these words tell us about the voice of the song and its addressees? Does the song present itself as the private thoughts of a solitary figure? Or is it an intimate address to a single person—a boyfriend, partner, or parent? Does the song present itself in a more public manner, explicitly addressed to a large group? Or do the modes of address change at some point, inhabiting a variety of different personas, from distant narrators to effusive lovers? Regardless of the situation, we will want to know how the music reflects the discourse, how it amplifies or even ignores various aspects of voice and address.

Aaron Copland's setting of Emily Dickinson's "The World Feels Dusty" offers a useful case study (Spotify playlist, track 76). This is a short, three-stanza poem that Copland set for voice and piano in 1949 as part of the *Twelve Poems of Emily Dickinson* (he later set eight of those poems for orchestra, including "The World Feels Dusty"). Here is the poem in its entirety:

> The World—feels Dusty
> When We stop to Die—
> We want the Dew—then—
> Honors—taste dry—
>
> Flags—vex a Dying face—
> But the least Fan
> Stirred by a friend's Hand
> Cools—like the Rain—
>
> Mine be the Ministry
> When thy Thirst comes—
> Dews of Thessaly, to fetch—
> And Hybla Balms—[9]

The poem begins with the first-person plural: "*We* stop to Die . . . *We* want the Dew . . ." This sounds like a voice issued to a wide audience. Though the text is strikingly "poetic," with its fascinatingly irregular uses of meter and rhyme, the tone is not altogether dissimilar to what we might expect from a rhetorically gifted pastor in a New England church. It feels *public*. As with most lyric poetry, almost nothing in this first stanza develops the "speaker" with distinct, novelistic detail. Indeed, we know little about the speaker altogether. But the poem's language, especially the emphasis on the pronoun "we," suggests a certain type of communal discourse—a rumination about death that appears to be addressed to a large group.

The tone changes over the course of the second stanza. It begins by extending the previous idea that public honors and patriotism are unwanted, even distressing, at the moment of death. The word "vex" sounds especially discordant. It is the first time that a line begins with two stressed syllables in a row, and it is the only line with four accented syllables in total ("**Flags— vex** a **Dy**ing **face**—"). Moreover, the pileup of fricatives—the *f*'s and the *v*'s— helps reinforce the implication of an almost wincing irritability. This effect is especially strong in contrast to what happens next, when the diction suddenly becomes much more folksy and plain: "the least Fan / Stirred by a friend's Hand / Cools—like the Rain." This change in diction coincides with a change in the rhyme scheme, which turns inward. The arrangement of the first stanza was *abcb*, but now the end rhymes are grouped in the middle, with "Fan" and "hand" bound together in a *deef* pattern. The language becomes more intimate as the rhymes are drawn closer together.

But these shifts lead to another remarkable shift in the third stanza. The second stanza changes its diction, but there is no distinct change of *address* (we could still imagine the words being addressed to a large group). With the third stanza, however, our assumptions are upended. This happens with the simple addition of the word "thy": "Mine be the Ministry / When *thy* Thirst comes—." This is complicated language, but the new pronoun suggests an intimate address to a specific individual. We might paraphrase it, crudely, as "when you're dying, it'll be my job to comfort you." This is no longer public language, but private. It fundamentally changes our sense of what the poem is about. The future tense—"When thy Thirst comes"—suggests that death is not necessarily the central concern here, despite its prominence in the first two stanzas. The poem is suddenly revealed as a statement of love and friendship, a commitment to be at someone's bedside at the hour of her or his death, whenever that may be.

If we were to rewrite this ending with the most clichéd paraphrase, the speaker of the poem would say, "I'll be there for you." But there is nothing trite or corny in the way Dickinson presents this particular sentiment. She dresses it, rather, in the stringent language of the King James Bible ("Mine be the Ministry..."). Indeed, not only is it *not* overly sentimental, it does not even come across as particularly affectionate. The result is a strange paradox: the direct address to a specific individual—the promise to quench "thy Thirst"—is an obviously intimate gesture, especially in comparison with the broad, first-person-plural statements of the opening stanza. But the use of archaic, quasi-biblical language creates an austere formality that sounds distinctly *less* personal than the easy folksiness of the preceding stanza's "Cools—like the Rain." The sudden address at the end—the introduction of an "I" and a "you"—creates intimacy, but the diction creates a sense of distance. How might a composer capture such moments in music?[10]

Copland's song expresses the poem in richly complicated ways, but I will confine myself here to a few observations about the song's basic sonic atmosphere. At the outset, the music is largely inert, with a restricted collection of notes that are gathered into a stagnant, airy haze (an orchestral version can be heard on the Spotify playlist, track 76). The accompaniment trudges along with a series of repetitive sighing figures, almost like labored breathing. Occasionally, the music brightens up, as can be heard most clearly at the word "Dew," about twenty seconds into the recording, but that moment of hopeful striving is temporarily overturned by a plummeting descent into the lower vocal register at the word "dry."

At two later points in the song, the voice drops down again in a similar manner to what we heard at "dry," but now with words that carry an opposite connotation: "Rain" and "Balms." At each moment, the music suddenly shifts into a far more positive, soothing space, with new harmonies that clearly reflect the meaning of the words—a sharp contrast to the dry, dusty music of the song's beginning (see the 0:58 mark and 1:27 mark, respectively). The word "rain" concludes the second stanza, and the song might have maintained those alleviating chords throughout the third stanza's subsequent direct address. But listen in particular to what happens *after* the word "rain" at the 1:05 mark. The music makes a sudden dark turn at the exact moment of direct address, a quick minor-mode shadow that briefly returns to the sounds of the opening but with a slightly more dissonant twist. This is how Copland interprets "Mine be the Ministry"—the paradoxically intimate outpouring that is expressed with bracingly pious language.

The moment is unsettling in part because Copland draws on a strange, dissonant symmetry for his choice of notes. This is perhaps best understood if we view the pitches on a keyboard, especially in relation to the sections both before and after the third stanza's opening. To appreciate this visually, or, better yet, to feel it under your fingers, look at example 5.5, which includes every note that Copland uses for the first two stanzas of the poem. As shown here, the song's most essential sound is generated from a five-note chord (the primary pentachord), which extends two notes upward for the first section and one note downward for the second section. These notes are based on a recurring, symmetrical pattern in which intervals alternate by four piano keys and then three piano keys.[11]

At "Mine be the Ministry," the central pentachord is retained, but for the first and only time, it is altered such that the interval skips now produce a 313313 pattern (example 5.6). This creates a much denser and more dissonant symmetrical pattern. The formal, biblical language of "Mine be the Ministry" is matched with a cramped, tightly packed symmetry that sounds far less "open" than the earlier music. But the dissonance only lasts a brief moment. At the phrase "thy Thirst comes," with its crucial appearance of the second-person pronoun, the music transforms into something similar to the opening section, and at "balms," the entire collection of notes shifts upward one key to the right, with the result that the ending shares very few notes with the beginning (musicians would refer to this as a "transposition"; see example 5.7). This upward shift in the source collection is matched by chords that stretch into the highest register of the piece thus far. In the orchestral version of the song, Copland even adds a harp to the concluding sounds, placing a "halo" of sorts on the newly achieved radiant sonorities.

Recognizing the precise changes in Copland's underlying pitch collections is difficult to do by ear, but the general movement between dusty, dissonant harmonies and brighter, more soothing balms is not hard to follow. What is perhaps most crucial is that the path toward intimacy, matched by distinct sonic shifts, is not entirely straightforward and unambiguous. The paradox of the poem—the way it moves toward a position of distance and one of intimacy at the same time—is strangely reflected in the music, which features several changes in pitch-collections that move, generally, in a "cooling" direction, but with a brief period of harsh, bracing dissonance before the ending's tender consolation.

■ I began this chapter with two questions: Who speaks to whom in a poem? and Who sings to whom in song? In *Theory of the Lyric*, the critical theorist Jonathan Culler justifiably worries about overemphasizing such questions:

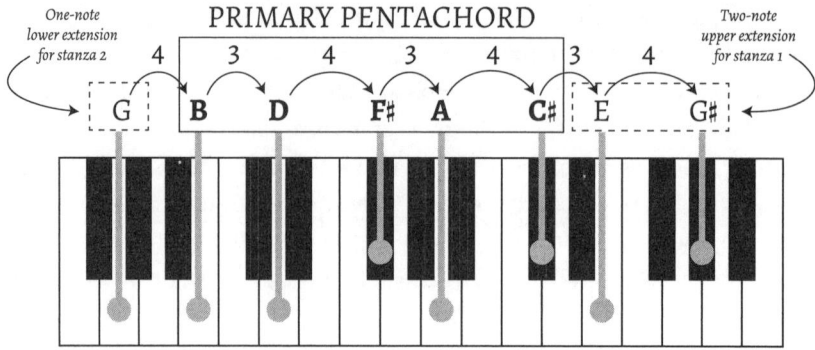

Example 5.5. Aaron Copland, "The World Feels Dusty," primary pentachord and its extensions

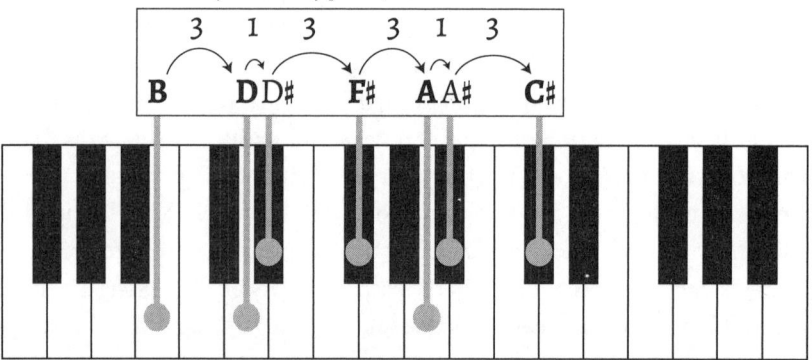

Example 5.6. "The World Feels Dusty," primary pentachord with added dissonant symmetry at "Mine be the Ministry"

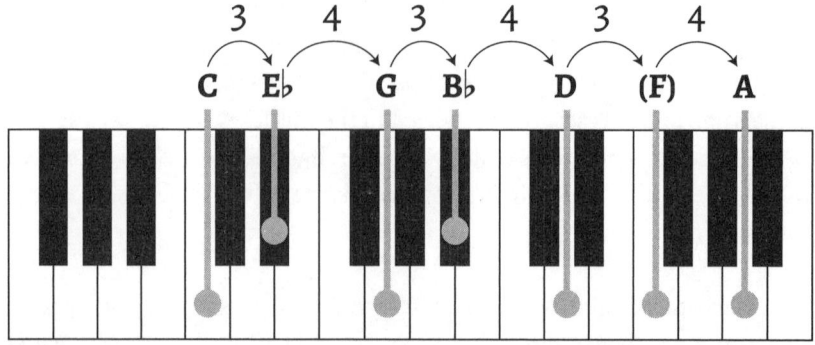

Example 5.7. "The World Feels Dusty," transposed pentachord with extensions at song's end

> This model deflects attention from what is most singular, most mind-blowing even, in [certain] lyrics, and puts readers on a prosaic, novelizing track: the reader looks for a speaker who can be treated as a character in a novel, whose situation and motives one must reconstruct. This model gives students a clear task but it is extraordinarily limited and limiting. It leads to neglect of the most salient features of many lyrics, which are not to be found in ordinary speech acts—from rhythm and sound patterning to intertextual relations.[12]

Culler, of course, is correct in raising these concerns, but as he himself has demonstrated on many occasions, we can productively ask questions about the effects of lyrical discourse without engaging in fruitless speculation about the identities of speakers and addressees. Indeed, it was with Culler's admonition in mind that I redirected the question "Who speaks to whom?" into several more pointed questions. Those questions were posed, admittedly, in bloodless, academic prose, but they are sufficiently useful in diverting us from the "novelizing track" to fully restate them here: How does the lyric present certain kinds of communicative acts? What are the expressive effects of the enacted discourse? and How would the poem be different if the modes of address were changed or altered? The goal, in other words, is not to dwell on things that we *cannot* know about the text (such as the potential backstories of its various "characters") but to focus on the things we *can:* how it moves between manners of speech in ways that we often find riveting and emotionally powerful.

When we engage with a song, we often identify with the voice in deeply intimate ways, singing along, repeating the melodies in our minds, or imagining the words as our own. Part of what draws us into such engagement is the way songs stage a certain kind of effusive emotional discourse, usually with charged, expressive connections between an "I" and a "you." As we have seen throughout this chapter, songs often involve multiple voices, shifting discourse, and ambiguous address. Such paths are worth tracking. When we analyze songs, we want to understand the language at its most detailed levels—including meter, rhyme, and diction—but we also want to know how all these elements come together in a fully communicative act. We cannot always know who sings to whom, but we can always benefit from asking.

CHAPTER SIX ||||||||||||||||||||||||||||||||||||||||||||||||||||||||||||||||||||

Form

> To find a form that accommodates the mess,
> that is the task of the artists now.
> —Samuel Beckett

This chapter is an introduction to form. It is not, however, an introduction to *specific* forms. In it I will not explain how sonnets work. I will not describe the intricacies of ghazals, sestinas, or haiku, nor will I explain how certain poetic forms may or may not relate to common song forms, such as binary form (AB), ternary form (ABA), or bar form (AAB). These are all important concepts, worthy of further study, but in this chapter I tackle something much broader, which applies to all songs and all poems: form as an *imposition of order*—an attempt to organize and shape the potentially chaotic elements of music and language while sometimes letting that chaos loose.

To begin thinking about how form might affect a poem or song, let us start with language in a state of disorder. Imagine words spilling forth on the page without punctuation or syntactic clarity—a muddle of unfettered verbal pandemonium. The result might look something like this:

> not solemnly almost and in swimmers verge the go the what phantom sea the strange and houses see I the land far winds pretend try myself change eye him seem self is someday the will the long final they yet the be should cannot shine could and swimmers of the some with dead as land see who there the strange repeats the see beautiful courage I'll go while going to it its I the leave is beside because swell thought of I friend among place of modest sound whose sea makes they he although my as cannot

To read this is an exercise in frustration. The words constantly disrupt our attempts to find meaningful syntactic relationships. Some of the language is evocative, but it is far too disorganized—far too formless—to make readers want to waste their time engaging with it. Yet if we reorganize the language into syntactically logical units, with helpful punctuation marks to indicate appropriate pauses, it quickly snaps into focus:

> I'll go among the dead to see my friend. The place I leave is beautiful: the sea repeats the winds' far swell in its long sound, and, there beside it, houses solemnly shine with the modest courage of the land, while swimmers try the verge of what they see. I cannot go, although I should pretend some final self whose phantom eye could see him who because he is not cannot change. And yet the thought of going makes the sea, the land, the swimmers, and myself seem strange, almost as strange as they will someday be.

This is now recognizable English. It is *ordered* language. But readers are still perhaps likely to find it difficult, cryptic—perhaps even a bit off-putting. There are several complex constructions that seem jumbled (for example, "whose phantom eye could see him who because he is not cannot change"), and, more important, the words sometimes create a "musical" rhythm that ill fits this stiff block of prose. What we need is the form Edgar Bowers actually created when he published these words in 1997 as a poem called "An Afternoon at the Beach":

> I'll go among the dead to see my friend.
> The place I leave is beautiful: the sea
> Repeats the winds' far swell in its long sound,
> And, there beside it, houses solemnly
> Shine with the modest courage of the land,
> While swimmers try the verge of what they see.
>
> I cannot go, although I should pretend
> Some final self whose phantom eye could see
> Him who because he is not cannot change.
> And yet the thought of going makes the sea,
> The land, the swimmers, and myself seem strange,
> Almost as strange as they will someday be.[1]

A sense of order now emerges that cannot be inferred from first contact with the prose version. The entire text is neatly divided into two equal halves that begin by opposing each other—"I'll go . . . ," "I cannot go . . ."—and the lineation draws attention to rhymes and repetitions ("sea" and "see"). It also exposes the iambic pentameter, which might have been felt intuitively while reading the prose version but probably not recognized as clearly as it is when we encounter it in distinct lines ("While swimmers try the verge of what they see"). And the phrase that was most puzzling in the prose version—"whose phantom eye could see / Him who because he is not cannot change"—is now made more clear, if for no other reason than that the lines invite us to slow down and read the text more carefully.

Yet, despite this neatness, there are still wonderful tensions: symmetries poised against asymmetries; balance against imbalance. The lines are grouped in two stanzas of 6 + 6, but the end rhymes are grouped as 8 + 4: *abababab* || *cbcb*. The first stanza is one sentence of six lines, but the second stanza is two sentences of three lines each. Some lines are enjambed, some are not. And the predictable iambic rhythm is sometimes thrown off kilter with metric variations (for example, the three accented syllables at "winds' far swell" in line 3). All these create a potentially unsettling effect. The poem's meditation on death, which makes familiar images seem strange, is reflected in the way the simple familiarity of balanced pentameter lines begins to twitch with tensions and energy that make it, too, seem strange.

Form, then, is an imposition of order on disorder, but a great deal of drama in poetry and song comes from the *tension* between the two: the way a sense of order wrestles with elements of disorder, the way an artist fashions disparate fragments into a contained chaos. Sometimes the goal is to restrict and reshape the disarray of unordered thoughts. Sometimes the goal is to uncork the chaos and let it loose. From an artist's standpoint, this can be an invigorating challenge. How much madness can be captured in a four-beat measure or an eight-bar phrase? What unruliness might a poet pack into balanced stanzas and four-beat lines?

With those questions in mind, imagine that you are tasked with composing music for the following poem:

> I was angry with my friend:
> I told my wrath, my wrath did end.
> I was angry with my foe:
> I told it not, my wrath did grow.
>
> And I water'd it in fears,
> Night & morning with my tears;
> And I sunnèd it with smiles,
> And with soft deceitful wiles.

And it grew both day and night.
Till it bore an apple bright;
And my foe beheld it shine,
And he knew that it was mine.

And into my garden stole,
When the night had veil'd the pole:
In the morning glad I see
My foe outstretch'd beneath the tree.[2]

This is William Blake's "A Poison Tree," from the *Songs of Experience*, a collection published in 1794. It is a bleak poem, but it has a childlike simplicity. The malicious growth of wrath spreads outward but is ultimately contained, quite neatly, in four stanzas, each with four lines, and each line thumping along with four palpable beats ("My **foe** out**stretched** be**neath** the **tree**"). Each stanza, moreover, is neatly subdivided with two rhyming couplets: *aabb*.

The form is clear, and if we were to translate this poetry into song, we might group the music in ways that reflect the basic structure of the poem. It could have four sections, one for each stanza. Each section could have two parts, with each couplet as a single large phrase that arrives at a significant resting point in the music (that is, a cadence), and each line as a smaller "subphrase" that ends with a weaker sense of closure. Our setting might look something like the outline in table 6.1.

But there is a potential downside to this simplicity: the neatness of the form might stifle the poem's more exciting and unruly elements. Notice how the second, third, and fourth stanzas begin with the word "and," suggesting a syntactic continuity that we might want to reinforce in the music.[3] We might find that there is good reason, in other words, *not* to break the song into four discrete sections. We might even recognize that the poem's story involves a subtle *three-part* structure that works in counterpoint with the four-part division of the stanzas (table 6.2).

The first stanza is set apart from the others because of its closed parallel construction: "I was angry with my friend . . . I was angry with my foe . . ." It sounds like an isolated aphorism, something that might plausibly stand on its own. The next two-and-a-half stanzas are different. They recount a series of events that happen over time, the growth of the tree and the foe's envy, which leads inexorably to the speaker's current state. The final two lines are the culmination of that story, but they are set apart not simply because they act as

150 Form

Table 6.1. Hypothetical subdivision of phrases for Blake's "A Poison Tree"

LARGE PHRASE 1	I was angry with my friend;	SUBPHRASE 1
	I told my wrath, my wrath did end.	SUBPHRASE 2
LARGE PHRASE 2	I was angry with my foe:	SUBPHRASE 1
	I told it not, my wrath did grow.	SUBPHRASE 2

Table 6.2. A hypothetical three-part division of Blake's "A Poison Tree"

I was angry with my friend: I told my wrath, my wrath did end. I was angry with my foe: I told it not, my wrath did grow.	**OPENING APHORISM**
And I water'd it in fears, Night & morning with my tears; And I sunnéd it with smiles, And with soft deceitful wiles. And it grew both day and night. Till it bore an apple bright. And my foe beheld it shine, And he knew that it was mine. And into my garden stole, When the night had veil'd the pole:	**GROWTH**
In the morning glad I see My foe outstretched beneath the tree.	**CONCLUSION**

a kind of punchline for the poem but because they shift from the past to the present tense: "In the morning, glad *I see* . . ." How, then, might we capture this aspect of the form? Is this more reason to abandon a simple four-part division?

Notice also that although the simplicity of the language is reminiscent of ballads and folksongs (it is a "song of experience"), the poem does not contain a refrain. There is no repeated text that could act as a kind of "hook" that might make the song more memorable or even, perhaps, invite people to sing along. This need not be a pressing concern, especially if we are composing something in the genre of modern art songs, which often lack recurring poetic lines. But refrains are so common among songs in general that a composer might consider *adding* repetition, even if it is not a feature of Blake's poem. Indeed, composers have been altering poetic texts for centuries, often by repeating phrases that are not repeated in the text. If we did this with Blake's poem, what would happen? Would it damage the poetic effect? Would it change the story?

Scholars of both poetry and music often struggle with a basic distinction between form and content. If we say that a rock song is structured as verse-chorus-verse-chorus-bridge-chorus, we may appear to be speaking only of form, not content. After all, many songs—many very *different* songs—share that same formal design. Each song section, then, might be viewed as an empty container that a songwriter could fill with different content—melodies, chords, lyrics, and so forth.

To a certain extent, this is true. But how do we know that something is a "verse" rather than a "chorus"? What would make a section of a song sound like a "bridge"? Scholars of popular music such as John Covach, David Temperley, Trevor de Clercq, and Drew Nobile often point to various musical and rhetorical features.[4] Among other things, the chorus is often the most memorable, catchy part of the song. It often incorporates the song's title, and the same words are usually repeated each time it occurs, often with more energy and a thicker texture than appear in the verse (frequently using backing vocals). The content, then, in some sense determines the form. The same issue arises in classical music. We often designate formal sections by neutral letters—for example, "ABA"—but we also talk about formal units in terms of things that the music *does:* introduction, transition, development, closing section. Form and content, in other words, are notoriously difficult to distinguish.

But there is more: the question of form also incorporates broader issues of style and tradition. A poet writing a sonnet, for instance, is likely to conceive it according to a certain abstract *form:* fourteen lines of rhymed iambic pentameter. Similarly, if you choose to write a blues song, you will likely adopt a specific musical form: three phrases of four measures each, where the second phrase repeats the lyrics of the first and the third concludes with a rhyme (all supported by a familiar harmonic pattern known as the "twelve-bar blues"). But the sonnet tradition and the blues tradition involve far more than these simple parameters. To adopt these forms is to place your original creation against a massive backdrop of similar works. Will your sonnet address the topic of love and devotion? Will it sound like Shakespeare? Or will it sound more like a modern sonnet, as we find in the work of contemporary poets such as Terrance Hayes? Similarly, if you were to write a blues song, would it be a lament? Would it sound like Ma Rainey or Muddy Waters? Would it sound like Stevie

Ray Vaughn? The terms "sonnet" and "blues," in this sense, signify much more than an empty shell. They carry with them a vast history of complex artistic choices, irreducible to any simple "form."

These tensions between form and content, style and genre contribute to the broader, overarching tension between order and disorder. And in song, the tension is often amplified when the words and music do not seem to "fit." Indeed, we often speak of the relationship between words and music in terms of a struggle. The music bends and twists the words into a certain shape—or the text pushes back, and shapes the music according to its own image. A poetic text might create an atmosphere of hypnotic repetition, but a composer might feel the need to introduce variation, contrast, and a dramatic arc. The music of pop songs might demand circular returns to familiar musical moments—a guitar riff or a catchy melody—but the lyricist might want to tell a linear story, one that is unhampered by repetition. These aspects of conflict, however, are often balanced by moments when music and words seem perfectly aligned, moments when the elements of disorder seem entirely contained. And in such cases, writers often discuss the relationship in cooperative terms, even speaking of a "marriage" between words and music.

But even if the music and the words fit together comfortably, the experience of hearing a song is always different from the experience of hearing a poem read aloud. Music not only shapes poetry into different forms, it creates a different kind of drama. It incorporates sounds, moods, tensions, and resolutions that are different from all the dramatic sounds, pacing, and meanings of the poem itself. To best understand how this works, I look at how two British composers, Ralph Vaughan Williams and Benjamin Britten, chose to set Blake's "A Poison Tree," and how their different decisions about form rechannel the poem's balance of order and disorder into remarkably different dramatic shapes.

Three Settings of Blake's "A Poison Tree"

The Ralph Vaughan Williams Setting

Sometime around Christmas 1957, Ralph Vaughan Williams, at the age of eighty-five (seven months before his death), began work setting ten poems by William Blake, all scored for voice and oboe. (They would be used in a film released the following year; see Spotify playlist, track 77). Table 6.3 offers an overview of the song's form.

Table 6.3. Ralph Vaughan Williams, "A Poison Tree," form diagram

OBOE INTRODUCTION			0:00–0:16
I was angry with my friend:	*Mournful music*	**A**	0:16–1:12
I told my wrath, my wrath did end.	*gradually*		
I was angry with my foe:	*rises upward*	(cycle 1)	
I told it not, my wrath did grow.	↓		
And I water'd it in fears,	*Melodic*		
Night & morning with my tears;	*highpoint (F)*		(0:58)
And I sunnéd it with smiles,			
And with soft deceitful wiles.	*Ends midrange*		(1:12)
OBOE INTERLUDE			1:12–1:20
And it grew both day and night.	*Mournful music*	**A'**	1:20–2:12
Till it bore an apple bright;	*gradually*		
And my foe beheld it shine,	*rises upward*	(cycle 2)	
And he knew that it was mine.	↓		
And into my garden stole,	*Melodic*		
When the night had veil'd the pole:	*highpoint (Eb)*		(1:47)
In the morning glad I see			
My foe outstretched beneath the tree.	*Ends on lowest note (D)*		(2:12)

Perhaps the most immediate thing to notice here is that Vaughan Williams divides the poem in two. Each half is preceded by a short oboe melody, and the two follow a similar trajectory: the voice begins on the lowest note of the piece (D), gradually rises upward toward a melodic highpoint, and then sinks back down, into the midrange in the first half and to the lowest note at the end. The overall sense of balance is clear, but, as with almost any other artistic form, the attempt to impose order also creates tensions. It inevitably struggles with elements of disorder.

One manifestation of this tension is that Williams's two-part form forces the third stanza to act as a *re-beginning* rather than a continuation. Recall that the third stanza of the poem opens with a syntactic continuity from the second: "And I watered it . . . ," "And I sunnèd it . . . ," "*And it grew . . .*" These repetitions have an incantatory force that drives the poem forward, arguably surging past the boundaries of the poem's neatly divided stanzas. But Vaughan Wil-

Example 6.1. Opening idea returns at midpoint in Ralph Vaughan Williams, "A Poison Tree"

liams halts all forward momentum at this point, emphasizing the gap between stanzas rather than the continuous linguistic flow. And because the second section returns to the song's opening phrase, with its slow, languid melody, it suggests a wearying cycle of growth, decay, return, and then growth yet again (example 6.1). This is not to say that the second half of the song is identical to the first—it is more of a "reimagining" than a direct repetition (hence the label "A'" rather than "A")—but there is an unmistakable feeling that the music loops back through something that has, in effect, already happened. In other words, at a moment when the poem begins to accelerate with extended, syntactic repetitions, the song quietly restarts itself. This is a tension that cannot easily be resolved.

These re-beginnings are not a feature of the large-scale form alone; they also happen at the level of the individual phrase. This creates a frequent, dread-inducing sense of déjà vu. Right from the start, the voice mimics the movements of the oboe, but it does so in a desolate, half-hearted manner. If the song had been written with a harmonic accompaniment—simple piano or guitar chords—the voice might have taken center stage unchallenged. But in Vaughan Williams's setting, the solo oboe establishes itself as a second "voice," moving about the musical space in an abstract dialogue with the singer. This is a purely musical doubling that resonates with a crucial doubling in the poem: the way the foe's feelings mirror the jealousy and rising anger of the speaker.

In the song, we might even imagine that the singer, in following the oboe's melody, reluctantly retraces the path of the dead foe's ghost.

By loosely mimicking the oboe, however, the singer creates an unpredictability that operates in tension with the balanced structure of the poem. As shown in example 6.2, the tenor begins by taking the oboe's last pitch (D) and rising upward, but he does so without the vigor of the oboe's earlier ascent, only reaching a minor third above (F). This seems almost like a failure, or perhaps an unwillingness to follow the oboe's lead. But the oboe responds with a slight rise to A♭, and the voice, seemingly guided by the oboe's coaxing ascent, does indeed reach the A♭ before sinking, slowly, back to the starting pitch.

That slow descent affects the proportions of the song. In the poem, the first two lines are presented with perfect balance: "I was angry with my friend; / I told my wrath, my wrath did end." But in the song, the lines are unmatched. The first is presented quickly, with a series of short eighth-note rhythms, but the second stretches out to a size nearly 50 percent longer (see the rectangles in example 6.2). One of the effects of this lengthening is to emphasize a sense of dejection and lethargy. When reading the couplet's neat conclusion—"my wrath did end"—we might sense an almost chipper satisfaction: we have no reason after those opening lines to imagine a future negative outcome. But by stretching out the second line, Vaughan Williams has already anchored the text with the heaviness and strain of what lies ahead. Indeed, it is precisely for that reason that the return of this phrase at the midpoint of the song effectively expresses the much more ominous conclusion: "And it grew both day and night. / Till it bore an apple bright." The poem begins with balance and order, but the music immediately shapes it into a less predictable form, one that branches off into asymmetrical pathways.

Britten's 1935 Setting

Britten set "A Poison Tree" to music twice: first when he was young and relatively inexperienced (1935), and then thirty years later, when he was a mature, world-renowned success (1965). A recording of his first, youthful version, can be heard in the Spotify playlist, track 78. The song arranges the poetry into a large, three-part form, with an arch-like palindromic symmetry (table 6.4).

The song begins with lurching, almost cartoonishly "wrathful" gestures in the piano, but they give way, after about twenty seconds, to quieter, stealthier movements as the song begins to turn toward the idea of growth (the song pivots into the B section at the word "grow," which is why that word is itali-

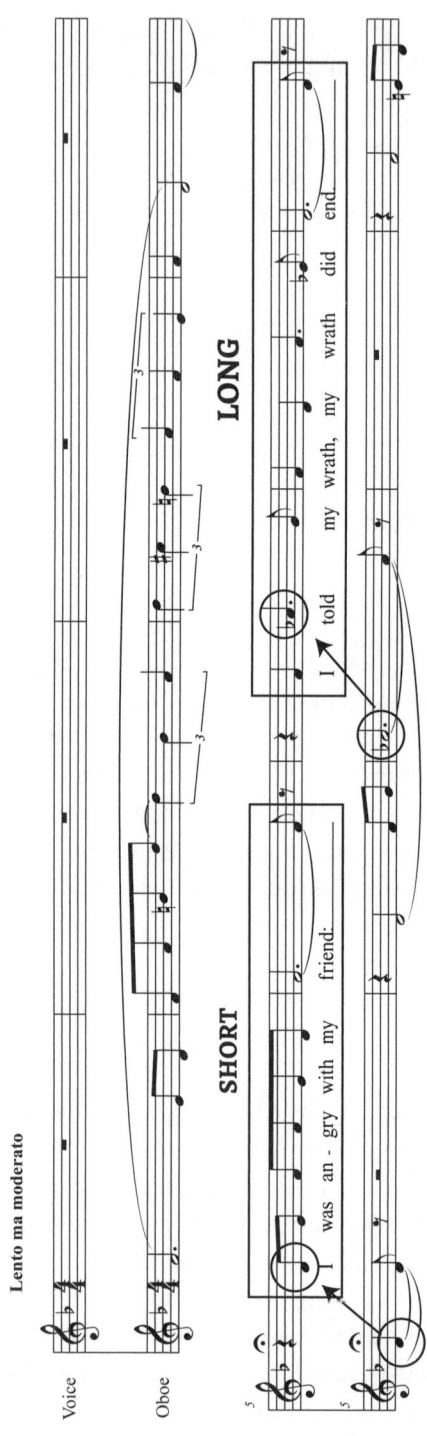

Example 6.2. Vaughan Williams, "A Poison Tree," opening lines

Table 6.4. Benjamin Britten, "A Poison Tree" (1935), form diagram

I was angry with my friend: I told my wrath, my wrath did end. I was angry with my foe: I told it not, my wrath did *grow* (trans.)	*Loud, angry* *gestures give way* *to quieter,* *"creeping"* *gestures*	**A**	0:00–0:20 0:20–0:45
And I water'd it in fears, Night & morning with my tears; And I sunnéd it with smiles, And with soft deceitful wiles And it grew both day and night. Till it bore an apple bright; And my foe beheld it shine, *And he knew that it was mine. (trans.)*	*Music gradually* *gets* *higher and louder* *over a low,* *rumbling bass* *("creeping"* *gestures retained)*	**B**	0:45–1:49 1:49–2:18
And into my garden stole, When the night had veil'd the pole: In the morning glad I see My foe outstretched beneath the tree.	*Quiet, "creeping"* *gestures gradually* *lead to loud, angry* *gestures*	**A**	2:18–2:34

cized in the table and marked as a transition to the next section). At the end of the song, the movement is reversed: the quiet stealthy gestures return after the line "and he knew that it was mine," eventually leading to an arrogantly triumphant return of the loud, lurching gestures from the beginning. At the center is the song's B section, in which the physical gestures from the opening are quietly transformed into more interior expressions, a brooding melody fertilized in the rich soil of a low, quiet, rumbling bass. From that ground, the music consistently rises, becomes increasingly loud, and ranges dynamically from the pianissimo opening line ("I watered it in fears") to a piercing, forte climax ("and my foe beheld it shine").

Unlike Vaughan Williams, who splits the poem in half, Britten emphasizes continuity across the poem's midpoint. The outer sections are not rigidly separated from the B section but instead bleed across boundaries with loose transitions. And by staging a dramatic buildup through the middle stanzas, Britten presents the narrator's continued enchantment with the apple's bloom as the driving force of the poem. Nevertheless, as with Vaughan Williams, the strong imposition of a symmetrical order creates tension with the more turbulent elements of both the music and the poetry. The overall design suggests a kind of musical palindrome: it has the same effect whether we follow it backward or forward—but the music, especially in the middle section, is *linear*, building up toward a distinct climax. Moreover, the return of the lurching gestures at the end suggests a victory rather than a return to the wrath of the song's opening (there is no déjà vu akin to what we experience in the Vaughan Williams song). In other words, a linear narrative works in tension with the broader, symmetrical order.

But the neatness of the form also contrasts with the emotional tone of the song. For Britten, the song's persona has none of the remorse and regret that hangs over the Vaughan Williams setting. And even though Britten's ending sounds different from his beginning, it is telling that the song, despite the orderliness of its layout, begins and ends with the loudest and most disjunct material. It is a triumph of chaos, packaged in the form of a balanced symmetry.

Britten's 1965 Setting

When Britten returned to this poem thirty years later, as part of *The Songs & Proverbs of William Blake*, op. 74, he decided to do something radically different. Instead of adopting the two-part grouping of Vaughan Williams or the three-part grouping of his earlier version, he now composed the song with different music for each stanza (what musicians call a "through-composed" form; see table 6.5). As shown in example 6.3, all four stanzas begin with a different, distinct vocal melody (the complete song can be heard on Spotify playlist, track 79).

By choosing this form, Britten essentially rejected the possibility that we would hear any specific moment as a reprise or "re-beginning," as happens in the Vaughan Williams setting (where the opening music returns halfway through) or in his earlier setting (where the opening music returns at the end). Instead, there is a clear pattern of growth in which: the A section involves slow rhythms in a restricted range; the B section maintains a restricted range, but adds more rhythmic complexity; the C section features prominent leaps and a wider range in the melody; and the D section involves a completely bifurcated melody that leaps dramatically between high and low ranges. These changes all clearly reflect a linear, directed sense of growth, without any distinct returns to an earlier section. And yet, ironically, this later setting is more obsessed with reusing familiar material than any other version of the song.

Table 6.5. Benjamin Britten, "A Poison Tree" (1965), form diagram

Text		Section	Time
I was angry with my friend: I told my wrath, my wrath did end. I was angry with my foe: I told it not, my wrath did grow		A	0:00–1:22
And I water'd it in fears, Night & morning with my tears; And I sunnéd it with smiles, And with soft deceitful wiles	*All sections use similar material, repeat similar motives, and repeat segments of text*	B	1:22–2:23
And it grew both day and night. Till it bore an apple bright; And my foe beheld it shine, And he knew that it was mine.		C	2:23–3:09
And into my garden stole, When the night had veil'd the pole: In the morning glad I see My foe outstretched beneath the tree.		D	3:09–4:23

Despite the clear differentiation, Britten adopts a rigorous compositional method based on recurring, organic motives that seem to spread uncontrollably across the piece, weaving themselves into the contrapuntal textures of both voice and piano.[5] And whereas the earlier versions left the poem unaltered, Britten now repeats certain poetic segments such that the text *itself* seems to mutate and grow along with the music. The most prominent example of this is the way Britten creates a "refrain" of sorts by returning to the phrase "my wrath did grow" four times after its initial appearance. All three settings create a sense of mounting dread by allowing the music to "grow" toward their respective climaxes. But in Britten's 1965 setting, the growth is especially palpable and leads toward a series of extraordinary vocal acrobatics as the voice begins to split between high and low ranges for the final section of the song (starting with the bottom melody in example 6.3). In short, this is no simple "orderly" path through the poem's four stanzas. As with the other settings, the song shapes the poem into a logical formal order—ABCD—but it constantly obscures its own boundaries.

What, then, do these three settings tell us about art songs in general? Given

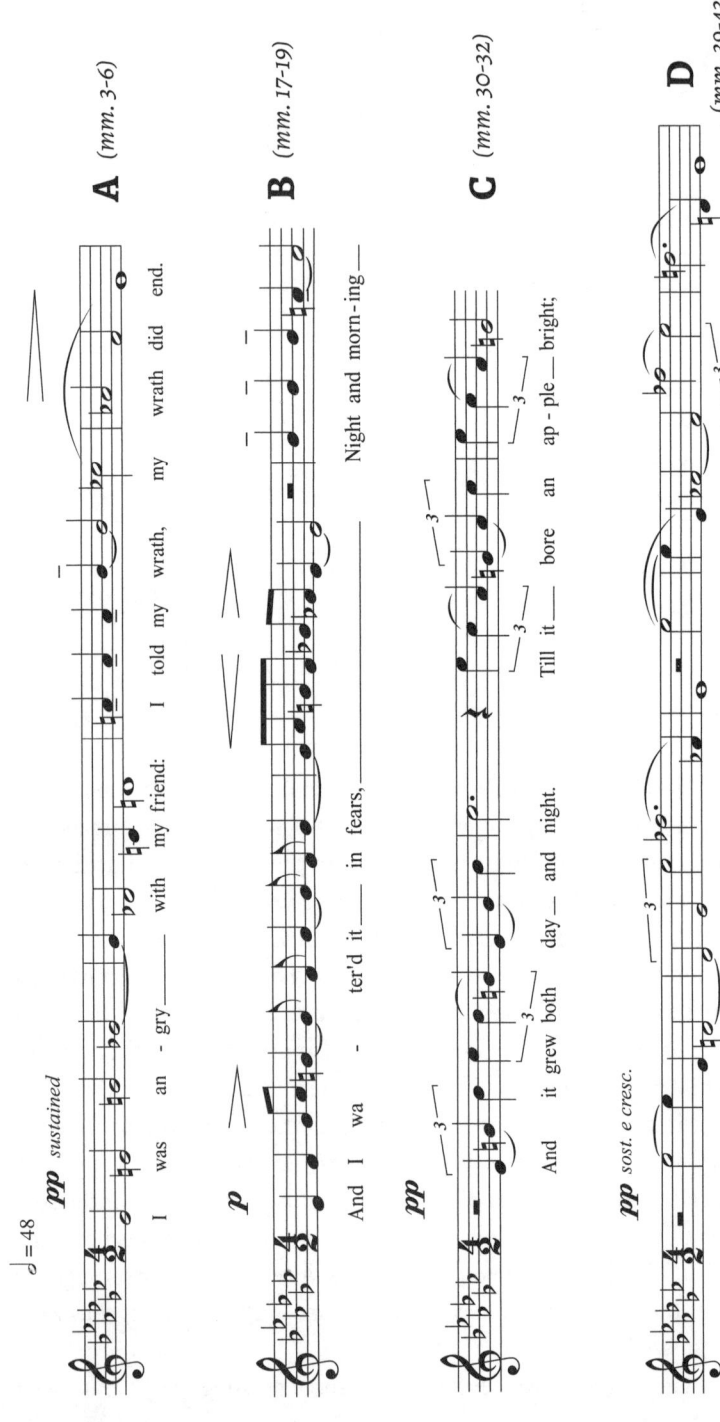

Example 6.3. Opening melodies for each of the four sections of Benjamin Britten, "A Poison Tree" (1965)

that they result in three very different forms, we might imagine that the possibilities are infinite, that composers could sculpt a poem into countless shapes and sizes. And although this is obviously true in theory, in practice, poetic forms tend to restrict compositional options more than we might imagine. Indeed, despite obvious differences, the three settings share important similarities: they all use dark, minor-mode themes and harmonies; each matches individual poetic lines with distinct musical phrases (even if, in Britten's final setting, he occasionally repeats certain segments); each stanza corresponds with a coherent musical section, even if the composers sometimes link stanzas together into larger shapes (as in the two large halves of the Vaughan Williams setting or the large central section of Britten's early version); and they all represent the idea of growth in relatively clear ways (by expanding in range, dynamics, and motivic development). The form and content of the poem, then, ultimately determine much of the form and content of these three settings, even if they need not have done so.

What is most important to me, however, is that there are *already* tensions in Blake's poem itself, especially between formal balance and chaotic growth. And no matter how the composers reshape the poem into different musical forms, those tensions are inevitably rechanneled into similar tensions within the songs. And such tensions are not unique to this poem or these three settings. Tensions between order and disorder are characteristic of almost any artwork, from Frida Kahlo paintings to Alfred Hitchcock films. Becoming attuned to those tensions is vital when pondering the role of form in any poem or song. So as we move forward, let us consider three questions: How does a poem or song impose a sense of order? How do certain elements resist or disrupt that sense of order? and How do these tensions relate to other poems and songs?

Rufus Wainwright's Shakespeare

I'm not an intellectual in this case—I can be in others—but not in this one because to try to match Shakespeare or challenge him in terms of wits is pretty stupid.
—Rufus Wainwright, quoted in "Rufus Wainwright Puts Shakespeare Sonnets to Music," Euronews, May 3, 2016

Art songs and popular songs often engage with form differently. Composers of art songs, especially since the nineteenth century, tend to shape their music in ways that they believe best suit the poetry, which may or may not involve repetitions of certain themes, sections, or ideas. Popular songwriters, on the other hand, tend to conceive lyrics with familiar formal designs already in mind, especially the alternation between verse sections, which tend to include relatively dense amounts of verbal information (perhaps even telling a story), and refrains, choruses, or hooks that are typically designed to be memorable and to invite participation (dancing, singing along). But the difference between pop songs and art songs is not always so stark. Before moving on to consider how pop songwriters grapple with issues of form, we might first consider a curious hybrid of the pop/art traditions: Rufus Wainwright's 2002 setting of Shakespeare's Sonnet 29 ("When in disgrace with fortune and men's eyes").

A recording of Wainwright's complete setting can be heard on the Spotify playlist, track 80. (An alternative arrangement, with Florence Welch singing, appears on the album *Take All My Loves: 9 Shakespeare Sonnets*.) It is an unusual song in that it maintains attributes of early Elizabethan music, including frequent lute-like flourishes and a brief use of a Renaissance-inflected harmony (what musicians call the "Mixolydian mode"). It is also ambitious enough to sound somewhat like an art song from the post-Schubert tradition, especially with its wide-arching vocal range, its setting of a famous preexisting poem, and its buildup of tension across the multiple sections of an ABA ternary form (which I discuss further below). But it also sounds in many ways like a modern pop song, with its prominent piano accompaniment, familiar repetitive chord loops, and Wainwright's textured and timbrally distinct voice, which eschews classical vocal technique. By gathering such disparate material together, the song imposes a certain order on disordered elements, not unlike the Blake settings above. But the tension in this case is often a *stylistic* tension—an attempt to reconcile language and sounds that seem to come from entirely different worlds.

As shown in table 6.6, Wainwright divides the sonnet into four parts: three quatrains and a closing couplet.

These are natural divisions, not only because they follow the poem's rhyme scheme (*abab* || *cdcd* || *ebeb* || *ff*) but also because they align with broader shifts of attention: the first quatrain describes the speaker's "outcast state," the second focuses on feelings of jealousy ("Desiring this man's art and that man's scope"), and the third turns toward the beloved ("Haply I think on thee..."). The final couplet then captures the poem's overall positive turn with a compact, two-line summation. Wainwright translates this into song with an ABA form followed by a coda. Many art song composers would no doubt pick a similar, highly *ordered* design. But, again, part of what makes Wainwright's song so

Form 163

Table 6.6. Rufus Wainwright, "Sonnet 29," form diagram

When, in disgrace with fortune and men's eyes, I all alone beweep my outcast state, And trouble deaf heaven with my bootless cries, And look upon myself and curse my fate,	**A SECTION** **FIRST QUATRAIN**
Wishing me like to one more rich in hope, Featured like him, like him with friends possessed, Desiring this man's art and that man's scope, With what I most enjoy contented least;	**B SECTION** **SECOND QUATRAIN**
Yet in these thoughts myself almost despising, Haply I think on thee, and then my state, (Like to the lark at break of day arising From sullen earth) sings hymns at heaven's gate;	**A' SECTION** **THIRD QUATRAIN**
For thy sweet love remembered such wealth brings That then I scorn to change my state with kings.	**CODA** **FINAL COUPLET**

intriguing is the way it seems to behave as both a pop song and an art song at the same time, sometimes expressing the words with remarkable elegance and beauty, but other times not quite fitting the antiquated diction and complex syntax of Shakespeare's text.

Example 6.4 clarifies the relationship between the ABA sections by grouping them in terms of pitch height.

The first quatrain (the A section) is set in a low, comfortable vocal range, with a simple three-chord progression. Each line is a distinct phrase, all fit neatly into four-measure groups with four beats each. If not for Shakespeare's distinctive language ("beweep," "bootless") it would sound like a traditional verse section from a popular song. The second quatrain (the B section, at 0:49) expands the range by leaping up to the pitch C-natural (C♮) at "wishing me like...." This is a somewhat troubling note, foreign to the song's key (it "should" be C#), and it creates a barrier of sorts. Every time Wainwright stretches up to that C♮, he subsequently slips back down the scale. The exception is at the end of that quatrain, the 1:10 mark, when he dramatically rises above the C♮ and reaches a high D at the phrase "contented least." This is a striking moment in that Wainwright clearly stages it as a victory—the achievement of a higher, stable platform—but it also sounds bizarre to have such a moment of triumph

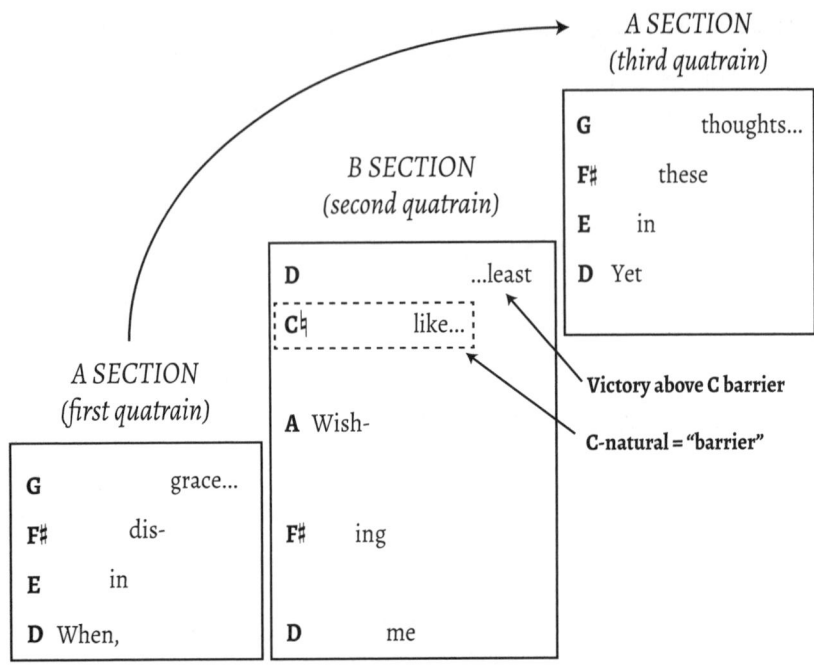

Example 6.4. Rising ABA form of Rufus Wainwright, "Sonnet 29"

occur with the phrase "contented least." The obvious intent is to set up the sonnet's turn, the moment when the language makes a distinct shift in tone and address, and Wainwright matches that by returning to the opening material (the A section), but now an octave higher, in a straining upper range.

The overall trajectory, then, is clear: the opening quatrain is in a low register (the "outcast state"), the second quatrain stretches higher, but with a touch of melancholy ("desiring"), and the third quatrain achieves the highest range ("Haply I think on thee"). It is a simple, logical dramatic arc. But again, notice how *oddly* these sections fit together. The phrase "contented least" is not only strange in the way it ironically resists the musical triumph of the moment—it is strange because the whole song still carries enough of the sheen of modern popular song that a syntactically archaic phrase like "With what I most enjoy contented least" cannot be absorbed into Wainwright's sound world. And yet, as with the Dunhill setting of Yeats in chapter 1, I find this discomfort to be a significant part of the song's appeal. It is an enchanting weirdness: a deftly realized dramatic arc that captures the overall shift in the poem's language but nevertheless struggles to match the poetic text, mostly because the language resists the style.

Form   165

Table 6.7. Ascent toward climax in the penultimate line of Wainwright's "Sonnet 29"

F#							brings
E						wealth	
D	For					uch	
C♮					su-		
B				membered			
A			love re-				
G		swee-					
F#	thy	ee-					
E			eet				
D							

Overcoming C♮

The song's greatest achievement, however, is the coda (the setting of the final couplet, at the 1:42 mark). Up until this point in the song, each poetic line is tethered to a predictable four-measure group—the strict adherence to regular phrasing is part of what makes the song reminiscent of pop music. But Wainwright clearly wants the final couplet to sound like an epiphany, and he partly achieves that effect by slowing everything down so that almost every individual word in the penultimate line is stretched out a full four measures ("thy ... sweet ... love ... remembered ..."). Moreover, the voice ascends in a way that summarizes the trajectory of all three previous sections, drifting slowly up an octave before ultimately settling back down to the voice's lower register (the ascent is diagrammed in table 6.7).

This rising melody, however, sounds entirely different from the previous ascent in the ABA section. Most important, it does not sound like a *struggle*. The voice seems to rise almost like a balloon. Notice how at the word "such," the music hits that barrier note once again—the C♮—but the voice is now bolstered by the swell of the accompanying voices into a lighter, softer, falsetto range, such that the whole ascent feels like an effortless rise, buoyed upward by external forces.

This is a climax not *achieved* but *granted*.[6] And the melodic highpoint, at the word "brings," is especially powerful. To begin with, it creates an enjambment that feels as if the song has finally broken loose from its strictures, in which every line corresponds with a distinct phrase of equal length. Here, the words stretch out with a transgressive freedom unlike anything we have heard thus far. The result is that this is the moment when the song most strongly achieves

Table 6.8. Dip schema draws the voice down after climax in Wainwright's "Sonnet 29"

VOICE:	F♯	Brings / that then	I -		
	E			I scorn	
	D				
	C♯				
	B				to
		D ↘ C♯ ↘ C♮ ↘ B			

its art song ambitions by ecstatically discarding the repetitive chord cycles of the previous sections. But even here we find a wonderful stylistic tension: at the climax of this ascent, Wainwright brilliantly deploys an extremely common pop music pattern, a chord progression similar to what we hear at the outset of Mötley Crüe's "Home Sweet Home." (The scholar Christopher Doll refers to it as a "dip" schema.)[7] As shown in table 6.8, the voice holds on to the melodic peak—the high F#—while the accompaniment sinks downward in a chromatic motion from D to C# to C♮ to B. It is an almost Beatles-esque reverie, somewhat reminiscent of the dreamy opening melody of "Something," which also uses the dip schema.

But it is also a device commonly used in classical repertoire, a sound that scholars such as Robert Hatten have discussed in terms of "abnegation."[8] It is a descending energy that seems to draw the voice part down alongside it, with everything eventually sinking back to the final chord at "kings." The descent does not feel like a failure or a lack of energy. It feels, instead, like a surrender into ecstasy, a giving of oneself over to the moment. And, most important, by slowing everything down, by articulating each word in the final couplet so slowly, the song finally seems to reconcile Shakespeare's diction with both pop and art song sensibilities.

There is a sense, then, in which the stylistic tensions in the song become resolved at the end, much as the poem itself dismisses all its earlier torment in the final couplet. And the fact that the climax of the song—the highpoint of the coda—has a Beatles-esque quality is telling. The Beatles were remarkably experimental with musical forms, and they especially relished tensions between order and disorder, often surprisingly tilting the balance from the one to the other. Since so many subsequent popular musicians have been influenced by their choices, they provide a perfect launchpad for questions about form in pop music generally speaking.

Order and Disorder in Popular Song: The Beatles

Casual music lovers might imagine that there is no category of song quite as neat and tidy as pop music. Formal paradigms change over time, of course—Cole Porter's tunes tend to take very different shapes from those of Maroon 5—but most popular songs feature predictable configurations of familiar elements: verses, choruses, and occasional contrasting sections such as bridges, instrumental solos, or intros and "outros." Even some of the most radical, antiestablishment songs in the pop music canon still follow familiar patterns: a song like "Anarchy in the UK" by the Sex Pistols, shockingly original in so many ways, nevertheless follows a quite conservative form.

Pop music, then, might be thought of as a recurring victory of order over disorder. Songwriters often express *disordered* energies and passions, but those passions tend to be packaged into neat little boxes: three to four minutes of music, generally conforming to a small collection of well-worn formal templates. (In fairness, the same generalization could be made of art songs.) There are exceptions, to be sure—Led Zeppelin's "Stairway to Heaven," Queen's "Bohemian Rhapsody," Travis Scott's "Sicko Mode"—but they tend to prove the rule. Even when trends change over time—when, for instance, guitar solos find their way into the dance hits of the 1980s, or EDM (electronic dance music) "drops" begin to appear in the pop songs of the 2010s—the general sense of orderliness holds remarkably steady.

These generalizations, however, obscure the tensions that can arise between lyrical content and musical form. Popular songs in all genres can be much more disorderly and much less well behaved than my summary suggests. And perhaps no band was better at capturing such tension than the Beatles. Some of their songs occupy extreme points on the order-disorder spectrum, with songs like "Love Me Do" on one side and "Revolution 9" on the other. But many of them find a thrilling balance between the two. I will briefly discuss four Beatles songs, each of which contains a certain level of chaos in the lyrics but nevertheless creates forms that often engage both the traditional and the truly bizarre.[9]

Table 6.9. The Beatles, "Penny Lane," form diagram

Section	Key	Time
Verse 1	B major	0:00–0:17
Verse 2	B major	0:17–0:33
Chorus 1	A major	0:33–0:50
Verse 3	B major	0:50–1:07
Solo	B major	1:07–1:24
Chorus 2	A major	1:24–1:40
Verse 4	B major	1:40–1:57
Verse 5	B major	1:57–2:14
Chorus 3	A major	2:14–2:30
Coda (Chorus 4)	B major	2:30–2:56

"Penny Lane"

"Penny Lane" was released as a single in early 1967 along with "Strawberry Fields Forever" (it also appeared on the *Magical Mystery Tour* album in November 1967). As should be clear on listening, the song has many familiar, *orderly* components (Spotify playlist, track 81). The verse sections adopt a narrative tone ("In Penny Lane there is a barber showing photographs . . .") and the choruses switch to a more intimate, lyrical first person ("Penny Lane is in my ears and in my eyes . . ."). These sections recur several times, as would be expected with pop songs, and there is only one significant contrasting section: a piccolo trumpet solo in place of one of the verses, played by David Mason, who was brought into the studio after Paul McCartney heard him performing J. S. Bach's Second Brandenburg Concerto on a BBC broadcast. The song's form is neatly summarized in in table 6.9.

But now let us look at the song's *disorderliness*. I have already noted the way the lyrics move from a narrative description of people and places in the verses to a more first-person state of mind in the choruses. But this shift is far less straightforward than it might at first appear. Consider, for instance, the simple words "there . . . I sit." The chorus begins with the phrase "Penny Lane is in my ears and in my eyes," a line that appears to be nicely balanced by the rhyme "there beneath the blue suburban skies." But what does the word "there" refer to? It would seem to refer to "Penny Lane" (in other words, if the question is "Where is Penny Lane?" the answer is *"there*, beneath the blue suburban skies"). But this turns out to be deceptive. The word "there" is actually the beginning of a much longer sentence, with a syntax that not only stretches across musical phrases, but also across the "neat" boundaries of chorus and verse: "*There* beneath the blue suburban skies *I sit*, and, meanwhile, *back in Penny Lane* there is a fireman . . ." (example 6.5). The phrase "back in Penny Lane" is crucial. It suggests that the "there" of the song's chorus is *not* Penny Lane, despite the scene being "in my ears and in my eyes." The lyrics, in other words, transgress boundaries and cause confusion. They introduce a sense of disorder into the orderly form of the song.

The question of place—Where is the "there" of the song?—might best be addressed as an issue of memory. The song is largely autobiographical, written in Paul McCartney's characteristic storytelling style, and Penny Lane is a real place in Liverpool. The barber, the banker, and the fireman were apparently real people whom John Lennon and McCartney remembered.[10] But memory is complicated, and the elements of this song are jumbled together in ways that create a somewhat surreal scene, a "very strange" place, where "blue suburban skies" hang above a rain-soaked fireman; where a "four of fish" are enjoyed in "summer," despite a nurse selling "poppies from a tray," something that is commonly associated with England's Remembrance Day on November 11. The nurse herself seems to sense this strangeness. She "feels as if she's in a play." And in what might be the most wonderful line of the song, we learn that "she is anyway."

The song, then, presents tensions between real and unreal, rain and sun, summer and winter—all lyrical tensions that are reflected by important *musical* tensions. Despite the orderliness of the song's form, it contains multitudes. Familiar pop harmonies and descending bass lines intermingle with a gradually unfolding circus of orchestral instruments and sound effects (for example, bells and bus sounds). Instrumental solos are, of course, nothing new, but here the baroque figures of the piccolo trumpet suggest a clash of styles similar to what we heard in the Rufus Wainwright setting of Shakespeare—a sense of the old and new freely juxtaposed, with neither effectively absorbing the other.

This disorderliness of style is matched by some strange movements in terms of chords and keys. It is frequently observed that the song features rather unusual key changes: B major in the verses and A major in the choruses (the exception is the coda, which is an altered version of the chorus in B major). For many listeners, this aspect of the song would be difficult to perceive in a distinct and conscious way, but certain musical shifts and detours are perfectly clear. The first occurs in the verse section, where the opening line is supported by simple, familiar harmonies that have been used in countless other songs:

Example 6.5. Syntactic continuity from chorus to verse in the Beatles, "Penny Lane"

notice, especially, the descending bass line at "Penny Lane there is a barber showing photographs." This provides a template from which the second line noticeably diverges. At the word "know," the song surprisingly runs aground on a melancholy B-minor-seventh chord (this happens approximately seven seconds into the song). It is an odd musical turn that coincides with a somewhat bizarre expression in the lyrics, which describes the barber showing photos of "every *head* he's had the pleasure to know." "Every *man*" would have been less interesting but also less oddly distant. The lyrics, which are so focused on providing snapshot images, are themselves a strange kind of photograph, and the objectified "heads" reinforce the peculiarity of the picture, which is reinforced in turn in the music as it shades from the sunshine of B major to the darker, "rainier" B minor.

The song recovers B major at the beginning of the next verse, when the camera shifts to the banker who never "wears a mac" in the "pouring rain." The music makes the same move from major to minor, but this time it transitions into the chorus, which returns to a major key, but a surprisingly *different* major key (A). Again, many listeners would not be able to follow these tonal shifts in a conscious way, but there is nevertheless a distinct musical connection that *can* easily be perceived: As the music theorist Walter Everett points out, the chorus opens with the same words and a similar three-note figure from the song's verses ("Penny Lane"), except the chorus is now a step higher (example 6.6).[11] This reinforces the bizarre feeling that the choruses are somehow in the same place as the verses but also *not* the same. The opening of the verse is also the opening of the chorus, and the end of the choruses stretches syntactically into the verses. The two different keys, moreover, suggest two different places and times (the chorus as "now/here" and the verse as "then/there"). But the point of the song is *not* to allow such neat divisions.

At the end of the song we finally hear the chorus in B major, which sounds noticeably higher, an excited upward displacement of the A-major chorus (see the right side of example 6.6). But it could also be interpreted as a way of reconciling the earlier shifts and disjunctions. Indeed, for the first and only time, the main couplet of the chorus—"Penny Lane is in my ears and in my eyes / There beneath the blue suburban skies"—is successfully sealed off as a closed entity. "Here" and "there" are finally brought together. It is, perhaps, a victory of order over disorder, but the song's energy derives not from one or the other, but from the tension between the two.

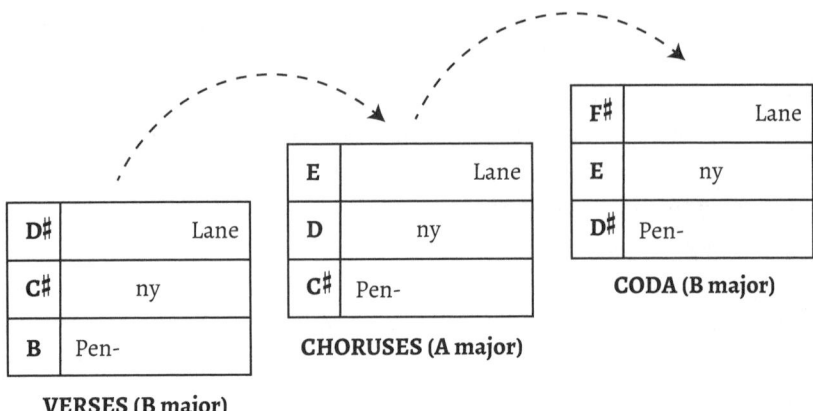

Example 6.6. Rising melodic incipits in verses, choruses, and coda of "Penny Lane"

"I Am the Walrus"

Dylan got away with murder. I thought, well, I can write this crap, too. You know, you just stick a few images together, thread them together, and you call it poetry.

—John Lennon

"I Am the Walrus" was recorded in September 1967, less than a year after "Penny Lane," and the songs share some subtle similarities (Spotify playlist, track 82). Both songs involve verses that describe strange urban scenes where you might "get a tan from standing in the English rain." Both choruses, too, shift toward first-person statements (for example, "In my ears and in my eyes" and "I am the eggman . . . I am the Walrus"). They also both involve somewhat chaotic mixes of rock and orchestral instruments. And they even have a brief harmonic similarity: "I Am the Walrus" begins with a B-major chord that quickly sinks down to the key of A major, briefly echoing the tonal movement between verse and chorus in "Penny Lane."

But they have a significant difference: although both songs express a strange and wonderful balance between order and disorder, they arrive at very different outcomes. Whereas McCartney's "Penny Lane" ultimately ends with a triumph of orderliness, Lennon's "I Am the Walrus" ends with entropy and centrifugal madness—a triumph of disorder.

The lyrics of "I Am the Walrus" are perhaps the most obvious agent of chaos. Lennon cites Bob Dylan as a source of mischievous inspiration ("I can write this crap, too"),[12] but Lewis Carroll's *Through the Looking-Glass* and the

Table 6.10. The Beatles, "I Am the Walrus," form diagram

Section	Time
Intro	0:00–0:21
Verse 1 (two parts)	0:21–0:55
Chorus 1	0:55–1:04
Verse 2 (two parts)	1:04–1:52
Chorus 2	1:52–2:00
Bridge	2:00–2:24
Chorus 3	2:24–2:36
Verse 3 (two parts)	2:36–3:09
Chorus 4 (extended)	3:09–3:25
Coda	3:25–4:35

poems of Gertrude Stein also seem to have left a distinct imprint. And though one hesitates to analyze the lyrics too closely, especially given that academic scholars are an obvious target of ridicule ("expert textperts ... don't you think the joker laughs at you?"), it has sounds and images that are well worth savoring. Lennon has a good ear for verse, and the song cunningly shifts between tongue-twisting assonance and alliteration ("Mister city p'liceman sitting pretty little p'licemen in a row") and startlingly bizarre diction ("crabalocker fishwife pornographic priestess").

But all the disordered language is ultimately packaged and contained in fairly predictable pop music groupings. Table 6.10 shows a diagram of the song's form, with its more or less standard sections: an intro and outro, repeated verses and choruses, and a contrasting bridge section, which is based on the music of the intro ("sitting in an English garden ...").

This is not to say that the musical elements of the song are "normal" in any way—they aren't: most of the vocal phrases are three measures long, rather than the more conventional four, and the song's seven underlying chords are all major, a feature that threatens to undermine the song's tonal stability—but there is a formal familiarity to them, despite the craziness of the lyrics. Indeed, the song is arguably *more* contained than "Penny Lane." It has nothing like Penny Lane's syntactic enjambment that spans chorus and verse, nor does it have any large-scale key changes. And though both songs use orchestral instruments, there are no musical intrusions in "I Am the Walrus" that sound as though they come from a different piece of music altogether, as does Penny Lane's baroque trumpet solo.

174 Form

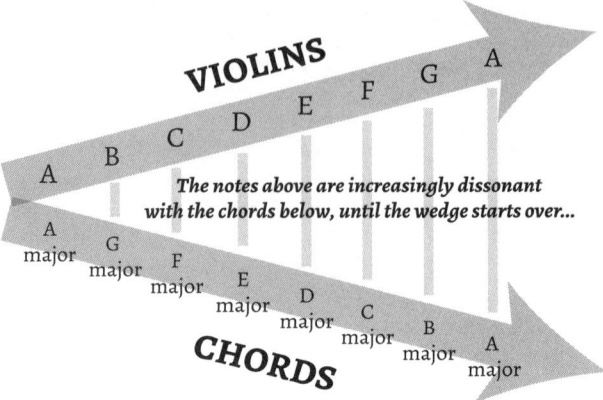

Example 6.7. Increasing dissonance in the wedge-like coda of the Beatles, "I Am the Walrus"

The crucial difference, however, is that whereas "Penny Lane" ends with an affirmation of order, "I Am the Walrus" ends with pandemonium. The song's coda features a centrifugal wedge motion, in which chords descend by step against a gradually ascending stepwise line in the violins (example 6.7).

With each octave loop, the two parts begin with the same note (A) but then gradually fight against each other with more and more dissonance until the process begins again, while the gap grows even wider. As this happens, we hear a chorus of voices chanting nonsense ("oompa, oompa, stick it up your jumper") and extracts from a BBC production of *King Lear*, the ultimate drama of unraveling madness. In that sense, both "Penny Lane" and "I Am the Walrus" use common pop forms to contain chaotic impulses, but with markedly different results. In the words of George Martin, "'I Am the Walrus' was organized—it was organized chaos."[13]

"A Day in the Life"

"A Day in the Life" was written and recorded in a brief period in 1967 between "Penny Lane" and "I Am the Walrus," and it feels in some sense like a bizarre, hybrid child of the two. (It was released on *Sgt. Pepper's Lonely Hearts Club Band* in May 1967; Spotify playlist, track 83.) To begin with, it fuses highly differentiated musical fragments that seem to be drawn from two different songs, one by Lennon, the other by McCartney. And although the lyrics are not as psychedelic as those of "I Am the Walrus," they are stranger than those of "Penny

Table 6.11. The Beatles, "A Day In the Life," form diagram

Section	Time
Verses (Lennon)	0:00–1:39
Buildup / Crescendo	1:39–2:15
Middle Section (McCartney)	2:16–2:49
Transition / Dream Sequence	2:49–3:18
Verse (Lennon)	3:18–3:45
Buildup / Crescendo	3:45–4:20
E-major Chord and Aftermath	4:20–end

Lane." Lennon's sections feature oddly detached descriptions of unrelated newspaper stories and film clips; McCartney's peppier central section tells a personal story, but it nonsensically unfolds as a weird palindrome: it begins with the narrator waking up, going downstairs, and rushing out, only to then go upstairs, have a smoke, and fall into a dream.

Again, we sense a blending of reality and unreality, a tension between order and chaos. But notice in table 6.11 how this song, unlike the other two, projects an unconventional song form.

Lennon's parts sound like plausible "verses" ("I read the news today, oh boy..."), but the song lacks a chorus in any traditional sense. There are certainly contrasting, energetic moments—for example, the crescendos at "I'd love to turn you on" and the dream sequence at the end of the McCartney section—but these ultimately behave more like transitions than as independent sections. And to even use the term "transition" for the crescendo buildups is perhaps inappropriate. These are ominous orchestral swells that threaten to unravel with the same centrifugal chaos we hear at the end of "I Am the Walrus" (moments that are also reminiscent, perhaps, of the uncontrollable growth in Blake's "A Poison Tree"). At the end, the spiraling chaos is decisively punctuated with a colossal E-major chord. But a question arises: Does this chord represent a victory of order over chaos or outright annihilation?

Regardless of how we interpret the ending, the song clearly represents a case in which the "disorder" of the lyrics has a pronounced effect on the song's form. This is even more true with "A Day in the Life" than it is with "Penny Lane" or "I Am the Walrus." The lyrics of "A Day in the Life" are *irreconcilable* in a way that sets it apart from the other songs. The lyrics for "I Am the Walrus" are bizarre, but they are *consistently* so. The song shuttles from one weird image to another, interspersed with the first-person assertions of the choruses ("I am

Table 6.12. The Beatles, "Happiness Is a Warm Gun," form diagram

Section	Key	Time
A: "She's not a girl . . ."	E minor to A minor	0:00–0:44
B: "I need a fix . . ."	A major/minor	0:44–1:13
C: "Mother Superior . . ."	A major/minor	1:13–1:34
D: "Happiness . . ."	C major	1:34–2:44

the eggman"). "Penny Lane" has many lyrical oddities, but the song maintains a firm grip on its central subject: Penny Lane. The various sections of "A Day in the Life," however, have very little to do with one another. The newspaper stories, the film, McCartney's middle section—the only thing that binds them is the way the disparate images are expressed with dreamlike detachment and ironic absurdity. To try to package these fragments into a conventional pop form would be a mistake. These are lyrics that demand a more idiosyncratic design, something that paves the way for the more extreme experimentation that we later find on *The White Album*.

"Happiness Is a Warm Gun"

Walter Everett describes the lyrics of "Happiness Is a Warm Gun" as "less coherent than anything else produced by the Beatles."[14] It has lines that would not sound out of place in a more conventional song, such as "She's not a girl who misses much" or "I need a fix 'cause I'm going down." But these lines are completely undeveloped and are interspersed with nonsensical digressions about "Mother Superior" and psychedelic ruminations about a pervert with mirrors on his "hobnail boots." Whereas "A Day in the Life" still featured several unmistakable verses (the Lennon sections), the chaos of the words in "Happiness Is a Warm Gun" results in the complete dissolution of any familiar pop song form (Spotify playlist, track 84). As shown in table 6.12, there are no repeated sections. There is no verse or chorus or bridge—just a sequence of clearly differentiated sections, several of which are in different keys. Moreover, the song is so disruptive with regard to meter that it required as many as seventy takes to get the rhythm right: the A section, for example, is in duple meter, but the B section unfolds as a stoned, drunken waltz, and many other metric shifts occur as well.[15]

The title of the song comes from a punchline in a *Peanuts* cartoon of 1966

A SECTION	B SECTION	D SECTION

G
E
C
A
She's |not| *a girl...*
	G
	E E E
	                (D)
	    (C♯) C C
	           A A
	I need a fix 'cause I'm goin' down...
		G
		E E E
		           (D)
		         C
		     A
		Happiness is a warm gun

Example 6.8. The "A-C-E-G" motive, first as a chord, then as melodic ideas in the Beatles, "Happiness Is a Warm Gun"

("Happiness is a warm puppy"). The phrase became a pre-internet meme of sorts, eventually appearing on the cover of a gun magazine as "happiness is a warm gun."[16] Lennon transforms that violent usage into something more sexually suggestive, but the dark humor and absurdity of the whole episode—the way the language is transformed and repurposed in pop culture—feeds into Lennon's broader project of cultivating chaos in both music and language.

This, then, would seem to be a decisive victory of disorder: a song that matches fragmented, nonsensical lyrics with a fragmented, nonsensical form. But even here, there are several features that bind the song together and maintain a certain level of coherence. For one thing, there is a consistent buildup of textural density over the course of the song, from the simple guitar picking of the opening to the dense, layered sounds of the doo-wop conclusion.

Moreover, as Everett points out, there are familiar musical motives that recur throughout the song; as seen in example 6.8, the opening chord, with the notes A, C, E, and G, is later transformed into melodic themes.

Perhaps more important, the song ends in a way that might be viewed as a reassertion of order despite its ironic absurdity. The C-major doo-wop conclusion, no matter how satirical it might be, is the most comfortably "familiar" section from a pop music perspective. It even acts as a bizarre kind of chorus in the way it features the song's title, thickens the texture, and invites listeners to sing along with its catchy tune. And yet we would have to be remarkably inattentive not to realize how deliberately strange it is to juxtapose this music with that of the earlier sections, and also to match it with lyrics that so mischievously caricature the 1950s era sound world (something that becomes especially clear when we hear "bang bang, shoot shoot" from the back-up singers). As George Martin said of "I Am the Walrus," the song is chaos, but it is organized chaos.

❧ If we listen to these four Beatles songs in a row they might suggest a linear narrative: the songs become progressively less traditional in terms of form, and the lyrics become progressively less coherent. But this straightforward story is itself a kind of order that does not capture the messiness of the complete group, not to mention the songs' place in relation to all the other Beatles songs from this period. The point of thinking about songs in terms of a binary such as "order versus disorder" is not to come up with final judgments about where a song falls on a given spectrum, but rather to enjoy the continually shifting tensions at play over the course of any particular song.

We might also recognize that the balance between order and disorder applies to more than questions of large-scale formal organization. Indeed, to some extent, *every* chapter in this book has dealt with a clash between order and disorder. Most of my examples in the diction chapter feature juxtapositions of different words and sounds: Latinate versus Anglo-Saxon, or "high" poetic styles versus "low" poetic styles. The chapter on meter introduces ordered patterns of accent but also shows how poems and songs frequently resist those patterns. And similar tensions emerge with rhyme, syntax, lines, and address—they all involve ways of organizing language into predictable units, but also ways of breaking patterns and disrupting expectations.

In some ways, this chapter itself has embodied the tensions it discusses. It is designed with a simple form—a collection of Blake settings in the first half, a collection of Beatles songs in the second half, and one art song–pop song mix in the middle—but each of the selected songs is too rich with individual details to capture in a quick overview. A full interpretation would require much more focused analytical engagement with all aspects of the chosen songs. Up to this point, it has not been important to delve into any particular song at that level of detail, but we now have enough of a foundation to do just that. In the final chapter I analyze two complete songs from every perspective I have covered in the book thus far.

CHAPTER SEVEN ||||||||||||||||||||||||||||||||||||||||||||||||||||||||||||||

The Complete Song

The title of this chapter is "The Complete Song." It is not "The Complete Interpretation." I am not sure what a "complete" interpretation would look like, but I know that I cannot provide it. What I *can* offer are sample analyses that engage with a full song rather than focus on isolated, individual moments. Diction, rhyme, meter, lineation, syntax, voice, address, and form are all helpful avenues for getting started, but an emphasis on individual details can sometimes feel like an aimless exercise. What good is it to notice a particular enjambment or metrical disruption if it has nothing to do with what else is happening in the song? How do these disparate features fuse together into something larger, compelling, and complete?

In this chapter I offer a close reading of two songs: Benjamin Britten's "Since She Whom I Loved," which sets a poem by John Donne, and "Thunder Road" by Bruce Springsteen. My goal is to engage every aspect of the book that I have introduced thus far but in a somewhat casual, introductory fashion rather than as a comprehensive scholarly analysis. I will take no deep dives into John Donne's theological background, offer no discussion of how Britten's song fits into a broader compositional context, and pose no ruminations about how "Thunder Road" accrues meaning against the backdrop of 1970s America. Those issues, like many others, are certainly worthy of further attention. But my aim here is rather to consider how certain poetic and musical details resonate with one another, interlock with other elements, and ultimately take shape within larger dramatic trajectories.

Neither of the analyses below follows a systematic method, but the general approach will be familiar from my earlier chapters. Each is an exercise in sustained attention—an attempt to discover how every facet of a song might speak out and say something meaningful beyond individual, fleeting moments. Indeed, we would do well to remember that one of the basic aims of analysis is simply to bring us closer to the poems and songs we love. It is not a search for definitive, summary explanations, but rather a quest for deeper connections, more possibilities, and more questions. With that in mind I again ask that readers unfamiliar with these songs take the time to listen to them beforehand, ideally several times. There is little benefit in reading an interpretation of a song without hearing it first.

Benjamin Britten, "Since She Whom I Loved"

Donne's "Holy Sonnets" include nineteen poems, most of which were written between 1609 and 1611. The sonnet I focus on here—beginning with the line "Since she whom I loved hath paid her last debt"—seems to have been written later, in 1617, after Donne's wife died in childbirth.[1] We have good reason, then, to read this poem, at least in part, as an autobiographical text. A speaker addresses God after the death of a loved one:

	Rhyme	Line
Since she whom I loved hath paid her last debt	A	1
To nature, and to hers and my good is dead,	B	2
And her soul early into Heaven ravishèd,	B	3
Wholly in heav'nly things my mind is set.	A	4
Here, the admiring her my mind did whet	A	5
To seek thee, God: so streams do show the head.	B	6
But though I've found thee, and thou my thirst hath fed,	B	7
A holy thirsty dropsy melts me yet.	A	8
But why should I beg more love, whenas thou	C	9
Dost woo my soul, for hers off'ring all thine?	D	10
And dost not only fear lest I allow	C	11
My love to Saints and Angels, things divine,	D	12
But in thy tender jealousy dost doubt	E	13
Lest the world, flesh, yea, Devil put thee out?[2]	E	14

The First Quatrain

The first four lines are designed with a "since / then" construction, which might be rewritten as

> Since (1) she whom I loved hath paid her last debt to nature
> [and since] (2) my good is dead

[and since] (3) her soul early into heaven [has been] ravishèd
[then...] wholly in heav'nly things my mind is set.

The lines might be paraphrased as a simple statement to God: "Since my beloved is dead, I can now devote myself fully to you." But that sentiment, with its straightforward expression of faith and devotion, is arguably undercut by the emotional trajectory of the three "since" statements. The first presents the death in positive terms—the speaker's loved one has "paid her last debt," a metaphor that casts her death as a successful financial transaction. The second is a darker, more somber expression—"my good is dead"—a possible punning allusion to the much more shocking sentiment "my God is dead."[3] The third comes close to outright hostility: it declares that the loved one's soul has been taken—indeed, "ravishèd"—prematurely.

The word "ravishèd" is used in several other Donne poems, and the connotation usually suggests sexual violence rather than a euphoric state of rapture.[4] Readers sensitive to diction and rhyme, moreover, will notice that the word has a marked sound in this context. For modern ears, the pronunciation is archaic and strange (the last syllable is accented in order to rhyme with "dead"). But the word stands out even without the three-syllable pronunciation. The rhyme scheme is *abba*, but "ravishèd" is the only multisyllabic end rhyme. It is also the most evocative and uncommon word in the passage, which otherwise uses simple, plainspoken English. Donne has arranged the poem to give this word maximal impact. It is an *arresting* word, one to which a sensitive composer would undoubtedly want to give careful thought.

But what does it say about our speaker's attitude toward God? Does it suggest anger? Is he less focused on "heavenly things" than the poem's fourth line suggests? Is the speaker sincere in his statement of devotion? Or is he actually expressing resentment and perhaps even sarcasm? Is it possible that he is doing both? These are important questions for any reader, but they would have been especially pressing for Britten. Art songs typically translate poetry into an elevated dramatic performance, in which the singer takes on the role of the poem's "speaker" and the accompaniment transforms the voice into an especially expressive medium for the words, heightening emotions and implications beyond what might be possible with the spoken word. What kind of persona, then, did Britten want to create when he sat down to compose this song in 1945? (See the Spotify playlist, track 85, for a complete recording.)

If we listen to the setting of the opening line (the first sixteen seconds), and filter it through a binary of "sincere devotion" versus "sarcastic anger," it would

182   The Complete Song

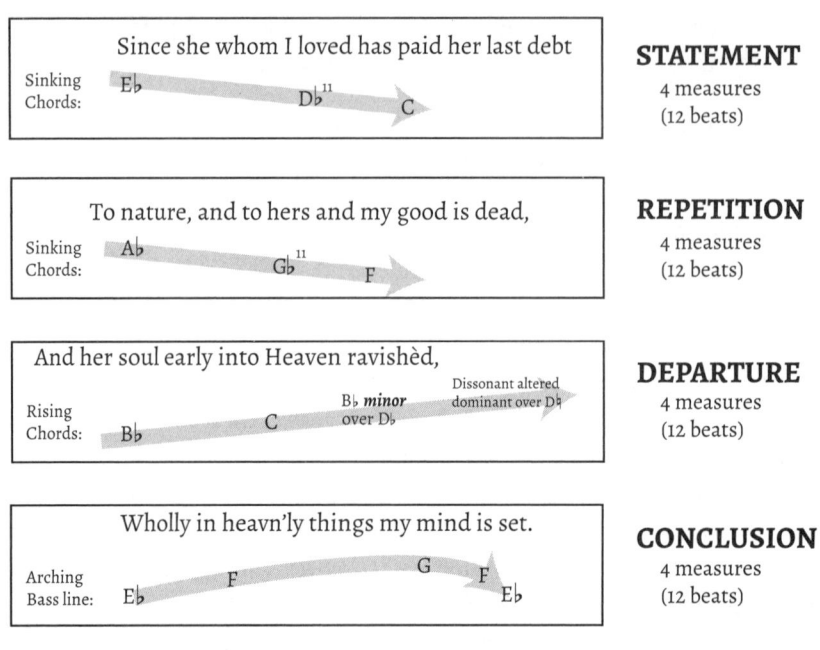

Example 7.1. Benjamin Britten, "Since She Whom I Loved," form and harmonies of opening quatrain

seem that Britten has chosen unambiguously to represent the former over the latter. There is nothing angry or resentful in this music. It is in a major key, the tempo is slow, the music is quiet, and the melody and chords sink downward with a meek, almost soporific effect. At the end of the phrase, the voice changes course and stretches upward ("paid her last debt"), but it sounds more like a hopeful gesture—a turning upward in prayer—than a defiant or confrontational expression. The only dissonance in the harmonies happens at the word "loved," when the pianist's right hand holds on to the note G, which is dissonant against the prevailing chord (D-flat major). But this subtle friction barely ruffles the overall idyllic sound. For a song written in 1945, the dissonance hardly even registers as a problem.

The next phrase repeats the same music—same melody, same chord progression—but with two important differences: it is louder (*forte* rather than *pianissimo*), and the music is transposed; the melody begins on a higher pitch and the bass on a lower pitch (a diagram of the first quatrain, showing the relationship between phrases, is presented in example 7.1). The expressive effect of this is that the music retains its broadly positive atmosphere, but it now sounds confident and self-assured rather than meek. And when the voice rises upward, now at the phrase "my good is dead," it approaches the highest range of the tenor voice (see the 0:26 mark). The space of the music is expanding in both upper and lower directions.

All of this leads to a triumphant point of arrival at the outset of the third line ("and her *soul* . . ."). Musicians will recognize this as a dominant to tonic progression in the key of B-flat major, but even non-musicians can recognize the music as a kind of achievement—the tenor announcing the soul's arrival into heaven with the loudest, highest, most energetic melodic motion thus far. The song has taken a turn not from meekness to anger but from the humble to the heroic. The arrival in heaven is presented as an almost ecstatic fanfare.

Everything collapses, however, at the word "ravishèd." This moment is crucial. We saw how conspicuous the word "ravishèd" is in the context of the poem, and Britten draws considerable attention to it musically (the 0:42 mark). Not only does the voice drop down with a significant leap, but the chord in the piano is the first minor chord of the song. It is also the first "inverted" chord, which is to say that the bass note, unlike all the previous bass notes, is no longer the "root" of the chord, and this makes the harmony somewhat unstable. The sense of triumph crumbles into quiet descent, and the B-flat-*major* chord, which propped up the word "soul," buckles into a corrupted B-flat-*minor* chord at "ravishèd." The subsequent harmony in the piano is even more dissonant (marked as an "altered dominant over D♮" in example 7.1), and it softly ushers in a return to the opening music. It does so, however, with a palpably bitter sense of discord, completely unlike the rooted major chords of the song's beginning.

We hear clear moments of dissonance, then, but none of them necessarily suggests a lack of faith or sincerity, which, I think, we can reasonably associate with the quiet, consonant sounds of the song's idyllic opening. The fourth line of the poem is set with a return to the opening melodic idea and a return to the home key (E-flat major). It is also anchored firmly to the home tonic with a simple, arching bass line that rises up from E♭ and then falls back down. Thus, although there is a painful stab of anguish at the word "ravishèd," the general atmosphere of quiet devotion is quickly recovered. Indeed, the overall shape of this opening quatrain is an arch: the melody gradually moves higher and higher, the music gets louder and louder, then it retracts at "ravishèd" and settles back to its original state.

In chapter 6, we considered how form can be heard as an imposition of order against disorder. That dynamic is very much in play throughout this song. The poem's opening quatrain constitutes a single grammatical sentence, neatly organized in rhymed pentameter lines. Britten matches this structure by carefully parsing the music into four phrases of four measures each. The design, moreover, perfectly matches what Walter Everett refers to as an "SRDC" pattern: "statement, repetition, departure, and conclusion" (marked on the right side of example 7.1).[5] This type of design frequently occurs in popular song. Think, for instance, of the chorus in the Beatles' "From Me to You":[6]

- STATEMENT: If there's anything that you want
- REPETITION: If there's anything I can do
- DEPARTURE: Just call on me and I'll send it along
- CONCLUSION: With love, from me to you

Britten's setting of Donne sounds nothing like the Beatles, but the music is unquestionably familiar and "orderly." The swelling up of emotion that we hear in the setting of the third line, and especially the breakdown at "ravishèd," is successfully contained by the song's balanced proportions and the return to the opening music.

This is not to say, however, that there are no subtle moments of friction and resistance. Consider the enjambment that happens at the end of the first line: "Since she whom I loved hath paid her last debt / to nature." As we learned in chapter 4, enjambments like these create a tension between the regular, balanced patterns of the line and the irregular, unbalanced proportions of the syntax. By parsing this opening quatrain into four measures per line, Britten clearly favors a line-oriented grouping. But notice two subtle details in the melody shown in example 7.2.

First, Britten sets the word "to" as an upbeat to the second phrase, but instead of making it a short upbeat, he holds it for the full length of a dotted quarter, such that the weak syllable "to" is held longer than the stressed syllable in "**na**ture." The result is that the second line essentially stretches back into the space of the first line, allowing a subtle thread of musical continuity to reinforce the poem's syntactic continuity. Second, Britten draws a slur all the way from the opening of the first line to the word "hers" in the second line. Slurs are indications to performers to group notes into a single, continuous phrase. Britten's slur, however, contradicts the song's form. Measure 5 is clearly a repetition of the same idea heard in measure 1. It sounds distinctly like a re-beginning rather than the continuation of an earlier phrase. But Britten's slur suggests something else—it suggests that the performer should, perhaps, focus on the continuity of the syntax rather than the division of the lines. There are undoubtedly a number of effective strategies for doing this, and lis-

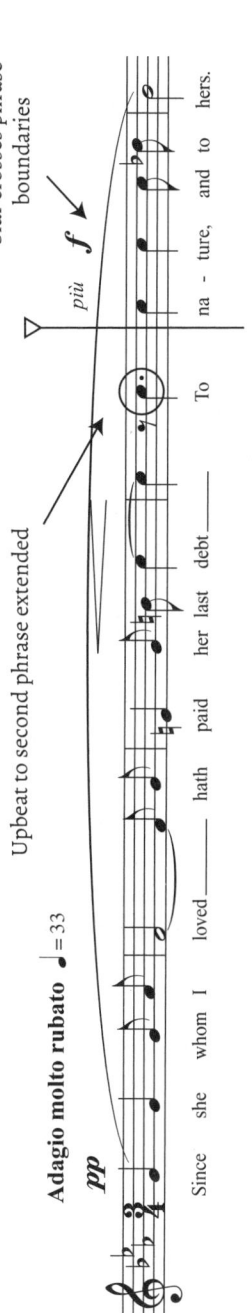

Example 7.2. "Since She Whom I Loved," opening enjambment

teners can consult different recordings to hear various solutions, but the tension itself is representative of broader issues. As we saw throughout the previous chapter, supposedly tight formal boundaries can be transgressed with subtle musical and linguistic continuities.

There are also slight tensions in the way the musical accents relate to the poetic accents. As already established, most of this music is orderly and well behaved. Accented syllables in the poem are accented in the music; unaccented syllables in the poem are unaccented in the music. But there are small exceptions. Notice, for instance, that the second and fourth lines end with parallel constructions: "my good is dead" and "my mind is set" (example 7.3). The former is an expression of despair, the latter an expression of constancy. Both of these would be read naturally with an iambic pattern: ta-TUM-ta-TUM. But Britten unexpectedly places the "my" of the first phrase on an accented downbeat, whereas the "my" of the second phrase is placed more "appropriately" on an unaccented upbeat.

The reasons for this might seem logical. "My good is dead" is a negative sentiment, sung with a complex, out-of-sync rhythmic interaction between piano and voice (quarter-note triplets against eighth-note triplets). "My mind is set" is a more positive sentiment, sung with sturdier rhythms and a sense of resolve. But there is much more *harmonic* dissonance in the second phrase. The chord at "mind" is an inverted chord that harshly superimposes notes from C major and C minor at the same time. The piano, in other words, raises questions about narrative reliability. Is the song's speaker telling the truth? If so, why are those sturdy rhythms in the voice undercut by such harmonic instability? This is a brief moment, but it is reflective of broader trends—a lurking presence of disorder within highly contained and regulated music.

Before moving on to the next quatrain, I would like to return to the word "ravishèd," specifically to view it through the binary of order/disorder. I have already explained the way the harmonies change at that word into less stable, dissonant sonorities. But listen especially to what happens with the piano's bass notes. The bass for all previous measures had been steadily descending. This descent is characteristic of the song generally speaking—descending motion is pervasive, starting with the immediately slouching chords of the song's opening (E-flat major to D-flat major to C major). Britten almost seems to have seized on the idea of "melting" as the persona's primary psychic state ("a holy thirsty dropsy melts me yet"). There are two moments, however, when the bass rises. The second will be discussed momentarily, but the first happens at "ravishèd," and it arguably suggests a counter-struggle to the prevailing meekness

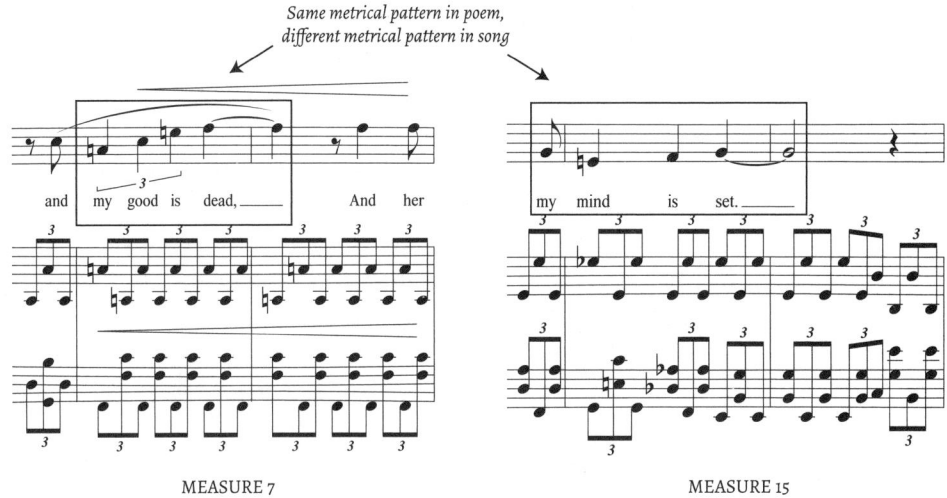

Example 7.3. "Since She Whom I Loved," contrasting approaches to an iambic pattern

of the song's quiet descents. Is this a sign of rising frustration? Or is it something worse—something that, if unleashed, might explode into outright blasphemy? Nothing especially blasphemous happens in the first quatrain—the bass ascent quickly yields to the prevailing descending energies—but for a moment the bass line upsets and unsettles the song's almost narcotic and sedated expression of faith. Order is restored, but not permanently.

The Second Quatrain

The language of the second quatrain is more complicated than that of the first. It begins with an enjambed line that addresses God directly for the first time. As we learned in chapter 5, any changes in the "I-you" relationship can be significant. A first-time reader might assume, from the first quatrain, that the poem is simply a first-person narrative addressed to a general reader. But things change at the outset of the second quatrain: "Here, the admiring her my mind did whet / To seek thee, God." This is a relatively complex construction, but it can be paraphrased as, "Loving my wife has prepared me to love you." And the subsequent analogy—"so streams do show the head"—reinforces that idea: just as a stream indicates a larger source of water, so too does the love for a wife lead toward the greater love of God.

Yet the next two lines of the quatrain introduce a problem in terms of both meter and meaning. The metric problem occurs in line 7, which seems to pack in more accents than we would expect in a standard pentameter line: "But **though** I've **found thee,** and **thou** my **thirst** hath **fed.**" If we accent both "found" and "thee," which strikes me as a reasonable way to read the line, we have six accented syllables rather than the usual five (and the accents are reinforced by the density of fricatives: four accents begin with *th* and two with *f*). Some readers, however, might prefer to elide "thee" with "and" as a single weak syllable in order to maintain a predictable rhythm, which Britten does in his melody by matching "thee-and" to a single note (1:34 mark). But even with such normalization, the line has a certain disruptiveness. It is easy to trip up on it when reading the poem for the first time. And notice how that disruptiveness wonderfully prepares the next line, which is both metrically regular and extraordinarily songlike: "A holy thirsty dropsy melts me yet."

There is an appealing musicality in the assonance of that final line with the pinging of the high *e*'s against the lower accented vowels. Indeed, the sound is so striking that it might distract from the meaning of the words. But the meaning is important. As suggested above, it introduces a problem. Dropsy was a condition associated with alcoholism. Fluid collects in the tissue of the body, which can make the sufferer look bloated and as if plagued with sagging, "melting" flesh.[7] The speaker, then, is telling God that he is sick with an unquenchable craving. Though the love of God should be fully satisfying ("thou my thirst hath fed"), it isn't—he wants something more. The speaker represents this as a "holy" sickness rather than a sinful one, but the overall sentiment is potentially blasphemous: "You, God, are not enough."

Musically, this section is more consistently subdued than the previous section. But, like the earlier music, it leads to a loud outpouring of emotion in the third line of the quatrain (at the 1:32 mark). The difference is that there is no gradual crescendo or any gradual ascent to the high tenor range. The music instead lurches into a sudden outburst without warning or preparation at the phrase "But though I've found thee..." This reflects a broader issue—the fact that there is a crooked asymmetry to the rhythmic and metric groups. As explained above, the first quatrain is set with a simple four-by-four pattern: four phrases, each four measures long. But, as shown in example 7.4, the phrasing for the second quatrain is much less predictable. The first phrase—the setting of the fifth line—is only three measures long. Since there are three beats per measure, the phrase includes nine beats in total. The sixth line of the poem is also nine beats long, but it is subdivided into asymmetrical groups of four beats and five beats. The seventh line is shorter—seven beats long—and the

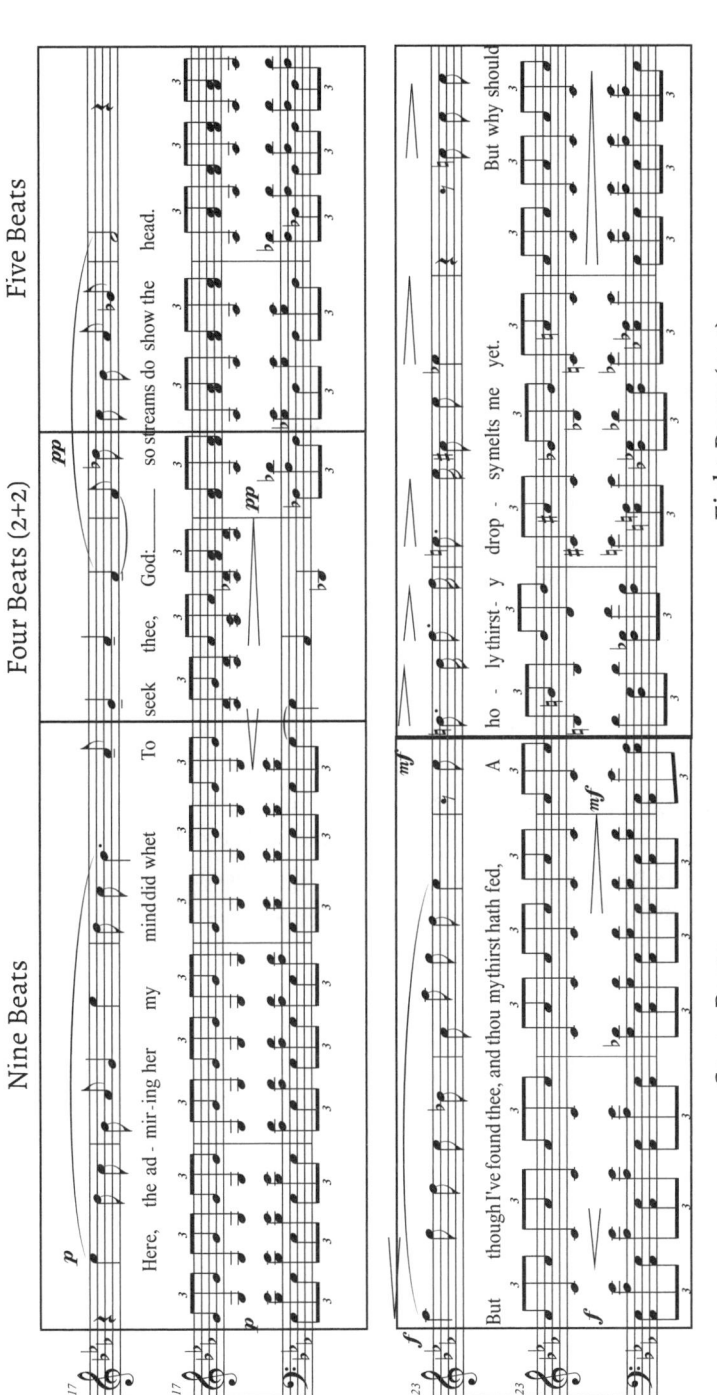

Example 7.4. "Since She Whom I Loved," asymmetrical phrasing of second quatrain

eighth line is eight beats, although it, too, is split into two smaller groups (two groups of four).

The whole section, then, suggests a cockeyed asymmetry, and it all gets thrown off balance, not insignificantly, with the revelation of a direct address—the first utterance of God's name ("to seek thee, God"). Up to that point, the music had been moving at the pace of a slow idyllic waltz, with three beats per measure. The turn toward direct address, however, changes our sense of time. The left hand of the piano, for the first and only time before the song's end, stops the steady stream of eighth-note triplets. Beats are grouped in two groups of two rather than three groups of three, and the effect of this is that the music suddenly slows down into a hushed reverence at "seek thee, God" (1:18 mark). The earlier rhythm picks up again at "so streams do show the head," but by that point we have already lost our sense of predictable phrasing, which is why the loud outburst at "But though I've found thee" is so startling. We no longer have any way of gauging when and where a phrase will begin or end.

Two poetic factors seem to motivate the sudden warping of musical time: the shift toward direct address, especially the mention of God's name; and the enjambment ("whet / To seek thee . . ."), which Britten acknowledges with not precisely a line-oriented grouping or a syntax-oriented grouping but something in between. Both issues lead toward the disruptive shift from triple groupings in the music to duple groupings (the 3 + 3 + 3 at the outset becomes 2 + 2). The subsequent lines reassert some triple groupings, but disruptive duple groupings return, especially at the end of the quatrain with "A holy thirsty dropsy melts me yet." And whereas the first shift was motivated by factors discussed in chapters 4 and 5 (lineation, syntax, and address), the second is motivated more by factors covered in chapters 1 and 2 (diction and meter). "A holy thirsty dropsy . . ." is by far the most "musical" line of the poem, with a pulsing iambic rhythm that reinforces the bounce between the high *e* vowel and lower vowel sounds like "oh" and "aw." Britten emphasizes this by shifting back into the heavily marked duple grouping he used at "to seek thee, God," but he also changes chords with each metrical foot: five poetic beats are articulated with five separate chords (1:40). Hitherto the quatrain had largely floated along with only three chords, each sustained for several beats (E-flat major, D-flat major, and A-flat major). But here we have a quick sequence of five chords in a row, some of which are completely unrelated to the others and all of which occur in an unstable "second inversion": G major, B-flat major, A major, G-flat major, and A-flat major.

This is all quite disorienting—the odd temporal disjunctions, the bizarre

Table 7.1. John Donne, "Since She Whom I Loved," enjambments

Since she whom I loved hath paid her last debt	A	**ENJAMBMENT**
To nature, and to hers and my good is dead,	B	END-STOPPED
And her soul early into Heaven ravishèd,	B	END-STOPPED
Wholly in heav'nly things my mind is set.	A	END-STOPPED
Here, the admiring her my mind did whet	A	**ENJAMBMENT**
To seek thee, God: so streams do show the head.	B	END-STOPPED
But though I've found thee, and thou my thirst hath fed,	B	END-STOPPED
A holy thirsty dropsy melts me yet.	A	END-STOPPED
But why should I beg more love, whenas thou	C	**ENJAMBMENT**
Dost woo my soul, for hers off'ring all thine?	D	END-STOPPED
And dost not only fear lest I allow	C	**ENJAMBMENT**
My love to Saints and Angels, things divine,	D	END-STOPPED
But in thy tender jealousy dost doubt	E	**ENJAMBMENT**
Lest the world, flesh, yea, Devil put thee out?	E	END-STOPPED

sequence of chords—but, again, the overall mood of this quatrain is still remarkably placid, almost beatific. The confession of a "holy" craving for something beyond God's love does not twist the music into something dissonant, violent, or tinged with the minor mode (every chord in the second quatrain is major). But a problem nevertheless has been introduced, and the music has clearly diverged from the orderly design of the first quatrain. What, then, might we expect of the closing sestet?

The Sestet

To this point, the rhyme scheme has been *abba / abba*. For the closing sestet (the sonnet's last six lines) Donne introduces new end rhymes: *cdcdee*.[8] He makes other changes as well. The two quatrains had each begun with mild enjambments, but the sestet features *three* enjambments, one every two lines (table 7.1).

These enjambments accelerate the pace of reading, pushing us along from one line to another. They also increase the tension between lines and syntax, which signifies that the poem is heading in a startlingly new direction. Sonnets often feature a crucial shift in tone, rhetoric, or address, usually described as a turn or volta, and it often happens at the outset of the closing sestet. In the Shakespeare sonnet discussed in chapter 6, the turn occurs when the speaker shifts his attention toward the beloved ("Yet in these thoughts myself almost despising, / Haply I think on thee . . ."). In Donne's sonnet, the turn also happens at the outset of the closing sestet, but in quite a different manner. The language becomes more explicitly blasphemous than that of the first two quatrains, and the changes in rhyme and syntax help underscore the emotional tension. There is also a rhetorical shift: whereas the first two quatrains involved direct statements, the sestet poses a question, one that might be paraphrased as follows: "Why is it, God, that I'm unsatisfied, given that you're acting like a jealous suitor who's afraid that I might give my love to saints, angels, or—worse—the world, flesh, and the devil?"

This is a remarkable shift in tone. Sonnets are traditionally love poems in which *the speaker* is often in the position of a desperate suitor. But here, *God* is presented as the fearful, jealous lover. It is a shocking role reversal, and perhaps more than anything else in the poem, it offers evidence that the speaker might not be addressing God from a position of sincere devotion. There is an implication of bitter sarcasm: "You took my beloved 'early' because you were jealous, so *of course* I want more than what you're offering." But not all readers of the poem see it this way. The phrase "tender jealousy" in line 13 is important. If we read it as sincere, free of sarcasm, it suggests that the speaker still views God with love and respect (as a "tender" rather than a wrathful God). But subtle details nonetheless hint at a more troubling emotional state, not least of them the sequence of end rhymes, which begins with "godly" words ("thou," "thine," "allow," "divine") but sharply moves away from them, concluding with the closed couplet of "doubt" and "out."

Britten sets the entire sestet as a single phrase, diagrammed in example 7.5, and it is structured in three parts: it states a simple melodic/harmonic phrase in the key of C major; it repeats that idea with a more extended anacrusis (a longer lead-in to the repeated motive); and it then builds up to a climax at the phrase "tender jealousy"—marking a return to the opening music, now an octave higher—before dissolving with a slow, chromatic descent.

This maps onto an expressive trajectory that is more turbulent than anything else in the song. The atmosphere at the outset is still beatific, a sound we have become accustomed to, with major chords and quiet, lilting melodies (God's intention to woo the speaker's soul in place of the beloved is presented, it seems, as a straightforward act of grace; see the 1:48 mark). But at the beginning of line 11—"and dost not only fear . . ."—the music becomes louder and

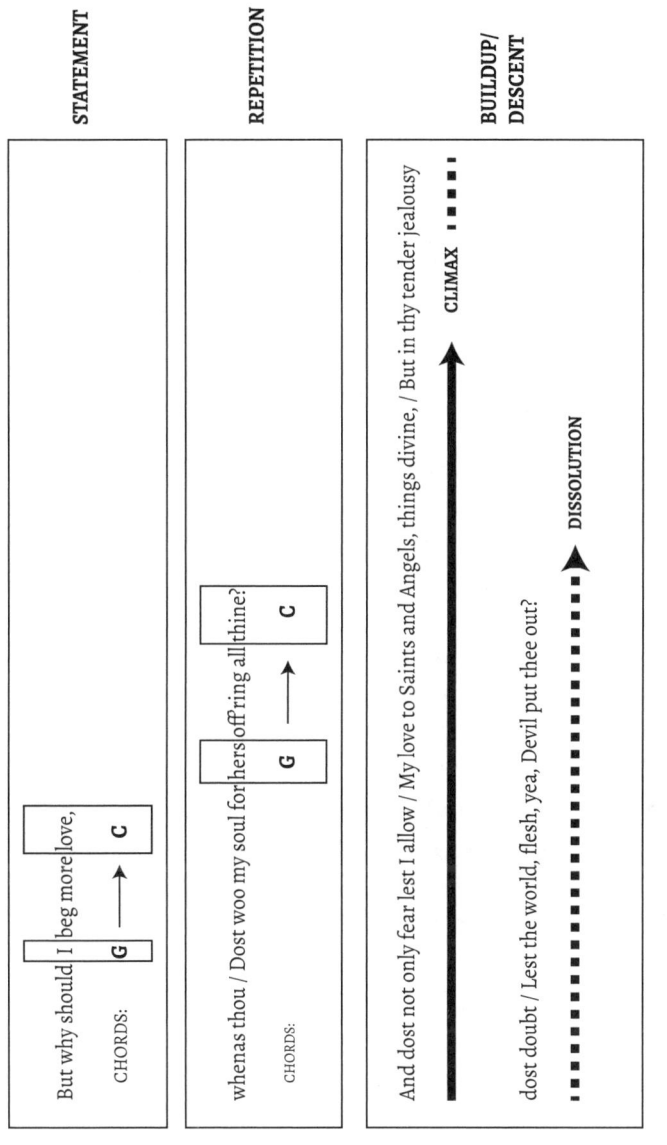

Example 7.5. "Since She Whom I Loved," sestet, three-part design

Table 7.2. Benjamin Britten, "Since She Whom I Loved," descent versus ascent

Since she whom I loved . . .	Voice descends	↓	0:00–0:10
	Bass descends.	↓	
And her soul . . . ravishèd	Voice descends	↓	0:35–0:50
	Bass ascends	↑	
And dost not only fear . . .	Voice ascends	↑	2:12–2:26
	Bass ascends	↑	
dost doubt / lest the world . . .	Voice descends	↓	2:26–3:10
	Bass descends	↓	

more agitated (*crescendo ed agitato*, in Britten's words). For the first time since the opening quatrain, specifically at the word "ravishèd," we hear dissonant, minor chords. And whereas most of the song features consistently "drooping" harmonies, this part drives resolutely upward. Indeed, it becomes so chaotic that for the first time in the song, it is almost impossible to hear each poetic line as a distinct phrase. The musical groupings are even less predictable than those of the second quatrain, and Britten responds to the increased pace of enjambments with an increasingly disorderly, "syntax-oriented" phrasing.⁹

Yet all the upward-rushing energy dissipates at the words "tender jealousy" (2:25). If the speaker had been expressing a genuine anger in the measures leading up to that moment, he unquestionably pivots at this point back into the idyllic, devotional expression we heard at the outset. The difference is that now the "melting dropsy" fully takes over, with chords continually sinking lower and lower, and poetic fragments dispersed in shorter and shorter groups:

> But in thy tender jealousy (8 syllables)
> Dost doubt lest the world (5 syllables)
> Flesh, yea, Devil (4 syllables)
> Put thee out (3 syllables)

Perhaps the most important aspect of this conclusion, then, is the way it directly juxtaposes agitated, upward motion (a rising sense of disorder) against quiet, yielding descent (a reassertion of the song's primary "order"). Table 7.2 shows how this conflict unfolds across the entire song.

The opening immediately establishes the motive of stepwise descent, a sound that will become pervasive. The combination of major-mode chords with gradually descending motion gives the song an aura of consistent abnegation, a giving oneself over to God. But at the word "ravishèd," a new sound arises in the bass: an upward stepwise chromatic motion, linked with more dissonant, minor-mode harmonies. The effect is to give a feeling of willful resistance. Nevertheless, the voice *descends* at that point, as if the bass's rise mirrors an unconscious emotion that has not been fully processed or accepted by the conscious mind. What makes the sestet so important, then, is the way the voice *joins in* with the ascending energy before ultimately yielding once again ("And dost not only fear . . ."). Indeed, the agitated uprising in the sestet features the right hand of the piano playing the same ascending notes we heard in the bass at "ravishèd." But here it now spreads to *all* parts of the musical texture, with the voice and the bass rising in an especially jagged, erratic fashion. Then comes the reversal at "tender jealousy," where the motion returns to outright descent in both voice and piano. How, then, do we make sense of all of this?

Devotion or Anger?

A basic question that I have returned to several times throughout this discussion is the question of sincerity: Is the speaker expressing a sincere devotion to God? Or does the poem actually express an understandable grief and anger at the loss of a loved one? And does Britten's setting choose one possibility over the other? Needless to say, neither the poem nor the song needs be interpreted as *fully* representing either side of this binary. Feelings of love, grief, anger, and faith are complicated, and John Donne's poems—especially the Holy Sonnets—move through complex thought processes, often working out a variety of attitudes and emotions over the course of a single poem. "Since She Whom I Loved" is highly reflective of that approach; it might best be read as an attempt to connect with God, to assert a sincere faith and devotion, but in a way that cannot wholly cover up the speaker's feelings of bitterness and resentment.

In Britten's song, the question of willfulness strikes me as especially important. The slow, languid descents are indicative of a nearly narcotic state, so much so that the sudden moments when the music swells upward almost have the effect of a medication wearing off. But such moments are short-lived, and the intoxicating stupor of God's grace always reasserts itself with quiet, descending harmonies. Never is this clearer than in the sestet, when every part of the musical texture rises up amid the speaker's blasphemous accusations of fear and jealousy. It is a moment that shockingly reveals sentiments that the previous music had only hinted at. But the arrival at "tender jealousy" is like a sudden opiate infusion. It reasserts the major key, and the music slowly declines into muted rapture. This ironically happens as the speaker expresses the very possibilities that would most trouble God: the fact that he, the speaker, might be seduced by the world, flesh, or the devil. On the page, these words can be read as a veiled threat—"you, God, *should* be afraid"—but in the music, the threat simply dissipates. The rising outbursts sound like temporary moments of willfulness, but the dominant—and ultimately conclusive—expressive mode is one of complete and utter surrender in the face of the divine.

My interpretation can be inferred from a rather casual encounter with Donne's poetry and Britten's music. But it is significantly bolstered by an attention to the subtle details of each. A close reading of the song uncovers fascinating complexities. We might notice the way poetic tensions between lines and syntax lead to an increasingly unpredictable and asymmetrical phrasing in the music. Or we might admire the way certain words, such as "ravishèd," have an especially powerful effect, both because they strongly contrast with other words in the poem, and because Britten dresses them with startlingly novel sounds. Like many other songs and poems, "Since She Whom I Lov'd" involves shifts of address, complex metrical interactions, elaborate rhyming patterns, and a complex engagement with form. My analysis only scratches the surface of what we might say about such issues, but it also points to the importance of giving each element careful consideration.

Bruce Springsteen, "Thunder Road"

The enduring success of "Thunder Road," widely regarded as one of the great rock songs of all time, is somewhat surprising, considering the song's form. Unlike most of Springsteen's other massive hits—"Born in the U.S.A.," "Dancing in the Dark," "Born to Run"—it has no clear chorus, no distinct, recurring hook. In chapter 6, we saw how the Beatles wrote songs without a traditional chorus ("A Day in the Life," "Happiness Is a Warm Gun"), but they feature radically contrasting sections that help keep the songs novel and interesting. "Thunder Road" is different. It has seven distinct sections, with varying degrees of contrast in texture, harmony, and melodic/lyrical design, but there are also consistent similarities between sections, and a listener might be forgiven for hearing the song as a series of related "verses," all seeking a chorus that never quite materializes. (The complete song can be heard on Spotify playlist, track 86.)

Let us revisit, then, what constitutes a song's chorus. This is still a topic of debate, but certain features are commonly associated with the concept. Most important, choruses often present a recurring, memorable tune with simple repeating lyrics, often featuring the song's title. This is true of the Springsteen songs mentioned above—"Born in the U.S.A.," "Dancing in the Dark," and "Born to Run"—but also of many of his others, including "Glory Days," "Rosalita," and "Tenth Avenue Freeze Out." Typically, choruses have more energy than the verses, with a thicker texture, louder dynamics, and a higher vocal range. For that reason, the verses often build tension and energy as they lead into the choruses (sometimes with a surging pre-chorus section), and the choruses then function as a satisfying *release* of that energy.

But if "Thunder Road" has no chorus, does that mean it lacks satisfying moments of arrival? Does it never achieve the goal that each individual phrase seems to be pushing itself toward? Such a result would jibe well with the lyrics. The song, like many others by Springsteen, is a working-class carpe diem anthem. It features a persona who wants to escape the confines of small-town life. He spends the majority of the song imploring a woman named Mary to join him, and, because we never hear her response, it would be appropriate for the music to remain unresolved, just as the lyrics are.[10] But the truth is that the song *does* achieve a climactic release of energy, not in the form of a recurring chorus, but in the triumphant saxophone celebration at the song's conclusion (the 3:50 mark).

That conclusion is unquestionably the climax of the song, but several other moments foreshadow its grand arrival. The most significant of these occurs at the 2:32 mark when Springsteen sings, "sit tight, take hold, Thunder Road!" Those words cap the fifth section of the song, which repeats the phrase "Thunder Road" five times (example 7.6).

The fifth section—marked in the example as a second B section—does not ultimately work as a chorus. We never hear the words "Thunder Road" again. And yet, because we expect the song's title to be a prominent part of the chorus, the repetition of "Thunder Road" unavoidably takes on a chorus-like status. The section is also significant because its culminating moment—"sit tight, take hold, Thunder Road"—arrives at a stable cadence, with Springsteen hitting the tonic note in the highest register of his voice (this is why the section is marked "closed" in the example).

But notice some of the strangeness of this form. The fifth section is marked as a second B section because it has the same melodic and harmonic content as the third section (both are based on the melody and chords of the piano and harmonica introduction). But it also shares similarities with the final A' sec-

A / OPEN	16 measures	0:19 - 0:47
A / OPEN	16 measures	0:47 - 1:14
B / OPEN	16 measures	1:14 - 1:42
A / OPEN	16 measures	1:42 - 2:09
B / CLOSED	**18 measures**	2:09 - 2:39
C / OPEN	16 measures	2:39 - 3:06
A' / CLOSED	**26 measures**	3:06 - 3:50

OPEN sections end with a dominant chord
CLOSED sections end with a tonic chord

Example 7.6. Bruce Springsteen, "Thunder Road," form diagram (excluding intro and coda)

tion: both stretch beyond previous sixteen-measure boundaries, and both end with decisive, unequivocally closed cadences (the cadence in the final section launches the saxophone's denouement: "It's a town full of losers / I'm pulling out of here to win"). The A sections are all based on the same sixteen-measure scheme, but they share many similarities with the B sections in terms of both chords and thematic motives. And the lone C section, which sounds somewhat like a traditional bridge, is also similar to earlier music. Moreover, the boundary lines between these sections are not especially sharp, and part of the artfulness of the song's design is the way Springsteen's vocals gradually rise in a continuous trajectory that pushes toward the upper end of the vocal range over the course of the song.

Example 7.7 shows vocal snippets from each of the seven sections. The opening A sections mainly feature lines that descend from Springsteen's middle range (the note C). The first B section starts in the lower range but gradually ascends with the line "hey, what else could we do now ..." And this leads to the song's first climax at the beginning of the third A section, "except roll down the windows and let the wind blow back your hair" (see the 1:41 mark). This is the same chord progression that we heard in the previous A sections, but now with a full texture, much louder dynamics, and a melody that descends from a high F rather than the lower C. It is the song's first hint at a victory, and much of the remainder of the song involves repeated surges up into that higher range, ultimately clinching and stabilizing that high, triumphant F at the end of both the second B section and the final A' section.

These melodic ascents in the voice are often accompanied by a specific "rising" gesture in the accompaniment (example 7.8). This musical idea occurs in every section of the song—it is one of the reasons the sections all sound similar—but it is deployed at different times and in different ways. It is a simple and familiar chord progression that musicians would refer to as a "IV-V-I" progression (subdominant, dominant, tonic). The first time we hear it, it launches the beginning of a small subphrase, "Roy Orbison singing for the lonely..." (at the 0:33 mark). Listen carefully to the accompaniment at that point and you will hear the rising surge in the music. But you will also notice that it does not create a powerful sense of resolution. It appears at a similar place in the next section at the words "show a little faith, there's magic in the night...," and that also coincides with the first time that Springsteen hits the high F (see the 1:00 mark). More significant, it appears in the B section, but now at the *conclusion* of a phrase, the lead-in to the subsequent A section ("Hey, what else can we do now..."). And this time it *does* create a powerful surge into a fuller texture and a higher vocal range at the song's first climax ("except roll down the windows and let the wind blow back your hair"). By the time it appears at the end of the song, it has been stretched out and transformed into its most triumphant guise, with the B-flat and C-major chords held twice as long as usual: "It's a town full of losers. I'm pulling out of here to win."

The reason I discuss these rising gestures in some detail is that they are representative of the song as a whole, which continually loops back to similar ideas in recurring waves of tension. Phrase after phrase, the music builds up toward a series of climaxes, with the saxophone breakout at the end as the most obvious sign of a redemption achieved. These trajectories, moreover, reflect the general theme of the lyrics—the desire to break free of past failures ("don't turn me home again, I just can't face myself alone again"). Many listeners might find such climaxes a bit hokey—Nick Hornby, a great admirer of the song, admits that it is "overwrought, both lyrically... and musically"[11]— but the song would not have achieved its staggering success if it did not also include subtle moments of beauty and elegance to match the broader, more melodramatic gestures of carpe diem Americana.

To get a better sense of this subtlety, we can compare the opening section with the closing section, focusing especially on lyrical attributes that relate to topics covered throughout this book. Springsteen himself often explained that he wanted to make this song "cinematic" and "theatrical."[12] He wrote the

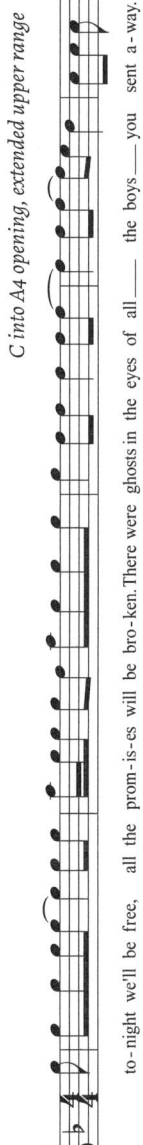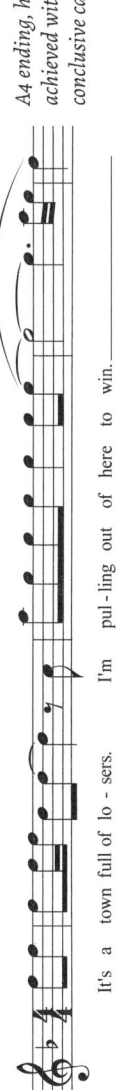

Example 7.7. Vocal snippets from each section of "Thunder Road"

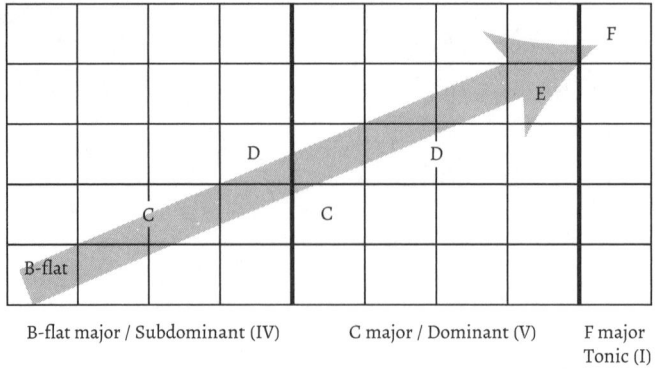

Example 7.8. Recurring rising gesture in the bass in "Thunder Road"

song—along with the rest of the *Born to Run* album—at the piano, which he says helped him expand his expressive palette beyond guitar-driven formulas.[13] He and his producers also created a certain "rock opera" effect by deftly layering a wide range of instruments into the final mix, such as piano, glockenspiel, harmonica, and saxophone. But the "cinematic" effect is most clearly established at the outset in the *lyrics*, which begin by describing "Mary" from a removed, third-person position:

> The screen door slams. Mary's dress waves.[14]
> Like a vision she dances across the porch as the radio plays

Notice how the syntax creates a gesture of opening with its "short: short: long" pattern: two quick sentences followed by a much longer sentence. And notice also the metrical differences between the two lines. The first line, if we read it aloud as plain speech, creates a pile-up of accented words, with six accented syllables compared to just two that are unaccented:

> The **screen door slams. **Mary's** dress waves.**

But now compare that to the flowing energy in the subsequent line, with its pervasive anapestic, triple groupings:

> Like a **vi**sion she **dan**ces a**cross** the **porch** as the **ra**dio **plays**

There are still six accented syllables in this line, but they are mixed in with *eleven* unaccented syllables. And notice how the rhythm speeds up and "dances" in a way that reinforces the lyrical imagery.

The slant rhyme of "waves" and "plays" creates the effect of a closed couplet, especially since the musical phrasing parses each line into distinct four-measure groups. If we were hearing this song for the first time, we would probably assume that "plays" is the end of a sentence. But "plays" turns out to be a transitive verb in search of an object, and the syntax surprisingly pushes past the boundaries of the balanced couplet with a wonderful enjambment: "the radio plays / Roy Orbison singing for the lonely." This moment is a microcosm of the song as a whole in the sense that it stages a transgression beyond restrictive barriers. And it is precisely at this moment, when the syntax pushes past the limits of a closed couplet, that two crucial things happen: the music activates the first "rising" gesture (see example 7.8), and the lyrics shift from a more distant third-person description to a more intimate direct address ("Hey, that's me and I want you only"). It also speeds up the pace of the rhymes to create smaller, two-measure units ("lonely" and "only"), establishing early on that the rhymes in this song may not fall in predictable places. Indeed, the subsequent line surprisingly seems to "fail," both by using identical words at the end of each rhyming unit ("home again" and "alone again"), and by placing those words in unusual, asymmetrical spots in the phrase so that the language ultimately projects a sheepishness that reflects the pathetic implication of the words:

> Don't turn me home again.
> I just can't face myself alone again.[15]

The final section is based on the same music as the opening section, but the overall tone of the lyrics has changed (3:06). Indeed, it is unlike anything else in the entire song. To begin with, the language is more self-consciously "poetic." None of the words would send a reader scurrying for a dictionary, and the diction retains the general streetwise, colloquial feel of the earlier lyrics ("you ain't a beauty but hey, you're alright"). But the words now take a turn toward something much darker and more somber than anything that had been implied thus far:

> There were ghosts in the eyes of all the boys you sent away.
> They haunt this dusty beach road in the skeleton frames of burned-out Chevrolets.

This is language that not only strives for a higher poetic register; it shifts its attention to something beyond the immediate scene. To this point the lyrics of the song have mainly featured four types of statements:

1. Descriptions of Mary ("so you're scared and you're thinking that maybe we ain't that young anymore").
2. The protagonist's self-descriptions ("I ain't no hero, that's understood")
3. Statements of opportunity ("The night's busting open. These two lanes will take us anywhere").
4. Imperatives ("Climb in back. Heaven's waiting down on the tracks").

But this final turn in the song offers something different. It focuses on Mary, but it does so by describing her past in ways that seem to put the speaker in an almost omniscient position. The description of the ghosts of boyfriends past is a strange turn for the song, but more important is the way the language zooms in on an especially intimate, isolated moment:

> And in the lonely cool before dawn
> You hear their engines roaring on
> But when you get to the porch they're gone

This is a level of intimacy unlike anything we have heard before. And since Springsteen explicitly claims that he conceived this song cinematically, we might even imagine this scene as a kind of flashback, one that focuses entirely on Mary. But given that it retains the crucial second-person "you," it has the effect not of a direct address but rather of a leap into Mary's mind, with a second-person narrator who can read her thoughts and knows her past. There is no change of pronouns, but the *tone* of the address is new.

The voice snaps back, however, to the original style of direct address at the moment Mary's name appears. We heard her name at the opening of the song, as part of the initial third-person description. But now the reappearance of "Mary" breaks a spell. The talk of ghosts and loneliness and the empty town dissipates, and the song returns to its main theme:

> So Mary climb in.
> It's a town full of losers. I'm pulling out of here to win.

Rhetorically, this is a powerful shift toward a renewed sense of optimism. And it is especially persuasive in that it appears after first exposing, with an almost omniscient power, Mary's desperate loneliness. But the effect of this moment relies on more than just the shift in the tone of the address. It is also carefully staged with other uses of artfully designed language.

Notice, for instance, how Springsteen's use of end rhymes—and rhymes in general—evolves over the course of the song. The opening section has three end rhymes, but they are not used in the same way: "waves" and "plays" is a slant rhyme that marks the ends of the four-measure units; "lonely" and "only" is a perfect rhyme that marks quicker, two-measure units; and "again" and "again" is an identity, with the two appearances of "again" slightly unbalanced (they appear at different parts in their respective measures). The first B section, however, begins with yet another scheme:

> You can hide 'neath your covers and study your pain,
> Make crosses from your lovers, throw roses in the rain,
> Waste your summer praying in vain
> For a savior to rise from these streets.

The first three lines—all parsed into two measure-groupings—feature important internal and end rhymes: "covers" / "pain," "lovers" / "rain," "summer" / "vain." The last line breaks the pattern, but it does so by switching from traditional rhymes to an emphasis on alliteration: "savior" and "streets" resonates with the word "summer" in the third line. These groups of threes work in tension with lines that are predominantly grouped in twos and fours. And they recur at crucial moments in the song. The first climactic arrival on a stable tonic, for instance, is marked by a three-part grouping: "road," "hold," and "road."

> Oh, oh, oh Thunder Road.
> Sit tight. Take hold.
> Thunder Road.

The final section of the song, however, is the most conspicuous in its use of an altered rhyme scheme. And it interacts in fascinating ways with both a shifting sense of address and a tension between lines and syntax.

It begins with a balanced couplet that rhymes "away" and "Chevrolet." These words resonate with the rhymes of the opening couplet ("waves" and "plays"), and this is not insignificant; it invites us to hear the final A section in comparison with the first, with a focus on similarities and differences. Both sections feature important enjambments, and both pair them with shifts in address. One of the features that is noticeably different at the end, however, is the switch to tercets, the grouping of rhymes into threes instead of twos:

> And in the lonely cool before dawn.
> You hear their engines roaring on
> But when you get to the porch they're gone

This is the first of two triple groupings at the end. Also, notice that the last line—"but when you get to the porch they're gone"—has a similar status to the enjambed line at the beginning of the song: "Like a vision she dances across the porch as the radio plays / Roy Orbison . . ." Here, the word "gone" could be the end of a sentence, much like "plays" might have sealed off the earlier line. But the syntax, once again, surprisingly pushes past a rhyming barrier: "they're gone / on the wind . . ."

This is a crux moment for three reasons. First, it pivots from one triple-rhyme group to another. "Dawn," "on," and "gone" lead to this:

> On the wind.
> So Mary climb in.
> It's a town full of losers. I'm pulling out of here to win.

The song had been gradually hinting that these triple rhymes might overtake the more common duple groupings, and here they finally do so in triumphant fashion.

Second, the enjambment is precisely the moment when the final section definitively stretches out beyond the limits of the other sections. As already shown in the form diagram of example 7.6, five of the seven sections in this song are sixteen measures long. The second B section stretches to eighteen measures in order to achieve the song's first climactic closure. This final section reaches eighteen measures exactly at the word "gone." In some ways, it represents an anticlimax, especially in comparison with the end of the previous B section, and it would have been a disappointment if the song ended there. But the enjambment—"gone / on the wind."—allows the section to move into uncharted territory, ultimately stretching out to *twenty-six measures* precisely because the enjambment allows for one last triple-rhyme grouping.

Third, this enjambment can be heard as the place where the language snaps back from the "omniscient narrator" position, with its cinematic flashback effect, to the present-tense, carpe diem moment. It is the ultimate, most rhetorically reinforced assertion of the song's basic goal—to get Mary into the car. And just as the song opens with a "short: short: long" lyrical pattern—

> The screen door slams. Mary's dress waves.
> Like a vision she dances across the porch as the radio plays

—so too does it end with a similar gesture, racing, with its final line, into the apotheosis of the saxophone conclusion:

On the wind.
So Mary climb in.
It's a town full of losers. I'm pulling out of here to win.

Tension Versus Triumph

It is easy to get lost in the details when analyzing a song. There are so many different things to discuss in both music and language that it can be difficult to tie the disparate elements together. But we have seen how "Thunder Road" continually repeats similar gestures, with the music often confined to symmetrical, squared-off phrases and simple, balanced rhymes. What makes the song work, though, is the way that it repeatedly creates breakthrough moments that become more and more momentous as the song proceeds. And these breakthroughs involve features at all levels of music and lyrics: syntax, rhyme, address, chord progressions, vocal range, texture, dynamics, and much else. It is a song about escape that continually escapes its own strictures.

But before I conclude, I want to point out that my analysis of "Thunder Road" has focused entirely on the version that was recorded for track 1, side 1 of the *Born to Run* album. The song went through many different iterations before that recording, including a version that the band apparently called "Angelina" or "Angelina's Dress Sways," in which the lyrics were quite different ("Mary" was preceded at one point by "Angelina" and "Christine").[16] Moreover, the song has been performed live by Springsteen thousands of times and has been covered by many other musicians. I will not launch into analyses of any of these different versions here, but it is worth mentioning how few of them retain the level of triumph that we hear in the 1975 recorded version. Springsteen himself frequently performs the song with smaller groups of musicians and in a much more subdued manner. Similarly, cover versions—by singers like Chris Cornell or Frank Turner, or bands like the Cowboy Junkies or Tortoise—often echo the subdued sound and eschew the heroic breakthroughs of the original (in the case of Tortoise, the entire song is shifted into a minor key). The simplest explanation for this change of tone is that musicians often prefer that the live versions or cover versions not sound too similar to a classic recorded version—the goal is often to reveal some new dimension of the song.

But perhaps the extraordinary optimism of the conclusion to "Thunder Road" was considered unsatisfying, even for its deepest fans—even, perhaps, for Springsteen himself. In 2010, Springsteen released a song called "The

Promise," which is a sequel of sorts to "Thunder Road." What we learn is that the supposed "triumph" of the earlier song did not lead to a happy ending:

> I followed that dream through the southwestern tracks
> That dead ends in the two-bit bars.
> The promise was broken, I was far away from home,
> Sleeping in the back seat of a borrowed car.

The song then finishes with one of the bleakest lyrics Springsteen ever wrote: "Thunder Road, take it all and throw it all away."

This is a dark reaction to the original song. But its darkness ultimately reminds us just how brightly "Thunder Road" shines. The song lingers on personal flaws and bad circumstances, sometimes with an almost comical directness—how many other love songs would deliver a line like "you ain't a beauty, but hey you're alright"?—but we never lose sight of the fact that these are all obstacles to be overcome. The song's narrator boxes himself in with repetitive phrases, balanced rhymes, and a restricted range, but does so only to break through those boundaries again and again. The sense of victory is so complete, so total, and so flagrantly triumphant that we can understand why almost all subsequent versions would shy away from the exultation of the studio album. A redemption like that is hard to sustain.

▌▌▌ What more could be said about these songs? What else is there to learn about Britten's "Since She Whom I Loved" or Springsteen's "Thunder Road"? The answer, of course, is a great deal. I have said almost nothing about historical context. What did it mean, for instance, for Britten to set Donne's Holy Sonnets in early August 1945, with atomic bombs falling on Japan, and so soon after he had visited the recently liberated Bergen-Belsen concentration camp? (He performed there with the violinist Yehudi Menuhin.) Europe was in ruins, London was a city of rubble, and here was Britten, writing songs that grapple with faith, love, sin, and forgiveness.

Springsteen's circumstances were far less apocalyptic—even small-town New Jersey could not have been *that* bad—but his was nevertheless music from a post-Vietnam, Watergate-obsessed America. It was a time of disillusionment, a time when hippy optimism was rapidly receding. As Springsteen himself put it in 2005, "Everybody experienced a radical change in the image they had of their country and of themselves."[17] Yet still, in the face of such change, he sat down at the piano and wrote lines that offered everyone "one last chance to make it real / to trade in these wings on some wheels." Surely a deeper analysis of the song would want to consider these issues more closely.

This chapter, then, is only a start. But it offers a way forward, a way of approaching complete songs by gathering together observations about diction, meter, rhyme, lines, syntax, and everything else discussed in this book. As I have emphasized throughout, every aspect of a song takes on meaning in relation to everything else. And although we can pull songs apart and place each element under a microscope, we will ultimately want to know how each fragment resonates with the music and words around it. Exploring such resonances takes time and patience, but the exercise is well worth the effort. It brings us closer to the songs we love best.

CONCLUSION ||||||||||||||||||||||||||||||||||||||||||||||||||||||||||||||||||||||||

Some Thoughts About Poetry, Meaning, and Word Painting

There is no chapter in this book specifically about meaning—nothing devoted exclusively to the challenge of determining what a poem or song is "about." In that way, it is like many introductory poetry texts. Authors often invite us into the world of poetry by revealing its sounds and rhythms, its structure and form. They rarely pull us aside and say, "Here's how you figure out what a poem *means*." For some readers, this might be puzzling. Isn't meaning the most *basic* thing that people struggle with when first encountering a poem? Shouldn't the experts help with that?

Billy Collins, the former U.S. Poet Laureate, once wrote a poem called "Introduction to Poetry." He begins by describing some playful ways he encourages his students to engage with poems—for example, "I want them to waterski / across the surface of a poem / waving at the author's name on the shore." What Collins offers his students is a way of reading poetry that is both joyful and enthralling, an activity that they would be fools to pass up. The poem ends, however, by describing their response, and it is not pretty:

> ... all they want to do
> is tie the poem to a chair with rope
> and torture a confession out of it.
>
> They begin beating it with a hose
> to find out what it really means.[1]

If this is how poetry teachers experience questions about a poem's meaning, we can understand why they would be reluctant to dwell on the issue.

Collins paints a comically extreme scenario, but his general viewpoint is shared by many poets. In 1933, T. S. Eliot used a different metaphor to similar ends. He compared the meaning of certain poems to the "nice meat" that a burglar throws at a watchdog, something that provides a useful distraction while the poem "does its work."[2] Though not the same as the Collins metaphor, it arrives at a similar conclusion. For Collins, the poem is an innocent victim, subjected to the violence of unimaginative students. For Eliot, the *poem* is the criminal; it invades the mind of the reader, and uses meaning as a blunt subterfuge to sneak in behind our backs. In both cases, finding out what a poem is "about" is beside the point. For Collins, the search for meaning is an impediment to pleasure; it is crude and brutish—certainly not *fun*. For Eliot, meaning is no more than a diversion, something unrelated to the real work of poetry.

I suspect that thousands of teachers across the world would respond to both these metaphors with a deep sense of recognition and agreement. After all, most poetry teachers are also poetry *fans*—they are drawn to poems as a source of enjoyment. When students insist on determining what a poem is "about," it can be disheartening—almost like watching someone ride a rollercoaster, exit the ride unmoved, and then ask, "What did that mean?" If the search for an explanation does not include a visceral, emotional connection, why even bother?

But this characterization is perhaps unfair. Indeed, it seems especially unreasonable when we consider the situation from the perspective of a struggling student. People use language in all manner of ways, but most of us spend our days dealing with words and sentences that we understand. We are often trying to communicate something *specific*, whether in conversation, emails, texts, or our own minds. A person can hardly be blamed, then, for looking at a strange line of poetry and wondering, "What does this mean?" It is a natural reflex for anyone who reads.

In chapter 1, I quoted a line from Robert Lowell's translation of Eugenio Montale: "The porcupine sips a quill of mercy." I immediately set aside any attempt to explain it, and I have no intention of doing so here—a convincing account of that line, which occurs at the end of "News from Mount Amiata," would require an extended discussion of the complete poem. But I can understand why a reader would be prompted to *ask* what it means. It is not normal language. I can think of no real-world context in which we would encounter such an utterance. For many readers, this is precisely what makes the line so exciting. This is part of what makes it poetry. But it would be inconsiderate of us to dismiss out of hand a student's justifiable confusion about what such a strange sentence might mean.

It is also unfair to suggest that the search for meaning is necessarily an impediment to pleasure. Poetry lovers often weigh one interpretation against another, and many would argue that doing so is part of the fun. In fact, many poetry lovers, at some point in their lives, have probably returned to a poem after a long period and discovered a completely new meaning in it. This is one of the great joys of the art form. A line that we once found enigmatic might suddenly strike us as having a very specific meaning. And something that we once read as unambiguous might later become clouded with confusion, wonder, and complex connotations.

But let us now think a little more carefully about what we mean by "meaning." In some cases, when students say that they don't know what a poem "means," they are referring to a lack of specific knowledge: Who is Heraclitus? What does "preternatural" mean? What's a grackle? This is an understandable and common form of confusion, but it is also relatively easy to overcome with a search engine, a dictionary, or an encyclopedia. In other cases, the vocabulary is not the problem but the syntax and lineation; if a poem unfolds as a single sentence of more than a dozen lines, inexperienced readers might understandably get lost: What is the subject of this sentence? Where's the verb? Why is there a question mark at the end? *How is this even a question?*

Most frequently, though, concerns about meaning arise when students assume that poems must have a deeper significance beyond the language on the page. If a poem describes a butterfly, it cannot just be about a butterfly; it must be about beauty or death or the passage of time. After all, many of the poems that students are taught in high school and college do indeed point toward meaning beyond the literal; few would read William Blake's "The Sick Rose" and see it as nothing more than a poem about a rose and a worm. But this particular concern can be problematic for multiple reasons: it is a potential source of anxiety—students often feel inadequate if they cannot identify a hidden meaning that clarifies what the poem is "really about"; the search for meaning beyond the words often distracts attention from the very features that make us want to read a poem in the first place—after all, we would hardly obsess over potential layers of meaning in clumsy, bland, or unimaginative poetry; and there is no reason to assume that a poem necessarily has a complicated subtext at all—it really might just be about a butterfly—in which case the search for a deeper meaning, as in the Billy Collins metaphor, is like trying to extract information from a suspect who cannot supply it.

But perhaps the biggest problem with people trying to find out what a poem means is that such a search often suggests laziness and lack of engagement. If a poem is treated like a riddle, then all we need to do is solve it and move on. Once we have found out what it's "about," our job is done. Such an analytical approach allows us to sidestep the most fundamental prerequisite for good interpretation of art: *an act of sustained attention*. Analysis requires that we read and reread, listen and then listen again. In doing so, we might indeed discover meanings on multiple levels. We might even uncover a complex symbolic logic or an inspiring ethical message. But most likely, we will simply begin to marvel, more and more, at how each element of a poem or song interacts in a dynamic and complex balance that continues to impress us years after an initial encounter.

If this is a special challenge in the poetry classroom—if English teachers really do struggle to get their students to move beyond a hasty paraphrase—is that also true for students of song? We might think that music students would be less obsessed with meaning. They have melodies, chords, and rhythms to worry about, and modern song lyrics are often far less cryptic than modern poems. Nobody needs to rack their brain to decipher what Taylor Swift is getting at when she sings "We Are Never Ever Getting Back Together." And even in the art song repertoire, composers often choose to set poems that are fairly easy to grasp.

But meaning is ultimately no less pressing for music analysts than it is for poetry analysts. In fact, the most popular interpretive approach among music academics is to identify instances of "word painting," moments when the music seems to depict or reflect various aspects of the text. If a poem mentions physical or spiritual anguish, we quickly seek out instances when the music sounds pained. If the poem mentions a sunrise, we catalogue every ascending line that might plausibly paint the scene. And if the gold standard for song analysis is to find out how the music reflects the words, then the first step for the analyst is to identify what the words *mean*—and, more broadly, what the poem or lyric is about. How else could we properly judge the musical response?

I have pointed out many instances of word painting throughout this book, but I have also consciously tried to deemphasize it as a general topic. I do not give it a chapter of its own, though not because I think there is anything inherently wrong with word painting. It has been an essential attribute of song for centuries, and it would be absurd for us to ignore its impact and expressiveness. (The term "madrigalism" is synonymous with "word painting," and derives from musical practices that stretch back to the Renaissance.) The reason I deemphasize word painting, rather, is that analysts often embrace it to the exclusion of all else. In order to explain why a song is "good," an analyst must first show how the music expresses the words and, in so doing, prove that the composer was sufficiently "sensitive" to the text.

There is nothing necessarily harmful in this approach—indeed, finding examples of word painting can be a real source of pleasure—but students of song should also recognize two basic concerns: first, word painting comes easily: bad composers do it just as easily as good composers. Pointing out an instance of word painting has little value in and of itself; we need to know why such an instance is particularly artful—why it creates an effect that people want to experience again and again. And to do that, we need to relate it to other aspects of the song. Second, word painting is often appreciated more on an intellectual level than a visceral, emotional level. For instance, in chapter 4, I pointed out an instance of word painting in the song "Little Talks" by Of Monsters and Men. I explained how, after some tensions between musical grouping and syntax, the music arrives at a stable cadence that coincides with the words "safe to shore." This is a nice detail, I think, and not without significance. But it is unlikely to have an impact on the way most people experience the song in real time, even on an unconscious level. Much more powerful are the syntactic disruptions, the rhymes, and the changing vowel sounds, all of which interact with the accompanying rhythms and harmonies in ways that would be effective even without the word painting. The fact that the music *does* reflect the meaning of the words matters, but there is much else to discuss and discover.

These issues reinforce a broader point: great poems and songs are more than mere vehicles to communicate meaning. We can ask what a poem or song is "about"—there is no harm in doing so, and it might lead to fruitful discoveries—but many other questions deserve our attention as well. How do the song's rhyming patterns affect its form? What about changes in diction? Who is addressing whom? How are the lines, phrases, and syntax aligned or misaligned? And how might they have been arranged differently?

People will continue to ask about meaning, of course, and there is much that is encouraging about that. In fact, entire websites, such as "genius.com" and "songmeanings.com," provide venues for large numbers of people to come together to debate and discuss what a given lyric might mean, presumably for no purpose other than their own enjoyment and understanding. What I find heartening about such activities is that they reflect an urge among listeners to find deeper intimacy with their most beloved songs. These websites suggest a desire for more attentive listening. Even a quick scan of the discussions on these online forums shows a recognition that we all might benefit from careful thought about even the smallest details of a poem or song.

Some might object that this emphasis on details is misguided. Shouldn't we sometimes adjust our lens *outward* instead of inward? Shouldn't we think more carefully about how a poem or song operates within the context of history and culture and society at large? Yes, we should. Indeed, great analysts typically move in *both* directions, sometimes dwelling for hours on the significance of a simple comma, sometimes stepping back and holding a poem or song up against the whole sweep of human history, including all the complex dynamics of race, gender, ideology, reception history, and aesthetics.

In this book I am working on the microscopic level, not because I object to the more macro-oriented approaches, but because the close reading of small details is a good way to start engaging with songs. And more than anything else, this is what I hope readers will have taken away from this book: a desire to get started; a desire to find a cherished song and think about it from as many angles as possible, to get lost in beats, rhythms, and syntax, and to find meaning wherever we might look—in form, lines, meter, and rhymes. Put simply: I hope it triggers a desire to grapple as thoroughly as possible with poetry and song.

APPENDIX ||||||||||||||||||||||||||||||||||||||||||||||||||||||||||||||||||||||

Transcribing Lyrics

Suppose that a famous songwriter dies. The people managing the estate want someone to produce a book that transcribes all the writer's lyrics onto the printed page. Unfortunately, there are no surviving primary documents on paper—all sketches and notebooks have been destroyed and there is no definitive, author-sanctioned version of the written lyrics. The only guide, then, is what can be deciphered from audio recordings. Given this hypothetical (but not implausible) scenario, what criteria should be used to arrange the song lyrics into lines?

This might not strike readers as an especially vexing problem, and in some cases it would not be. Songs are often sung with discrete melodic phrases that can easily be transcribed into distinct poetic lines. But a person charged with the task of transcribing lyrics in a professional capacity would want to give the issue some serious thought. Moreover, anyone *reading* the printed lyrics might want to know why the words were arranged in one way and not another, especially since those decisions could theoretically have an effect on how to process and understand the song.

Below is a list of potential factors that might consciously or unconsciously guide a would-be transcriber. They are not ranked in any particular order, because each factor might take on more or less significance depending on context.

- *Vocal caesuras:* When there is a significant pause in the vocal part, it often makes sense to treat that as a line ending.
- *Musical meter and phrasing:* If the vocal phrases are parsed into predictable units of more or less equal length (for example, a four-beat measure in rap), then each unit might reasonably be equated with a single poetic line. If the vocal phrases spill beyond those units, they would be treated as enjambments.

- *End rhymes:* If rhymes predictably occur at the ends of musical phrases, it would stand to reason that the written lines should also end with a rhyme.
- *Syntax:* If the goal of the written lyrics is to make the words easy to read on the page, it would be advisable to avoid enjambments and parse the language into logical syntactic chunks (this goal, of course, might contradict the concerns regarding meter and phrasing above).
- *Parallel construction:* If the first verse of a song is transcribed in a certain way, it would probably make sense to transcribe the second verse in a similar way, even if the words are different. This would be true of subsequent parallel moments as well.
- *Poetic representation:* If the goal is to make the lyrics readable "as a poem," the words would have to be rendered in a way that would be satisfying from a poetic standpoint. (What qualifies as "satisfying" is, of course, subjective, but the point is that a transcriber might choose line endings based not on how we hear the words in the song, but on how we might read the lyrics as poetry.)

In the easiest cases, these guiding factors would reinforce one another without conflict. The phrases, syntax, rhymes, and parallel constructions would all point unambiguously toward a certain parsing of the lyrics. Ideally, that would also accord with what the transcriber deems to be the most "poetic" way of representing the language.

But we also saw in chapter 4 that there are frequently tensions, ambiguities, and misalignments between these above factors, and sometimes they would leave a transcriber with multiple opposing yet viable options. If the rhymes are in conflict with the syntax, which of the two should be privileged? Where should line endings occur? What if the rhymes are out of sync with a previously established metrical grouping? What makes one factor more important than another?

To better grasp these issues, consider a specific case: Cole Porter's "Anything Goes" from 1934. This is a useful example not only because the song is well known—and has been anthologized in books of poetry—but also because it involves complexities of rhyme, rhythm, phrasing, syntax, and parallel construction, all of which make it ideal as a challenge for would-be transcribers. Example A.1 shows one of the song's principal melodies as it appears with lyrics from three of the verses (the complete song is on Spotify playlist, track 87). If we look at Robert Kimball's compilation *The Complete Lyrics of Cole Porter*,

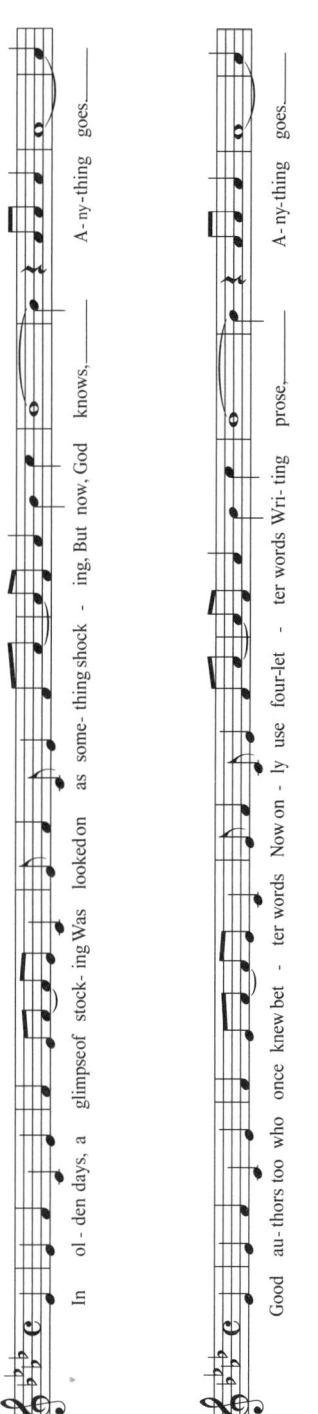

Example A.1. Cole Porter, "Anything Goes," different lyrics set to the same melody

we find these words presented with curious differences in lineation.[1] The first verse segment in the example (the top line) is represented as:

> In olden days a glimpse of stocking
> Was looked on as something shocking,
> But now, God knows,
> Anything goes.

This arrangement is both sensible and intuitive. Each line ends with a strong, standard rhyme ("stocking"/"shocking," "knows"/"goes"), and they are also distinct syntactic units. It would be hard to imagine many transcribers coming up with radically different ways of writing this verse. The second melody, however, is represented with a slight rearrangement of syllables (second line of example):

> Good authors too who once knew better words
> Now only use four-letter words
> Writing prose,
> Anything goes.

Note the subtle change: the first segment is transcribed as four lines with syllables that follow a 9-8-4-4 pattern. The second segment, *which is matched to exactly the same notes in the score*, is represented with the pattern 10-8-3-4. What accounts for the difference?

If the second segment had been treated the same as the first, it would have looked like this:

> Good authors too who once knew better
> Words now only use four-letter
> Words writing prose,
> Anything goes.

The standard rhymes ("better"/"letter," "prose"/"goes") would still be preserved, but the syntax would be disrupted by strong enjambments: "knew better / words," "four-letter / words." If it makes more sense to avoid these enjambments, would it then be better for the sake of consistency to go back and make the first segment correspond to the 10-8-3-4 syllable pattern? If we did so, the lines would look like this:

> In olden days a glimpse of stocking was
> Looked on as something shocking, but

Appendix 221

> Now, God knows,
> Anything goes.

The two segments would now be transcribed the same way, but the transcription would create more problems: it disrupts the standard rhymes ("stocking"/ "shocking") and also creates strong enjambments: "was / Looked on," "but / now God knows."

The most likely reason, then, that the transcriber, whether Kimball or someone else, used different syllable groupings for identical melodies is that he wanted to preserve standard end rhymes and syntactic clarity, but decided that if the two were in conflict, syntactic clarity would be privileged, which meant that parallel constructions would *not* be maintained if they disrupted the rhymes or syntax.

Such reasoning is perfectly sensible. But the system cannot avoid enjambments altogether. The final segment (bottom line of the example) is the most complicated to render on the page. In *The Complete Lyrics of Cole Porter* it is presented with a 9-8-4-4 syllable pattern, which comically hyphenates the word "enough":

> When Rockefeller still can hoard en-
> Ough money to let Max Gordon
> Produce his shows,
> Anything goes.

This version seems deliberately silly because of the hyphen (as well as the capital O for "Ough"), but notice that neither of the previous syllabic options can avoid a hyphenated word when applied to this text. The 10-8-3-4 option would require a hyphen for the word "produce":

> When Rockefeller still can hoard enough
> Money to let Max Gordon pro-
> Duce his shows,
> Anything goes.

Since neither option allows for unbroken syntactic units, the transcriber privileged the version that allowed for the simpler—but by no means simple—rhyme ("hoard en-"/ "Gordon").

Thus far, I have focused primarily on rhymes and syntax. But what about melodic groupings? "Anything Goes" has a brilliantly complex melody, which is part of what makes the transcription a potential challenge. How might the metrical subdivisions of the tune itself inform our arrangements of the words? Example A.2 shows how repetitive rhythmic units parse the tune into asymmetrical groups.

The melody starts off simply enough with a measure of four straight quarter notes, and we might expect another such measure that would make a larger group of eight (as shown with the "8" above the beginning of the melody). But the boxed units all have the same syncopated rhythm, which encompasses three beats. It is an example of a purely musical "rhyme" that works partly in conjunction with, and partly against, the lyrical rhymes. Melodies in common time, such as this song, would normally group measures in multiples of two (duple groupings). But here the repetition of a distinctive rhythmic pattern creates disruptive *three-beat* groups that impose a striking asymmetry. The result is a sense of reckless acceleration, perhaps mimicking the song's theme of a world gone crazy. As each lyric moves from a state of past innocence to modern chaos, the melody slips off the four-beat grid, starts speeding up in groups of threes, and rises in pitch, only to be reined in at the tune's end by a two-beat anacrusis—a gesture that resets the music into neat two-measure units (eight beats total).

How then do we transcribe these groupings into poetic lines? If we represented the words according to the beat-groupings above, the lines would look like this:

> When Rockefeller still
> Can hoard enough
> Money to let
> Max Gordon pro-
> Duce his shows,
> Anything goes.

This, it seems to me, is not necessarily an improvement on the other versions. It is not easy to read, and though it captures some of the disjunctions in the melody, it sacrifices rhyme and syntactic clarity in order to make the musical syncopations more palpable.

There is another problem: when we listen to the tune, we may not recognize the status of the three-beat groupings until *after* the boxed rhythm in the example above has been repeated. As a result, the first three-beat grouping will still feel experientially linked to the first five beats (hence the tentative eight-beat grouping above in the annotated example). For that reason, it might be better to group them together in a large ten-syllable line:

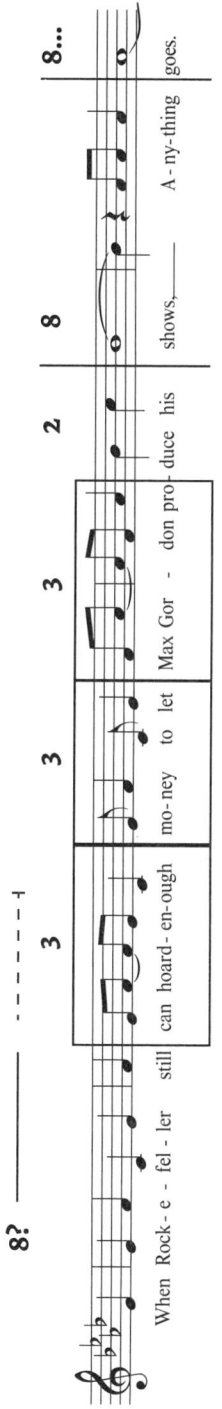

Example A.2. "Anything Goes," metrical complexity in melody

> When Rockefeller still can hoard enough (anacrusis plus eight beats)

The next two boxed rhythms—six beats altogether—assert themselves as distinct units, which could then be grouped together to emphasize the rhyme of "hoard enough" and "Gordon pro-" (pronounced: "pruh"):

> Money to let Max Gordon pro- (six beats)

The final lines would then involve a "reset" of duple patterns:

> Duce his shows,   (two-beat anacrusis and downbeat)
> Anything goes.   (two-beat anacrusis and downbeat)

Another option would be to use longer lines, so that all the syncopated turmoil and complex rhyming could be pushed into the middle. In that case, no line endings would draw attention to rhymes other than "shows" and "goes," which cap off two massively imbalanced lines:

> When Rockefeller still can hoard enough money to let Max Gordon produce his shows,
> Anything goes.

There are reasons to quibble with all of these options, but an obvious question arises at this point. Why does any of this matter? In poetry, lineation has a direct effect on how we read and experience lines. Long lines or short lines, enjambed lines or end-stopped lines—these choices affect pacing, create tension, and encourage us to accent certain words rather than others. The choices are rarely arbitrary, and even if a poet *does* choose to end lines in an arbitrary fashion, lineation still has a direct impact on the way we read the poem. To test this, change the lineation of any poem you love; you will quickly recognize that a different lineation alters or upsets your reading experience.

Lyrics, however, are different. In most cases, we only read lyrics after we have heard a performance of the song. If the tune is especially well known—like Porter's "Anything Goes"—we will probably "hear" the song in our minds while reading the words. A skeptic, then, would say that it does not matter how the words are arranged on the page. The only reason we look at lyrics in the first place is to learn the words, which we might otherwise forget or fail to process. We do not need the lineation to help tell us *how* to read the words, because the music has already told us how they go. Our only goal should be to keep things as clear and as readable as possible.

But such skepticism is too strong in its assumption that lyrics could not or should not be read as poetry. Hundreds of anthologies of English poetry include anonymous ballads from centuries ago—songs which were once sung but are now mainly appreciated as written poetry. Moreover, not everyone who flips through a book of lyrics knows all the songs by heart. Some people just enjoy reading lyrics by Bob Dylan, Joni Mitchell, Tupac Shakur, or Cole Porter regardless of whether they know the music well. In such cases, the lineation *will* have an impact on the way people experience the language. As Adam Bradley and Andrew DuBois point out in their *Anthology of Rap,* reading lyrics on the page allows us to "pause in contemplation" before returning to the music.[2]

But to what extent should this pause in contemplation be separated from the musical recordings? Transcription involves problems that go far beyond lineation. Some words might be difficult to decipher from a recording, which would force the transcriber to choose from likely possibilities without being certain what the composer and/or lyricist had in mind. Transcribers also face problems regarding repetition. Should every word be represented on the page, even if the same thing is sung dozens of times? What about nonsense syllables—"la, la, la" or "na, na, na"—should they be written down as well? And how should transcribers handle issues regarding spelling, slang, and pronunciation? If a songwriter sings the word "you," but it sounds more like "ya," how should it be written on the page? This is not a minor concern, because singers often dramatically alter the sounds of words, most frequently by amplifying, elongating, or altering vowel sounds. Should transcribers try to capture these vocal inflections in the way they print the lyrics? Should spellings be phonetic in order to expose the similar sounds in rhyming songs? Should backslashes indicate the beginning of a measure, or boldface stress patterns? Or should transcribers focus only on how they think the words would best be read aloud with a normal speaking voice?

These issues raise a fundamental and unavoidable question: How much should the printed lyrics try to reflect the actual sounds of a particular recording or performance? It can be charming to read through Porter's lyrics and appreciate his wit and verbal virtuosity. But what most people value are his *songs*, especially the way the words fit with the music. And the best way to fully appreciate them is to experience the words in relation to the melodies and harmonies they are associated with. Indeed, a skeptic might say that the only good transcription of lyrics is *a complete transcription of the entire score.* Any separation of words and music will inevitably be insufficient.

But even reading lyrics from a score does not solve all the problems. Many people cannot read music, of course, but even beyond that, scores themselves are abstractions. They give far more information than a lyric sheet, but they cannot fully capture the nuances of tone, timbre, dynamics, and micro-timing that go into an actual performance of a song. Reading a score is not the same as experiencing a particular performance at a particular time. And as a simple, practical problem, looking at a score is not an ideal way to appreciate lyrics. End rhymes, accent patterns, formal groups—these are all easy to see when verses are arranged into stanzas on a page, but they are significantly obscured when stretched out across the measures of a musical score.

For that reason, poetic arrangements of lyrics are both useful and desirable, and if we are going to represent lyrics as a kind of poetry, it makes sense to think carefully about how we might best arrange the details: lines, spelling, punctuation, stanza groupings, and so forth. The challenge, then, is to be attentive to the musical groupings in the song, but also to consider thoughtfully how various options might affect the way people read and process the language. When people want to learn lyrics, many search the internet and eventually find themselves on a website where the transcribers may or may not have strategically chosen how to represent the words on the page. As Cole Porter might say, "Anything goes." But what Porter's song makes clear is that choices about transcription can involve considerable subtlety and sophistication, just like the music itself.

Notes

INTRODUCTION

1. See Jonathan Cott, "Van Morrison: The Poet," *Rolling Stone*, November 30, 1978, 50–54. Morrison cites the success of his songs in non–English speaking countries, arguing that it shows "how irrelevant the words are" (52).

2. There is also a carefree ambiguity in the lyrics because of the use of homophones: Is it "sun" or "son"? "Won" or "one"?

CHAPTER 1. DICTION

1. Robert Lowell, "News from Mount Amiata," in Lowell, *Collected Poems* (New York: Farrar, Straus and Giroux, 2003), 294–95 (295).

2. This is not to say that Lowell's English translation is somehow better than Eugenio Montale's original (i porcospini / s'abbeverano ad un filo di pietà); the Italian language has its own unique history and beauty. The point is that the enchantment of poetry depends upon an appreciation of its basic *material*, its vocabulary and sounds. Helen Vendler, *Poets Thinking: Pope, Whitman, Dickinson, Yeats* (Cambridge: Harvard University Press, 2004), 54. Vendler uses this phrase within the context of a discussion of Whitman, but it applies equally well to Lowell's translation.

3. Percy Bysshe Shelley, "Adonais," in *Percy Bysshe Shelley: Selected Poetry and Prose*, ed. Kenneth Neill Cameron (New York: Holt, Rinehart and Winston, 1951), 266, 20.1–3.

4. Anne Sexton, "Praying on a 707," in *The Complete Poems: Anne Sexton* (Boston: Houghton Mifflin, 1999), 378.

5. Paul Zollo, *Songwriters on Songwriting* (Boston: Da Capo, 2003), 98.

6. See Stephen Rodgers, "Song and the Music of Poetry," *Music Analysis* 36/3 (October 2017): 315–49, Rodgers, "The Fourth Dimension of a Song," *Music Theory Spectrum* 37/1 (2015): 144–53, and Rodgers, "Music, Poetry, and Performance in a Song by Maria Scheider," *SMT-V: Videocast Journal of the Society of Music Theory* 3/3 (December 2017).

7. Robert Lowell, "For The Union Dead," in Lowell, *Collected Poems*, 376–78 (378).

8. Walt Whitman, "Out of the Cradle, Endlessly Rocking," in Whitman, *Leaves of Grass* (Franklin Center, Pa.: Franklin Library, 1981), 235, ll. 130–33.

9. John Keats, "To G.A.W.," in *The Complete Poems of John Keats* (New York: Modern Library, 1994), 30, ll. 9–10.

10. William Butler Yeats, "The Second Coming," in *Selected Poems and Four Plays of William Butler Yeats*, ed. M. L. Rosenthal (New York: Scribner, 1996), 90.

11. Peter Ladefoged and Keith Johnson, *A Course in Phonetics*, 7th ed. (Boston: Cengage Learning, 2011), 22.

12. Dinitia Smith, "The Music Is Sweet, the Words Are True," *New York Times*, January 7, 2007.

13. Adam Bradley, *The Poetry of Pop* (New Haven: Yale University Press, 2017), 15.

14. T. S. Eliot, "Sweeney Among the Nightingales," in *The Waste Land and Other Poems* (New York: Penguin, 1998), 52, ll. 37–40.

15. Yeats, "He Wishes for the Cloths of Heaven," in *Selected Poems*, 27.

16. It was originally written as part of a song cycle for tenor and orchestra called *The Wind Among the Reeds*; the recording in the Spotify playlist is a version for voice and piano.

17. Part of the complication here is that the poem creates a palpable tension between lines and syntax. The line endings suggest a 4 + 4 grouping: cloths, light, cloths, light / feet, dreams, feet, dreams. But the syntax suggests a 5 + 3 grouping, since the first five lines lead to a colon with an antecedent phrase ("if . . ."), and the next three lines complete the sentence by leading to a period with the consequent phrase ("but . . ."). Dunhill opts for the 5 + 3 grouping in terms of musical form, and it accounts for some of the oddness of the song's rhythm. In chapter 4 I cover such tensions in more detail.

18. It is worthwhile to compare the climax, "tread softly," with the earlier "dark cloths." The phrase "tread softly" *begins* a line with a double stress, whereas "dark cloths" *ends* a line with a double stress. "Dark cloths" withholds the climax, whereas "softly," with its fricative *s* and *f* and liquid *l*—along with the high vowel at its end—fulfills the climax with the opposite effect.

19. I borrow the term "vocality" from Jonathan Dunsby, *Making Words Sing* (Cambridge: Cambridge University Press, 2004), 4–6.

20. Despite the twelve-tone approach, Tavener does a great deal to make the song sound consonant and almost folklike (it is essentially in E-flat major). In addition to the persistent use of drones in the background, he uses twelve-tone rows that are more "tonal" sounding than others (the first row begins with the seven notes of an E-flat-major scale). That accounts, in part, for why the song often sounds like a tonal improvisation rather than a strict twelve-tone composition.

21. James Longenbach, *How Poems Get Made* (New York: Norton, 2018), 26.

22. John Donne, *The Poems of John Donne*, 2 vols., ed. Robin Robbins (Harlow, U.K.: Pearson Education, 2008), 2:65.

23. Edna St. Vincent Millay, "Lethe," Poetry Explorer, https://www.poetryexplorer.net/poem.php?id=1010773.

24. W. H. Auden, "Nocturne," in *The Dog Beneath the Skin; or, Where Is Francis?* (London: Faber and Faber, 1946), 116.

25. Robert Browning, "Childe Roland to the Dark Tower Came," in *Robert Browning: Selected Poems*, ed. John Woolford, Daniel Karlin, and Joseph Phelan (London: Routledge, 2013), 360–61.

CHAPTER 2. METER

1. The meter becomes more complicated over the course of the song, with an emergent ambiguity about where and when downbeats occur.
2. This method of metrical analysis is borrowed from Fred Lerdahl and Ray Jackendoff, *Generative Theory of Tonal Music* (Cambridge: MIT Press, 1983). My use of the term "real" accent is equivalent to what they call a "phenomenal" accent. My "virtual" accent is equivalent to their "metrical" accent.
3. Emily Dickinson, "My Life Closed Twice Before Its Close," in *Emily Dickinson's Poems: As She Preserved Them*, ed. Cristanne Miller (Cambridge, Mass.: Belknap, 2016), 686.
4. Edgar Allan Poe, "The Raven," in *Poetry: A Longman Pocket Anthology*, ed. R. S. Gwynn (New York: Addison-Wesley, 1998), 120.
5. Frank O'Hara, "The Day Lady Died," in *The Selected Poems of Frank O'Hara*, ed. Donald Allen (New York: Vintage, 1974), 146.
6. William Shakespeare, "Sonnet V" and "Sonnet LXXVII," in *The Complete Works of William Shakespeare* (New York: Avenel, 1975), 1192, 1203.
7. Any given reader, of course, could choose to stress certain syllables that others might not find natural or intuitive. We could imagine, for instance, someone reading the Shakespeare line by adhering to the accents of strict iambic pentameter: "Time's **thiev**ish **prog**ress **to** e**ter**nity." This involves intentionally weakening the articulation of the word "Time's" and strengthening the articulation of the function word "to." To my ears, this sounds unnatural, but there are often legitimate grounds for debate.
8. Sylvia Plath, "Edge," in Plath, *The Collected Poems*, ed. Ted Hughes (New York: HarperPerennial, 1992), 272.
9. I am grateful to Richard Desinord for bringing this song to my attention and sharing his transcription of the verse. For a more in-depth analysis, see his forthcoming dissertation, provisionally entitled "That Gospel Sound: Harmony as Genre in Contemporary Black Church Music" (Eastman School of Music).
10. Emily Dickinson, "Will There Really Be a 'Morning'?" in *Emily Dickinson's Poems*, 87.
11. Emily Dickinson, "The Loneliness One Dare Not Sound," in *Emily Dickinson's Poems*, 399.
12. The iambic pattern is so strong in the poem that we might hear the voice attempting to articulate an iambic pattern *against* the trochaic pattern of the piano (rather than hearing them both as trochaic).
13. Lawrence Kramer, *Music and Poetry: The Nineteenth Century and After* (Berkeley: University of California Press, 1984), 125–27. As Kramer explains it: "The relationship

between poetry and music in song is implicitly agonic; the song is a 'new creation' only because it is also a de-creation. The music appropriates the poem by contending with it, phonetically, dramatically, semantically; and the contest is what most drives and shapes the song" (127).

14. This distinction between "end-accented" phrases and "beginning-accented" phrases comes from David Temperley, "End-Accented Phrases: An Analytical Exploration," *Journal of Music Theory* 47 (2003): 125–54.

15. The word "'gram" is an abbreviation for "Instagram"— i.e., Lamar is not hanging out in Compton just to keep up his image on social media, but because he cares about the city.

16. There are many successful composers who have set their own poetry to music, including Gustav Mahler and Amy Beach, but unlike Campion, most have never achieved acclaim as poets in their own right.

17. Thomas Campion, "The Cypress Curtain of the Night," in *The English School of Lutenist Song Writers*, series 1, vol. 4, ed. Edmund Horace Fellowes (London: Stainer and Bell, 1922), 33. Although Campion is assumed to be the author of this poem and the composer of the music, the musicologist Erik Ryding has suggested that Philip Rosseter (1568–1623) might have collaborated on some of the musical accompaniments to Campion's songs, particularly in *A Book of Ayres* (1601), which includes "The Cypress Curtain of the Night." For more, see Erik S. Ryding, "Collaboration Between Campion and Rosseter?" *Journal of the Lute Society of America* 19 (1986): 13–28.

18. My discussion of this song was inspired by James Longenbach's treatment of similar issues in *How Poems Get Made*, 107–17. I am also indebted to Cathal Twomey and Andrew Cashner for their generous advice about the song. For a much more in-depth treatment of meter in English vocal music, readers should consult Twomey's "'To Catch the Song': Word-Setting, Creative Collaboration, and the Reader-Listener in Handel's English Language Works" (Ph.D. diss., Maynooth University, forthcoming).

19. Baroque music often features conflict between groupings of twos and threes. Musicians use the term "hemiola" to describe such occurrences.

CHAPTER 3. RHYME

1. Gerard Manley Hopkins, "Pied Beauty," in *Gerard Manley Hopkins: Poems and Prose*, ed. W. H. Gardner (Baltimore: Penguin, 1963), 30.

2. Matthew Arnold, "Dover Beach," in *Matthew Arnold: Selected Poems and Prose*, ed. Miriam Allott (London: Everyman, 1993), 76–77.

3. T. S. Eliot, "Burnt Norton," in Eliot, *Four Quartets* (Boston: Mariner, 1971), 18.

4. Alexander Pope, "An Essay on Criticism," in *Alexander Pope: A Critical Edition of the Major Works*, ed. Pat Rogers (Oxford: Oxford University Press, 1993), 28, ll. 350–51.

5. Adam Bradley, *Book of Rhymes: The Poetics of Hip Hop* (New York: BasicCivitas, 2009), 70.

6. Bradley refers to this type of rhyme as "transformative rhyme," ibid., 71–73.

7. The cynic, of course, would see this tendency as proof of the problem: the fact that rappers force novel rhymes is evidence that their options for originality are impossibly limited.

8. From Ross W. Duffin, *Shakespeare's Songbook* (New York: Norton, 2004), 342.

9. This tune appears in William Chappell, *The Ballad Literature and Popular Music of the Olden Time: A History of the Ancient Songs, Ballads, and of the Dance Tunes of England, with Numerous Anecdotes and Entire Ballads; also, A Short Account of the Minstrels*, 2 vols. (New York: Dover, 1965), 1:295.

10. See Michael R. Callahan, "Sentential Lyric-types in the Great American Songbook," *Music Theory Online* 19, no. 3 (2013): 1–31.

11. Gerard Manley Hopkins, "God's Grandeur," in *Gerard Manley Hopkins: Poems and Prose*, ed. W. H. Gardner (Baltimore: Penguin, 1963), 27.

12. Samuel Taylor Coleridge, "The Rime of the Ancient Mariner," in *Poems, Poets, Poetry: An Introduction and Anthology*, ed. Helen Vendler (Boston: Bedford/St. Martin's, 2002), 432.

13. Kenneth Koch, *Making Your Own Days: The Pleasures of Reading and Writing Poetry* (New York: Touchstone, 1998), 40.

14. Lester Bangs, "Astral Weeks," in *Stranded*, ed. Greil Marcus, 178–87 (New York: Knopf, 1979), 183–84, 180.

15. Greil Marcus, *When That Rough God Goes Riding* (New York: Public Affairs, 2010), 153.

16. Lester Bangs, "Astral Weeks," 181.

17. Richard Garnett, "Where Corals Lie," Oxford Lieder, https://www.oxfordlieder.co.uk/song/5344.

18. The cadence in D major is what musicians call a "plagal cadence" rather than an "authentic cadence." Plagal cadences are generally considered less strong than authentic cadences, but there is a clear sense of closure here regardless.

CHAPTER 4. LINES AND SYNTAX

1. Alexander Pope, "Elegy to the Memory of an Unfortunate Lady," ll. 9–10, Poetry Foundation, https://www.poetryfoundation.org/poems/44891/elegy-to-the-memory-of-an-unfortunate-lady.

2. John Milton, *Paradise Lost*, ed. Gordon Teskey (New York: Norton, 2005), 142–43, 6.386–89.

3. William Carlos Williams, "Paterson: Episode 17," in *The Complete Collected Poems of William Carlos Williams, 1906–1938* (Norfolk, Conn.: New Directions, 1938), 280, ll. 127–35.

4. Walt Whitman, "Out of the Cradle, Endlessly Rocking," in Whitman, *Leaves of Grass* (Franklin Center, Pa.: Franklin Library, 1981), 235, ll. 150–51.

5. Robert Frost, "To Earthward," in *Collected Poems of Robert Frost* (New York: Halcyon House, 1939), 279.

6. I borrow the term "counterpoint" from Charles O. Hartman, *Free Verse: An Essay on Prosody* (Princeton: Princeton University Press, 1980), 61–80. Robert Pinsky discusses this Frost poem and argues that a "natural" reading, akin to my syntax-oriented reading, is "more attractive," in *The Sounds of Poetry* (New York: Farrar, Straus and Giroux, 1998), 36.

7. Jay Z, *Decoded* (London: One World Publishing, 2011), 12.

8. Pinsky, *The Sounds of Poetry*, 39.

9. "The Waking" is a villanelle, a complex form that involves systematic repetition of certain lines over the course of the poem. Because of that, it is common for such poems to have lines that end with syntactic closure.

10. Theodore Roethke, "The Waking," in *The Collected Poems of Theodore Roethke* (New York: Doubleday, 1966), 104.

11. See chapter 1, above, for "descending" vowel sounds.

12. Giuseppe Verdi, letter to Goffredo Mazzini, October 18, 1848, as quoted in Robert Anthony Moreen, "Integration of Text Forms and Musical Forms in Verdi's Early Operas" (Ph.D. diss., Princeton University, 1975), 39. I am grateful to William Rothstein for bringing this to my attention.

13. John Keats, "To Sleep," in *The Complete Poems of John Keats* (New York: Modern Library, 1994), 270.

14. This type of tension is not especially relevant to popular music, since most listeners do not typically have a poetic reading of the lyrics in mind, especially before they hear the song.

15. Anne Sexton, "The Truth the Dead Know," in *The Complete Poems of Anne Sexton* (Boston: Mariner, 1999), 49.

16. Admittedly, this "rebellion" is not entirely successful. Four-beat lines are maintained along with a neat, balanced rhyme scheme. The poem never fully breaks away from the patterns that the opening lines establish.

17. The syntax of the fourth line is complicated in that its opening is perhaps best understood as a continuation of the previous sentence: "Mama Earth is dyin' and cryin' [and] rainin' cats and jackals." The next sentence begins in the middle of the fourth line's internal rhyming: "All shackles disintegrate to residue."

18. This section of the song prepares a subsequent EDM (electronic dance music)-"drop," which means that it has attributes of both a "prechorus" (in its preparatory role) and a chorus (in that, among other things, it is the most memorable part of the song and features the song's title).

19. The asymmetry of the sentences is reinforced by the odd way that each long sentence gradually veers away from physical intimacy (referencing, respectively, the car that the lover can't afford and the stolen mattress). This makes the subsequent one-line sentences feel almost like non sequiturs.

20. Lin Manuel Miranda and Jeremy McCarter, *Hamilton: The Revolution* (New York: Grand Central Publishing, 2016), 16.

21. This argument was developed in conversation with Seth Monahan, and I am grateful for his insights.

22. I am grateful to Victoria Malawey for raising this point about breathing (personal correspondence).

23. A subtle, but significant, aspect of this culminating melody is that Bowie hums the tune in the background of the second verse. As a result, when it appears at the end of the song it sounds vaguely familiar, like something we *already know*—a prelinguistic urge that now transforms into a dramatic utterance. The background humming can be heard clearly in isolated vocal tracks that are found online at YouTube or elsewhere.

24. In chapter 7, I shall offer two case studies in which tensions between line and syntax have a significant impact on the overall structure of songs by Bruce Springsteen and Benjamin Britten.

CHAPTER 5. ADDRESS

Epigraph. Bob Dylan, quoted in Paul Zollo, *Songwriters on Songwriting* (Boston: Da Capo, 2003), 79.

1. Charles Simic, "Old Couple," in Helen Vendler, *Poems, Poets, Poetry: An Introduction and Anthology* (Boston: Bedford/St. Martin's, 2002), 49. Vendler shares several insightful comments about the nature of address in this poem in the subsequent discussion (49–50).

2. My referring to her as a "wife" is an assumption. The poem does not specify the precise nature of the relationship.

3. Robert Hass, *A Little Book on Form: An Exploration into the Formal Imagination of Poetry* (New York: HarperCollins, 2017), 202.

4. Rosanna Warren, *Fables of the Self: Studies in Lyric Poetry* (New York: Norton, 2008), 270.

5. Carl Sandburg, "Baby Face," Bartleby, https://www.bartleby.com/300/923.html.

6. Dylan Thomas, "Do not go gentle into that good night," in *The Collected Poems of Dylan Thomas, 1934–1952* (New York: New Directions, 1957), 128.

7. This poem is a villanelle, the same form as Roethke's "The Waking," which was discussed in chapter 4.

8. Walt Whitman, "O Captain! My Captain!" in Whitman, *Leaves of Grass* (Franklin Center, Pa.: Franklin Library, 1981), 314–15.

9. Emily Dickinson, "The World Feels Dusty," in *Emily Dickinson's Poems: As She Preserved Them*, ed. Cristanne Miller (Cambridge, Mass.: Belknap, 2016), 244.

10. Copland used an inauthentic 1929 edition of Dickinson's poem, which replaces the characteristic em-dashes with more traditional punctuation and alters some of the words in the final two lines. An article by Michael Cherlin carefully addresses the differences between the two versions as well as the significant metric complexities of the third stanza. As Cherlin puts it, "The final stanza is the problem child. Compared to the other stanzas it remains awkward, even in the authentic version, and more so in 1929." See "Thoughts on Poetry and Music in Emily Dickinson's 'The World Feels Dusty' and Aaron Copland's Setting of It," *Intégral* 5 (1991): 67.

11. Symmetry is important for this song in general. The midpoint of the poem, for

instance, occurs at the exact midpoint of the song, a moment that is marked on the score with a change in time signature; the middle of the measure is the middle of the piece.

12. Jonathan Culler, *Theory of the Lyric* (Cambridge: Harvard University Press, 2015), 2.

CHAPTER 6. FORM

Epigraph. Samuel Beckett, quoted in Tom F. Driver, "Beckett by the Madeleine," *Columbia University Forum* 4 (1961): 23.

1. Edgar Bowers, "An Afternoon at the Beach," in *The Vintage Book of Contemporary American Poetry*, ed. J. D. McClatchy (New York: Vintage, 2003), 188.

2. William Blake, "A Poison Tree," in *Selected Poetry and Prose of William Blake*, ed. Northrop Frye (New York: Modern Library, 1953), 48.

3. The scholar Philip Gallagher relates this to the repetitive "ands" in the book of Genesis, which is one of several ways Blake's poem invites comparison with the story of Adam and Eve. But this itself is evidence of the tension between order and disorder. Blake's poem seems like a simple parable—a potential summary of a biblical story—but it ultimately behaves in ways that are startlingly unlike Genesis. Gallagher, "The Word Made Flesh: Blake's 'A Poison Tree' and the Book of Genesis," *Studies in Romanticism* 16, no. 2 (Spring 1977): 247.

4. See John Covach, "Form in Rock Music: A Primer," in *Engaging Music*, ed. Deborah Stein (New York: Oxford University Press, 2005), 65–76, David Temperley, *The Musical Language of Rock* (New York: Oxford University Press, 2018), 150–82, Trevor de Clercq, "Sections and Successions in Successful Songs: A Prototype Approach to Form in Rock" (Ph.D. diss., University of Rochester, 2012), and Drew Nobile, *Form as Harmony in Rock Music* (New York: Oxford University Press, 2020).

5. The opening melody, presented at the top of example 6.8, is a twelve-tone row not unlike what we saw in the Tavener setting of Yeats discussed in chapter 1.

6. I borrow this distinction from Robert Hatten's *Musical Meaning in Beethoven: Markedness, Correlation, and Interpretation* (Bloomington: Indiana University Press, 1994), 18.

7. Christopher Doll, *Hearing Harmony: Toward a Tonal Theory for the Rock Era* (Ann Arbor: University of Michigan Press, 2017), 155–156.

8. See Hatten, *Musical Meaning in Beethoven*, 56–63.

9. These overviews all benefit from the expert analyses of the relevant songs in Walter Everett's *The Beatles as Musicians: "Revolver" Through the "Anthology"* (New York: Oxford University Press, 1999), as well as advice that he generously shared in personal correspondence.

10. McCartney describes his memories of Penny Lane in an interview with Simon Harper of *Clash* magazine, September 9, 2009. Available at https://www.clashmusic.com/features/paul-mccartney-interview.

11. Everett, *The Beatles as Musicians*, 86.

12. Barry G. Golson, *The Playboy Interviews with John Lennon and Yoko Ono: The Final Testament* (New York: Berkley, 1981), 194.

13. Mark Lewisohn, *The Beatles: Recording Sessions* (New York: Harmony, 1988), 122.

14. Everett, *The Beatles as Musicians*, 182.

15. See Lewisohn, *The Beatles*, 157.

16. Everett, *The Beatles as Musicians*, 182.

CHAPTER 7. THE COMPLETE SONG

1. See *The Poems of John Donne*, 2 vols., ed. Robin Robbins (Harlow, U.K.: Pearson Education, 2008), 2:112.

2. *The Poems of John Donne*, 2:112–14. Britten used an earlier edition with more archaic spelling and alternate punctuation. For the sake of clarity, I use the more modern version here. None of the differences in spelling or punctuation is especially relevant to the analysis in this chapter, but interested readers should consult the Britten score to find the variations.

3. Gary Kuchar makes this claim in "Petrarchism and Repentance in John Donne's Holy Sonnets," *Modern Philology* 105, no. 3 (2008): 535–69 (566).

4. Robbins describes it as a "Christianized re-enactment of Pluto's abduction of Proserpina and Jupiter's of Ganymede." *Poems of John Donne*, 113.

5. For more SRDC, see chapter 6 of Walter Everett, *The Foundations of Rock: From "Blue Suede Shoes" to "Suite: Judy Blue Eyes"* (New York: Oxford University Press, 2008).

6. Drew Nobile discusses the SRDC pattern of this song in "Form and Voice Leading in Early Beatles Songs," *Music Theory Online* 17, no. 3 (2011): 1.2.

7. This is the seventeenth-century viewpoint, of course, not the modern medical explanation.

8. The rhyme scheme is a hybrid of the Petrarchan tradition (the *abba* quatrains) and the Shakespearean tradition (the *cdcdee* sestet).

9. A close analysis will show that Britten does take care to emphasize end rhymes in certain ways, but they are often caught in the flow of the larger three-part form. A first-time listener would struggle to identify where the poem's lines begin or end.

10. I am using the pronoun "he" because of the autobiographical implications in the lyrics and the fact that Bruce Springsteen is the singer on the album version of the song. Gender dynamics, however, can be quite fluid in popular music, and some cover versions of the song, such as the one by Cowboy Junkies (2004), use female singers.

11. Nick Hornby, *Songbook* (New York: Riverhead Books, 2003), 8.

12. See the 16:30 mark of the documentary *Wings for Wheels: The Making of "Born to Run,"* directed by Thom Zimny (Sony Music, 2005).

13. *Wings for Wheels*, 16:11 mark.

14. There has been considerable debate about whether the lyric should be "Mary's dress waves" or "Mary's dress sways." I am following the language of the official Spring-

steen songbook in opting for "waves," but Jon Landau, Springsteen's longtime collaborator, argues that it should be "sways." See David Remnick, "A Springsteen Mystery Solved," *New Yorker* July 17, 2021, https://www.newyorker.com/culture/cultural-comment/a-springsteen-mystery-solved.

15. The music also descends at this point in a way that might be seen as the opposite of the rising gesture.

16. People sometimes refer to the early version as "Wings for Wheels," but Max Weinberg, Springsteen's drummer, remembers it as "Angelina" or "Angelina's Dress Sways." See the section on "Thunder Road" in Brian Hiatt, *Bruce Springsteen: The Stories Behind the Songs* (New York: Abrams, 2019), 40.

17. As quoted in Hiatt, *Bruce Springsteen*, 43.

CONCLUSION

1. Billy Collins, "Introduction to Poetry," in *The Apple That Astonished Paris* (Fayetteville: University of Arkansas Press, 1988), 58.

2. T. S. Eliot, *The Use of Poetry and the Use of Criticism* (Boston: Harvard University Press, 1986), 93. I am grateful to James Longenbach for bringing this passage to my attention.

APPENDIX

1. *The Complete Lyrics of Cole Porter*, ed. Robert Kimball (New York: Vintage, 1984), 171–72.

2. Adam Bradley and Andrew DuBois, *The Anthology of Rap* (New Haven: Yale University Press, 2010), xxxv.

Further Reading

I have found the following sources especially helpful while working on this book. My lists are by no means exhaustive, but they might provide a helpful starting point for readers who are interested in further research.

POETRY

James Longenbach, *How Poems Get Made* (New York: Norton, 2018), and Robert Pinsky, *The Sounds of Poetry* (New York: Farrar, Straus and Giroux, 1998), offer excellent explanations of why poetry is worth reading. These are slim, highly engaging books written for broad audiences.

Mary Kinzie, *A Poet's Guide to Poetry* (Chicago: University of Chicago Press, 1999), and Helen Vendler, *Poems, Poets, and Poetry: An Introduction and Anthology* (Boston: Bedford/ St. Martin's, 2002), are larger introductions, but they are no less thoughtful and compelling.

Jonathan Culler, *Theory of the Lyric* (Cambridge: Harvard University Press, 2015), is also a larger volume, and perhaps more challenging for beginners (as is clear from the title, it offers a scholarly theory of lyric poetry), but it covers many of the fundamental issues that I discuss in this book.

Finally, for readers who want more extensive historical detail, every aspect of poetry in this book is carefully explained in *The Princeton Encyclopedia of Poetry and Poetics*, ed. Roland Greene and Stephen Cushman (Princeton: Princeton University Press, 2012).

POPULAR SONG

Adam Bradley, *Book of Rhymes: The Poetics of Hip Hop* (New York: BasicCivitas, 2009) and *The Poetry of Pop* (New Haven: Yale University Press, 2017), offers expert analysis of song lyrics that does not require readers to have special knowledge of music theory.

Allan Moore, *Song Means: Analyzing and Interpreting Recorded Popular Song* (Farnham, U.K.: Ashgate, 2012), is another accessible book for non-musicians, and includes detailed scholarly introductions to issues of music, lyrics, and performance.

David Temperley, *The Musical Language of Rock* (New York: Oxford University Press,

2018), and Walter Everett, *The Foundations of Rock: From "Blue Suede Shoes" to "Suite: Judy Blue Eyes"* (New York: Oxford University Press, 2008), both provide superb introductions to rock music with perceptive and engaging comments regarding lyrics and melody. These books will be easier to digest for readers with musical experience, but both authors provide copious audio examples to make things easier to follow.

ART SONG

Carol Kimball, *Art Song: Linking Poetry and Music* (Milwaukee: Hal Leonard, 2013), is primarily designed for singers, but it also provides a useful introduction for general readers.

Deborah Stein and Robert Spillman, *Poetry into Song: Performance and Analysis of Lieder* (New York: Oxford University Press, 1996), is a more complex, scholarly work, with detailed, insightful thoughts about German art songs.

Yonatan Malin, *Songs in Motion: Rhythm and Meter in the German Lied* (New York: Oxford University Press, 2010), focuses primarily on the temporal and rhythmic domains of German lieder, but it is also a skilled introduction to the genre of art songs for people with an advanced background in music theory and analysis.

SONGWRITERS

Stephen Sondheim offers insightful observations about the craft of songwriting in *Finishing the Hat* (New York: Knopf, 2010) and *Look, I Made a Hat* (New York: Knopf, 2011).

For rap fans, Jay-Z, *Decoded* (New York: Spiegel and Grau, 2011), provides a similar peek behind the scenes, with considerable attention given to the challenges of writing successful rap lyrics.

Paul Zollo, *Songwriters on Songwriting* (Cambridge, Mass.: Da Capo, 2003), is a massive compendium of interviews with rock, pop, and country singers, all talking about their songwriting techniques in loose and informal ways.

READINGS RELATED TO SPECIFIC CHAPTERS

Diction

Stephen Rodgers, "Song and the Music of Poetry," *Music Analysis* 36, no. 3 (October 2017): 315–49, is an indispensable introduction to phonetics and diction in the art song repertoire. The issue also comes up in many of his other publications, including "The Fourth Dimension of a Song," *Music Theory Spectrum* 37, no. 1 (2015): 144–53.

Kathryn LaBouff, *Singing and Communicating in English: A Singer's Guide to English Diction* (New York: Oxford University Press, 2007), is a helpful introduction to diction from the standpoint of a renowned vocal coach.

For more on the way cover songs can involve changes in language and sound, see

Victoria Malawey, "'Find Out What It Means to Me': Aretha Franklin's Gendered Re-Authoring of Otis Redding's 'Respect,'" *Popular Music* 33, no. 2 (2014): 185–207.

For more on the expressive uses of monotone, see John Fuller, "Britten, Auden and the 1930s," and Vicki Stroeher, "'Without Any Tune': The Role of the Discursive Shift in Britten's Interpretation of Poetry," in *Literary Britten: Words and Music in Benjamin Britten's Vocal Works*, ed. Kate Kennedy (Woodbridge, U.K.: Boydell Press, 2018), 31–48 and 144–70.

Meter

For poetic meter, Thomas Carper and Derek Attridge, *Meter and Meaning: An Introduction to Rhythm in Poetry* (New York: Routledge, 2003), is a great place to start. Attridge, *Poetic Rhythm: An Introduction* (Cambridge: Cambridge University Press, 1995), is also excellent, as is Paul Fussell, *Poetic Meter and Poetic Form*, rev. ed. (New York: McGraw-Hill, 1979).

Musicians who want to go beyond textbook introductions might want to grapple with the more sophisticated approaches of Harald Krebs, *Fantasy Pieces: Metrical Dissonance in the Music of Robert Schumann* (New York: Oxford University Press, 1999), and Christopher Hasty, *Meter as Rhythm* (New York: Oxford University Press, 1997).

Rhyme

John Hollander's classic *Rhyme's Reason: An Introduction to English Verse* (New Haven: Yale University Press, 2001) is an introduction to poetry generally speaking, but it includes a characteristically clever introduction to the topic of rhyme.

David Caplan, *Rhyme's Challenge: Hip Hop, Poetry, and Contemporary Rhyming Culture* (Oxford: Oxford University Press, 2014), is a well-conceived introduction to rhyme broadly speaking, but also to specific issues regarding rap.

For more on the relationship of the "CVC" chart to music, see Dai Griffiths, "Internal Rhyme in 'The Boy with a Moon and Star on His Head,' Cat Stevens 1972," *Popular Music* 31, no. 3 (2012): 383–400.

Lines and Syntax

The best recent discussions of lines and syntax in poetry come from two contemporary poets: James Longenbach and Ellen Bryant Voigt. See Longenbach, *The Art of the Poetic Line* (Minneapolis: Graywolf, 2007), and Voigt, *The Art of Syntax: Rhythm of Thought, Rhythm of Song* (Minneapolis: Graywolf, 2009). Another excellent source on the impact and importance of lineation is Charles Hartman, *Free Verse: An Essay on Prosody* (Princeton: Princeton University Press, 1980).

Readers interested in tensions between phrasing and syntax in rap should consult Kyle Adams, "On the Metrical Techniques of Flow in Rap Music," *Music Theory Online*

15, no. 5 (2009) and "Aspects of the Music/Text Relationship in Rap," *Music Theory Online* 14, no. 2 (2008).

A more technical discussion of line and syntax, as well as many other issues relating to this book, appears in Robert Snarrenberg, "On the Prosody of German Lyric Song," *Journal of Music Theory* 58, no. 2 (2014): 103–54, and "Linear and Linguistic Syntax in Brahms's O Kühler Wald, Op. 72 No. 3," *Music Analysis* 36, no. 3 (2017): 372–83.

Address

Many of the issues that come up in this chapter arise in an earlier article I wrote called "From Me to You: Dynamic Discourse in Popular Song," *Music Theory Online* 20, no. 4 (December 2014).

The issue of address also comes up in Rosanna Warren's excellent *Fables of the Self: Studies in Lyric Poetry* (New York: Norton, 2008).

There are also excellent discussions of distance and intimacy in relation to address in two of the books mentioned above: Jonathan Culler, *Theory of the Lyric* (Cambridge: Harvard University Press, 2015), and Allan Moore, *Song Means: Analyzing and Interpreting Recorded Popular Song* (Farnham, U.K.: Ashgate, 2012).

Form

For a discussion of form in poetry, see Robert Hass, *A Little Book on Form: An Exploration into the Formal Imagination of Poetry* (San Francisco: HarperCollins, 2017).

For more on form in the Beatles, see Walter Everett, *The Beatles as Musicians: "Revolver" Through the "Anthology"* (New York: Oxford University Press, 1999).

The Complete Song

Gordon Sly has an excellent overview of Britten's settings of John Donne in "Guilt, Deliberation, Affirmation: Britten's *The Holy Sonnets of John Donne* as Catharsis," in *Twentieth and Twenty-First-Century Song Cycles: Analytical Pathways Toward Performance*, ed. Gordon Sly and Michael Callahan (London: Routledge 2020).

For a broader sense of how "Thunder Road" fits within Springsteen's overall aesthetic, see Walter Everett, "Beyond the Palace: Casing the Promised Land," *Interdisciplinary Literary Studies* 9, no. 1 (Fall 2007): 81–94.

Acknowledgments

Until this moment, I hadn't suffered much from writer's block. The words for each chapter came relatively quickly. Now, however, I'm stuck. Finding the right words to thank everyone who inspired and assisted me over the past few years is a near impossibility. These next few paragraphs will have to stand, then, as my best attempt to express an inexpressible gratitude.

First, this book simply would not exist without James Longenbach. Almost everything I have written here has been shaped by things I learned from him, whether from his scholarship, his poetry, his teaching, or our informal discussions. The best moments in this book reflect his thinking; the worst, I'm afraid, are all mine.

Seth Monahan has been an ideal thinking partner for over a decade—everything I have written since 2009 has benefited from our ongoing discussions. His impact on this book is widespread, but I am especially grateful for his assistance with the many musical examples. They would have been hopelessly bungled without his input.

I am also deeply grateful to my many colleagues who read the manuscript and offered thoughtful feedback. In particular, I would like to thank Adam Bradley, who patiently responded to the book at every stage of the process and consistently offered invaluable, expert advice. I would also like to thank Harald Krebs, who provided brilliant and rigorously detailed commentary. I am extremely lucky to have had such wonderful readers.

I would also like to thank Joan Rubin, Gloria Culver, and the University of Rochester Humanities Center for providing funding for a manuscript workshop. With that support, I was able to invite Victoria Malawey, Stephen Rodgers, and Philip Rupprecht to campus to discuss this book. Their advice and encouragement has been indispensable.

Several other colleagues also read sections of the book and offered excellent feedback, including Cathal Twomey, Jake Arthur, Ryan Prendergast, Walter Everett, Ben Givan, and Rob Lagueux. I also received crucial advice and support from John Covach, Honey Meconi, Andrew Cashner, Kim Kowalke, Jonathan Dunsby, Michael Blankenship, and Kenneth Gross.

Many of the ideas in this book took shape during a fall 2016 class on music, poetry, and song. I would like to thank all of the wonderful students in that class for sharing their favorite songs and ideas. Several examples in this book were cultivated with them in mind. In particular, I thank Ezekiel Starling for expanding my repertoire and providing a model for thoughtful and exciting approaches to song.

At Yale University Press, Sarah Miller and Heather Gold have been ideal collaborators, and Susan Laity was the best manuscript editor I could have hoped for. Her careful edits and thoughtful suggestions improved this book in countless ways. I am also grateful to Ash Lago and Eva Skewes for their generous assistance.

I would also like to thank the Society for Music Theory for a generous subvention grant in 2020, and the Publications Endowment of the American Musicological Society, supported in part by the National Endowment for the Humanities and the Andrew W. Mellon Foundation.

Finally, I want to thank all of my family and friends who have encouraged me over the years. I couldn't have written this without you.

Credits

Poems and songs are listed in order of their appearance in the book.

BLAH, BLAH, BLAH (from "Delicious")
Music and Lyrics by GEORGE GERSHWIN and IRA GERSHWIN
Copyright © 1931 (Renewed) WC MUSIC CORP.
All Rights Reserved.
Used by Permission of ALFRED MUSIC.

Excerpts from Robert Lowell, "For the Union Dead" and "News from Mount Amiata" from COLLECTED POEMS by Robert Lowell. Copyright © 2003 by Harriet Lowell and Sheridan Lowell. Reprinted by permission of Farrar, Straus and Giroux.

Excerpts from Anne Sexton, "Praying on a 707"
Reprinted by permission of SLL/Sterling Lord Literistic, Inc. Copyright by Linda Gray Sexton and Loring Conant, Jr. 1981.

Bob Dylan, "Lay, Lady, Lay"
Copyright © 1969 by Big Sky Music; renewed 1997 by Big Sky Music.
Used by permission.

Patti Smith, "Dancing Barefoot"
Words and Music by Jay Dee Daugherty, Leonard Kaye, Ivan Kral, Patti Smith and Richard Sohl
Copyright © 1979 Mr. Fiyu Music, Hypnogogic Sounds, Estate Of Richard Sohl Music and (publisher unknown)
All Rights for Mr. Fiyu Music, Hypnogogic Sounds and Estate Of Richard Sohl Music Administered by BMG Rights Management (US) LLC
All Rights Reserved. Used by Permission.
Reprinted by Permission of Hal Leonard LLC.
Also used by permission of Ivan Kral / ASCAP / Bohemia Music LLC.

Holy Sonnet No. 3 ("O! might those sighs and tears return again") from "Holy Sonnets of John Donne" by Benjamin Britten

Credits

© 1946 by Boosey & Co. Ltd.
All Rights Reserved. Used With Permission.

Edna St. Vincent Millay, Excerpt from "Lethe" from *Collected Poems*.
Copyright 1928, © 1955 by Edna St. Vincent Millay and Norma Millay Ellis. Reprinted with the permission of The Permissions Company, Inc., on behalf of Holly Peppe, Literary Executor, The Millay Society, www.millay.org.

"Nocturne," copyright © 1974 by The Estate of W. H. Auden; from COLLECTED POEMS by W. H. Auden, edited by Edward Mendelson. Used by permission of Random House, an imprint and division of Penguin Random House LLC. All rights reserved.

Frank O'Hara, excerpts from "The Day Lady Died" from *Lunch Poems*. Copyright © 1964 by Frank O'Hara. Reprinted with the permission of The Permissions Company, LLC on behalf of City Lights Books, www.citylights.com. All rights reserved.

Five lines of "Edge" from *The Collected Poems by Sylvia Plath*.
Copyright © 1960, 1965, 1971, 1981 by the Estate of Sylvia Plath.
Used by permission of HarperCollins Publishers and Faber & Faber Ltd.

George Perle "The Loneliness One Dare Not Sound" from 13 DICKINSON SONGS, Volume III. Used by permission.

Section IV of "Burnt Norton" from T. S. Eliot, *Four Quartets* © 1943, 1971
Used by permission of Faber and Faber, Ltd.

Excerpt from "Burnt Norton" from COLLECTED POEMS 1909–1962 by T. S. Eliot. Copyright © 1952 by Houghton Mifflin Harcourt Publishing Company, renewed 1980 by Esme Valerie Eliot. Reprinted by permission of Houghton Mifflin Harcourt Publishing Company. All rights reserved.

HOMMAGE À T. S. ELIOT by Sofia Gubaidulina. Copyright © 2002 by Hans Sikorski Musikverlag GMBH. International Copyright Secured. All Rights Reserved. Reprinted by Permission of G. Schirmer, Inc.

Bob Dylan, "It's All Over Now, Baby Blue"
Copyright © 1965 by Warner Bros. Inc.; renewed 1993 by Special Rider Music.
Used by permission.

Bob Dylan, "Like a Rolling Stone"
Copyright © 1965 by Warner Bros. Inc.; renewed 1993 by Special Rider Music.
Used by permission.

"Madame George," Words and Music by Van Morrison
Copyright © 1969 UNIVERSAL MUSIC PUBLISHING INTERNATIONAL LTD.
Copyright Renewed.
All Rights for the U.S. and Canada Controlled and Administered by UNIVERSAL—
SONGS OF POLYGRAM INTERNATIONAL, INC.
All Rights Reserved. Used by Permission.
Reprinted by Permission of Hal Leonard LLC.

William Carlos Williams, from PATERSON, copyright © 1946 by William Carlos Williams. Reprinted by permission of New Directions Publishing Corp.

Theodore Roethke, "The Waking," copyright © 1966 and renewed 1994 by Beatrice Lushington; from COLLECTED POEMS by Theodore Roethke. Used by permission of Doubleday, an imprint of the Knopf Doubleday Publishing Group, a division of Penguin Random House LLC.
All rights reserved.

"The Waking" by Ned Rorem / Theodore Roethke
© 1961 by Henmar Press, Inc.
All Rights Reserved. Used With Permission.

"Serenade" by Benjamin Britten
© 1990 by Boosey & Hawkes, Inc.
All Rights Reserved. Used With Permission

Excerpts from Anne Sexton, "The Truth the Dead Know"
Reprinted by permission of SLL/Sterling Lord Literistic, Inc. Copyright by Linda Gray Sexton and Loring Conant, Jr. 1981.

The Chainsmokers, "CLOSER"
Words and Music by SHAUN FRANK, ANDREW TAGGART, ISAAC SLADE, ASHLEY FRANGIAPANE and FREDERIC KENNETT
Copyright © 2016 WARNER-TAMERLANE PUBLISHING CORP., REGICIDE ENTERTAINMENT, INC., SONY / ATV ALLEGRO, NICE HAIR PUBLISHING, SONGS OF UNIVERSAL, INC., 17 BLACK PUBLISHING, AARON EDWARDS PUBLISHING and EMI APRIL MUSIC INC.
All Rights on behalf of itself and REGICIDE ENTERTAINMENT, INC. Administered by WARNER-TAMERLANE PUBLISHING CORP.
All Rights Reserved.
Used By Permission of ALFRED MUSIC.

The Chainsmokers, "Closer"
Words and Music by Andrew Taggart, Frederic Kennett, Isaac Slade, Joseph King, Ashley Frangipane and Shaun Frank

Copyright © 2016 Sony/ATV Music Publishing LLC, EMI April Music Inc., Sony/ATV Music Publishing (UK) Limited, EMI Music Publishing Ltd., Nice Hair Publishing, Aaron Edwards Publishing, Songs Of Universal, Inc., 17 Black Music, Warner-Tamerlane Publishing Corp. and Regicide Entertainment, Inc.

All Rights on behalf of Sony/ATV Music Publishing LLC, EMI April Music Inc., Sony/ATV Music Publishing (UK) Limited, EMI Music Publishing Ltd., Nice Hair Publishing and Aaron Edwards Publishing Administered by Sony/ATV Music Publishing LLC, 424 Church Street, Suite 1200, Nashville, TN 37219

All Rights on behalf of 17 Black Music Administered by Songs of Universal, Inc.

All Rights on behalf of Regicide Entertainment, Inc. Administered by Warner-Tamerlane Publishing Corp.

International Copyright Secured. All Rights Reserved.

Reprinted by Permission of Hal Leonard LLC

ALEXANDER HAMILTON (from the Broadway musical "Hamilton")
Words and Music by LIN-MANUEL MIRANDA
Copyright © 2015 5000 BROADWAY MUSIC (ASCAP)
All Rights Administered by WC MUSIC CORP.
All Rights Reserved.
Used by Permission of ALFRED MUSIC.

Charles Simic, "Old Couple" from *Selected Early Poems*. Copyright © 1983 by Charles Simic. Reprinted with the permission of George Braziller, Inc. (New York), www.georgebraziller.com. All rights reserved.

Pink Floyd, "Wish You Were Here"
Words and Music by Roger Waters and David Gilmour
Copyright © 1975 Roger Waters Music Overseas Ltd. and Pink Floyd Music Publishers, Inc.
Copyright Renewed.
All Rights for Roger Waters Music Overseas Ltd. Administered by BMG Rights Management (US) LLC
All Rights Reserved. Used by Permission.
Reprinted by Permission of Hal Leonard LLC.

Excerpts from the poem "Baby Face" by Carl Sandburg (1918) printed by arrangement with John Steichen, Paula Steichen Polega and The Barbara Hogenson Agency, Inc. For more information about Carl Sandburg visit www.nps.gov/carl.

"White Moon" from *Five Songs for Contralto and Piano* by Ruth Crawford-Seeger © Copyright 1990 by C.F. Peters Corporation. Used by permission. All Rights Reserved.

"Do Not Go Gentle Into That Good Night" by Dylan Thomas, from THE POEMS OF DYLAN THOMAS, copyright © 1952 by Dylan Thomas. Reprinted by permission of New Directions Publishing Corp. Copyright held by The Dylan Thomas Trust. Reprinted by permission.

"An Afternoon at the Beach" from COLLECTED POEMS by Edgar Bowers, copyright © 1997 by Edgar Bowers. Used by permission of Alfred A. Knopf, an imprint of the Knopf Doubleday Publishing Group, a division of Penguin Random House LLC. All rights reserved.

"A Poison Tree" from "Ten Blake Songs" by Ralph Vaughan Williams © Oxford University Press 1958. Reproduced by permission. All rights reserved.

Benjamin Britten, "A Poison Tree"
"The Songs & Proverbs of William Blake, op. 74"
© 1965 by Faber Music Ltd.
All Rights Reserved. Used With Permission.

Benjamin Britten, "Since She Whom I Lov'd"
"Holy Sonnets of John Donne" by Benjamin Britten
© 1946 by Boosey & Co. Ltd.
All Rights Reserved. Used With Permission.

"THUNDER ROAD"
Words and Music by BRUCE SPRINGSTEEN
Copyright © 1975 (Renewed) BRUCE SPRINGSTEEN (ASCAP)
All Rights Reserved.
Used by Permission of ALFRED MUSIC.

"THE PROMISE"
Words and Music by BRUCE SPRINGSTEEN
Copyright © 1999 BRUCE SPRINGSTEEN (ASCAP)
All Rights Reserved.
Used by Permission of ALFRED MUSIC.

Billy Collins, excerpts from "Introduction to Poetry," from *The Apple That Astonished Paris*
Copyright © 1988, 1996 by Billy Collins
Reprinted with permission of The Permissions Company, LLC on behalf of the University of Arkansas Press, www.uapress.com.

ANYTHING GOES (from "Anything Goes")
Words and Music by COLE PORTER
Copyright © 1934 (Renewed) WC MUSIC CORP.
All Rights Reserved.
Used by Permission of ALFRED MUSIC.

Index

abnegation, 166
accents: linguistic, 44, 45, 46; patterns of, 33–38, 63; real, 36, 37, 38, 44, 45, 46; syncopation, 37, 38, 44, 47; virtual, 36–38, 44, 45, 46, 59. *See also* meter
address (who speaks to whom): and covert second-person narrator, 136–38; intimate forms of, 130–36; and movement toward distance, 138–40; in poetry and song, 126–30, 143, 145; in rap songs, 131–32; shifts of, 131–32; third-person narrative, 128–29; voice as factor in, 140–43. *See also* names of individual poets and artists
alliteration, 19, 65, 66, 68
André 3000, 117
Arnold, Matthew, "Dover Beach," 65
art songs, 5; lineation in, 104–5; meter in, 57–62; poetic address in, 132; rhyme in, 88–95. *See also* Campion, Thomas; Copland, Aaron; Elgar, Edward; Rorem, Ned; Schubert, Franz; "Since She Whom I Loved"; Vaughan Williams, Ralph; Wainwright, Rufus; Wolf, Hugo
assonance, 66
Auden, W. H., "Nocturne," 27, 29–30

Bangs, Lester, on "Madame George," 84, 88, 137
Barrett, Syd, 30
Beatles, 4, 178; "A Day in the Life," 174–76, 196; "From Me to You," 184; "Happiness Is a Warm Gun," 176–78, 196; "I Am the Walrus," 172–74, 175; "Love Me Do," 167; "Penny Lane," 168–71, 172, 174, 175; "Revolution 9,"

167; *Sgt. Pepper's Lonely Hearts Club Band*, 174; "Something," 166; *The White Album*, 176. *See also* Lennon, John; McCartney, Paul
beats (in music), 32–33. *See also* meter
Beckett, Samuel, 146
Beethoven, Ludwig van: Fifth Symphony, 36; Ninth Symphony, 40
Berio, Luciano, *Sequenza I*, 40
Beyoncé, 36
Bieber, Justin, 9; "Baby," 11–12, 17, 18
Big Boi, "Shutterbug," 83
Big Daddy Kane, 102
Björk, "Triumph of a Heart," 101
Blake, William: Britten's setting of "A Poison Tree" (1935), 155–58; Britten's setting of "A Poison Tree" (1965), 158–61; "A Poison Tree," 148–51, 175, 234n3; "The Sick Rose," 212; Vaughan Williams's setting of "A Poison Tree," 152–55
blank verse, 96
Blues Traveler, "Hook" 3
Bon Jovi, "Livin' on a Prayer," 129
Bostridge, Ian, 17
Bowers, Edgar, "An Afternoon at the Beach," 147–48
Bowie, David, 10, 122, 123, 233n23
Bradley, Adam, 71; *The Anthology of Rap*, 225; *The Poetry of Pop*, 18
Britten, Benjamin, 5, 15–16; Holy Sonnet No. 3 (Donne), 26–27, 28; "Nocturne" (Auden), 27, 29–30; *Peter Grimes*, 15–16, 17; "A Poison Tree" (Blake), 155–61; *Serenade for Tenor, Horn, and Strings*, 17, 113–15; "Sonnet"

249

Britten, Benjamin (continued)
  (Keats), 113–15. *See also* "Since She Whom I Loved"
Browning, Robert, "Childe Roland to the Dark Tower Came," 30

cadences: end rhymes as, 74–76, 79, 92; plagal, 231n18
Callahan, Michael, 78
Campbell, Lamar, & Spirit of Praise, "More Than Anything," 44, 46, 47
Campion, Thomas, 108, 230nn16,17; "The Cypress Curtain of the Night," 57–62
Carroll, Lewis, *Through the Looking Glass*, 172–73
Cash, Johnny, 6, 18–19; "Hurt," 19–20; "I Walk the Line," 101–2
Cashner, Andrew, 230n18
Chainsmokers, "Closer," 118–20
Cherlin, Michael, 233n10
choruses (in popular music), 70, 130–31, 151, 196–97; in "Penny Lane," 168–69, 170, 171, 172. *See also* form; *and names of individual artists*
Clarke, Rebecca, "Lethe" (Millay), 27–29, 30
Cole, J., "Who Dat?," 78–79
Coleridge, Samuel Taylor, "The Rime of the Ancient Mariner," 83
Collins, Billy, "Introduction to Poetry," 210–11
common meter, 39
consonance, 66
Copland, Aaron, 6; *Twelve Poems of Emily Dickinson*, 140; "The World Feels Dusty" (Dickinson), 140–43, 144, 233n10
Cornell, Chris, 207
Covach, John, 151
Cowboy Junkies, 207, 235n10
Crane, Hart, 53
Crawford, Ruth, 6; "White Moon," 132, 133, 134
Culler, Jonathan, *Theory of the Lyric*, 143, 145

Davis, Richard, 88
de Clercq, Trevor, 151
Delicious (film), 3
Desinord, Richard, 229n9
Dickinson, Emily, 10; "The Loneliness One Dare Not Sound," 51–53; "My Life Closed Twice Before Its Close," 38–40, 41–42, 47, 50; "Will There Really Be a 'Morning'?," 50–51, 53; "The World Feels Dusty," 140–43, 144, 233n10
diction. *See* poetic diction
Dinco D, 14
Doll, Christopher, 166
Donne, John, 5; Holy Sonnet No. 3, 26–27, 28. *See also* "Since She Whom I Loved"
Dowland, John, 58
DuBois, Andrew, *The Anthology of Rap*, 225
Dunhill, Thomas, "He Wishes for the Cloths of Heaven" (Yeats), 20–24, 164, 228n17
Dylan, Bob, 2–3, 6, 29, 126, 172; "It's All Over Now, Baby Blue," 72, 73; "Lay, Lady, Lay," 14–15; "Like a Rolling Stone," 79–80

Elgar, Edward, 6; *Sea Pictures*, 89–95; "Where Corals Lie" (Garnett), 89–95
Eliot, T. S., 6, 18, 32, 43; "Burnt Norton," 67–68; *Four Quartets*, 67–68; on meaning in poetry, 210–11; "Sweeney Among the Nightingales," 19
Eminem, "Lose Yourself," 103, 105, 131–32
end rhymes, 74–76, 79, 92; transcription of, 218
English language, history of, 9. *See also* phonemes; poetic diction
enjambment, 96; in Donne's "Since She Whom I Loved," 184, 190, 191, 194; etymology of, 104; in Frost's "To Earthward," 98–100; in Milton's *Paradise Lost*, 96–97; and poetic syntax, 101, 104–5, 112; in rap music, 102–4; in Roethke's "The Waking," 104–5; in Springsteen's "Thunder Road," 203, 205, 206; Verdi on, 113
Everett, Walter, 171, 176, 177, 184, 234n9

Farrell, Perry, 69–70
form: the Beatles' use of, 166, 167, 168–78; in Britten's 1935 setting of Blake's "Poison Tree," 155–58; in Britten's 1965 setting of Blake's "Poison Tree," 158–59, 160; as an imposition of order, 146–48; and tensions between order and disorder, 148–52, 161,

166, 167, 168–69, 178; in Vaughan Williams's setting of Blake's "Poison Tree," 152–55, 161; in Wainwright's setting of Shakespeare's Sonnet 29, 161–67
Franklin, Aretha, "(You Make Me Feel Like) A Natural Woman," 33
free verse, 43
fricatives, 13–14
Frost, Robert: "Stopping by Woods on a Snowy Evening," 4; "To Earthward," 98–100, 104, 108

Gallagher, Philip, 234n3
Garland, Judy, 78
Garnett, Richard, "Where Corals Lie," 88–89
genius.com, 214
Gershwin, Ira, "Blah, Blah, Blah," 3
Gilmour, David, 130
Goethe, Johann Wolfgang von, "Erlkönig," 139
Goodall, Reginald, 15
Gordon, Ricky Ian, "Will There Really Be a Morning?" (Dickinson), 50–51, 53
Great American Songbook, 78
Great Big World, "Say Something," 17–18
Gubaidulina, Sofia, 6; *Hommage à T. S. Eliot*, 68–69

Harnick, Sheldon, *Fiddler on the Roof*, 17
Harper, Simon, 234n10
Hass, Robert, on the origin of the lyric, 128
Hatten, Robert, 166
Helloween, "Keeper of the Seven Keys," 138
Holiday, Billie, 36, 43
Hopkins, Gerard Manley: "God's Grandeur," 80–81; "Pied Beauty," 65
Hornby, Nick, 199
Houston, Whitney, "How Will I Know?," 100–101

Imagine Dragons, "Whatever It Takes," 47, 49
internal rhymes, 79–83

Jackendoff, Ray, 229n2
Jagger, Mick, 3
Jane's Addiction: "Jane Says," 69–70; *Nothing's Shocking*, 69

Jay Z, *Decoded*, 104
Johnson, Keith, 17

Keats, John: "To G. A. W.," 15; "To Sleep," 17, 113–14, 115, 128
Kimball, Robert (compiler), *The Complete Lyrics of Cole Porter*, 218, 220, 221
King, Martin Luther, Jr., 131
Koch, Kenneth, 83
Kramer, Lawrence, 53
Kretzmer, Herbert, "Master of the House," 44, 45, 56

Ladefoged, Peter, 17
Lamar, Kendrick, 4, 108; *DAMN.*, 54; "Element," 53–57, 60
Led Zeppelin, "Stairway to Heaven," 167
Lennon, John: "A Day in the Life," 174–75; "Happiness Is a Warm Gun," 177; "I Am the Walrus," 172; "Penny Lane," 169, 172, 176
Lerdahl, Fred, 229n2
Les Misérables (Schönberg and Kretzmer), 44, 47
limericks, 76–78
Lincoln, Abraham, 138–39
lineation: in art songs, 104–5, 106, 107, 110–13; and poetic tensions, 113–14, 115, 124–25; in poetry, 97–100; in popular music, 100–102, 105, 108, 109; in rap music, 102–4; and rhyme, 95; and syntax, 96–97, 98; in transcribing lyrics, 220–21, 222. *See also* enjambment; *and names of individual poets and artists*
line-oriented reading (of poetry), 99, 103, 114
linguistic accents, 44, 45, 46
liquids (phonemes), 14–15
Longenbach, James, 25, 230n18
Lowell, Robert: "For the Union Dead," 13–14; translation of "News from Mount Amiata" (Montale), 9, 10, 11, 211, 227n2
lyric poetry, 126–27; address in, 130, 141; origin of, 128
lyrics: as poetry, 1–7; poetry as, 126–28, 139–43; in popular music, 1–7; as prayer, 128; transcribing, 217–26. *See also* Blake, William; Dickinson, Emily; Donne, John;

lyrics (continued)
  Eliot, T. S.; Goethe, Johann Wolfgang von; meaning; Millay, Edna St. Vincent; poetic diction; Roethke, Theodore; Sandburg, Carl; Sexton, Anne; Shakespeare, William; Simic, Charles; song; Thomas, Dylan; Whitman, Walt; Yeats, William Butler; *and names of individual artists*

madrigalism, 213
Malawey, Victoria, 233n22
Mameli, Goffredo, 113
Marcus, Greil, 87
Mars, Bruno, "When I Was Your Man," 138
Martin, George, 174, 178
Mason, David, 168
McCartney, Paul: "A Day in the Life," 174–75, 176; "Eleanor Rigby," 129; "Penny Lane," 168, 169, 234n10
meaning: Eliot on, 210–11; in poetry, 210–13, 215; in song, 213–15
Meet Me in St. Louis (film), 78
Menuhin, Yehudi, 208
Mercury, Freddie, 122, 123
"Merry, Merry Milkmaids," 76–78
meter: in art songs, 57–62; as beats, 32–33; common, 39, 52; in music, 32–38; as patterns of accent, 33–38, 63; in poetry, 38–43; in song, 43–53; subtlety in, 53; and transcription of lyrics, 217. *See also names of individual poets and artists*
Millay, Edna St. Vincent, "Lethe," 27–29, 30
Milton, John, *Paradise Lost*, 96–97
Miranda, Lin-Manuel: "Alexander Hamilton," 120–21; *Hamilton*, 120–21
Mitchell, Joni, 4
Mixolydian mode, 162
Monahan, Seth, 232n21
Montale, Eugenio, "News from Mount Amiata," 9, 11, 211, 227n2
Mörike, Eduard, "Auf eine Christblume I," 110
Morrison, Van: *Astral Weeks*, 84; "Brown Eyed Girl," 84; "Into the Mystic," 1–2, 7, 84; "Madame George," 84–88, 136–37; *Moondance*, 1; "Wild Nights," 84

Mötley Crüe, "Home Sweet Home," 166
Murphy, Heidi Grant, 22

nasals, 14
Nine Inch Nails, "Hurt," 19–20
Nobile, Drew, 151
Nowottny, Winifred, 18

Of Monsters and Men, "Little Talks," 105, 108, 109, 214
O'Hara, Frank, "The Day Lady Died," 40, 43
Oke, Alan, 16
Outkast, 6, "Da Art of Storytellin' (Part 2)," 103–4, 108, 117–18, 125

patterns of accent: meter as, 33–38, 63; in popular music, 43–50
Pearl Jam, 25
Perle, George, "The Loneliness One Dare Not Sound" (Dickinson), 51–53
Petty, Tom, "Breakdown," 78
phonemes, 12–13; fricatives, 13–14; liquids, 14–15; nasals, 14; plosives, 13; sibilants, 13–14; vowels, 15–18
Pink Floyd, 6; "Shine on You Crazy Diamond," 30; "Wish You Were Here," 129–30
Pinsky, Robert, *The Sounds of Poetry*, 104, 232n6
Plath, Sylvia, "Edge," 42–43
plosives, 13
Poe, Edgar Allan, "The Raven," 40, 41
poetic diction, 10–12, 18, 25; changes in (within one song), 25–26; and context, 30; as translated into song, 20–25, 26–30; as word choice, 18–20, 31. *See also names of individual poets and artists*
poetry: lineation in, 97–100; meaning in, 210–15; meter in, 38–43; metrical, 40–42; non-metrical, 42–43. *See also* lineation; meter; poetic diction; rhyme; *and names of individual poets*
Police, "Don't Stand So Close to Me," 131
Pope, Alexander, 96; "Essay on Criticism," 71, 72
popular music: choruses in, 70, 180–81, 151, 196–97; form as used in, 151, 167–78; lineation in, 100–102, 105, 108, 109; lyrics in,

1–7; patterns of accent in, 33–38, 43–50. *See also* address; rhyme; "Thunder Road"; *and names of individual artists*
Porter, Andrew, 15
Porter, Cole, 101; transcription of "Anything Goes," 218–24
Pound, Ezra, 19
prayer, poems as, 128
Public Enemy: *It Takes a Nation of Millions to Hold Us Back*, 81; "Louder Than a Bomb," 81, 82

Queen, 6; "Bohemian Rhapsody," 167; "Under Pressure," 122–24, 125

Radiohead, "Everything in Its Right Place," 34
Rakim, 102
rap music: enjambment in, 102–4; rhyme in, 71–72, 81, 104, 231n7. *See also names of individual rappers*
rappers. *See* Big Boi; Big Daddy Kane; Eminem; Jay Z; Lamar, Kendrick; Outkast; Rakim; Run DMC; West, Kanye
real accents, 36, 37, 38
Remedios, Alberto, 15
Reznor, Trent, 19–20
rhyme, 63, 64; in art songs, 88–95; broader uses of, 83–95; effectiveness of, 70–73; end rhymes as cadences, 74–76, 79, 92; and internal rhymes as syncopations, 80–83; and lineation, 95; in "Madame George," 84–88; musical functions of, 73–84; in rap music, 71–72, 81, 104, 231n7; slant, 64; standard, 66; as subphrases, 76–80; in "Thunder Road," 204–6; types of, 66–67; in "Where Corals Lie," 89–95. *See also names of individual poets and artists*
rhythms, of poetic syntax, 116–24. *See also* meter
Robinson, Rick, "More Than Anything," 44, 46, 47
Robyn, "Dancing on My Own," 34, 35, 36
Rodgers, Stephen, 12
Roethke, Theodore, "The Waking," 104–5, 106, 107, 232n9
"Rogero," 74, 75

Rolling Stones: *Exile on Main Street*, 3; "Ruby Tuesday," 131; "Tumbling Dice," 3
Rorem, Ned, "The Waking" (Roethke), 104–5, 106, 107, 108
Ross, Rick, "Sanctified," 71–72
Rosseter, Philip, 230n17
Run DMC, "King of Rock," 102
Ryding, Erik, 230n17

Sandburg, Carl, 6; "Baby Face," 132
Schoenberg, Arnold, 23, 78
Schönberg, Claude-Michel, "Master of the House," 44, 45, 56
Schubert, Franz, "Erlkönig" (Goethe), 139–40
Scott, Travis, "Sicko Mode," 167
Sex Pistols, "Anarchy in the UK," 167
Sexton, Anne, 6; "Praying on a 707," 10; "The Truth the Dead Know," 116–18
Shakespeare, William: meter in, 42, 229n7; Sonnet 5, 42; Sonnet 8, 5; Sonnet 29, 161–67; Sonnet 77, 42
Shelley, Percy Bysshe, "Adonais," 10
sibilants, 13–14
Silvestri, Charles Anthony, 4
Simic, Charles, "Old Couple," 126–28, 129
Simon, Paul, 10; "Boy in the Bubble," 13, 14; "You Can Call Me Al," 131
Simon and Garfunkel, "The Boxer," 138
"Since She Whom I Loved" (Britten/Donne), 235n2; as addressed to God, 180–82, 188, 190, 192–96; circumstances surrounding, 180, 208; close reading of, 179, 180–96, 208; dissonance in, 183, 186; enjambments in, 184, 190, 191, 194; first quatrain of, 180–87; form in, 183–84; musical accents in, 186; rhyme scheme of, 180, 191; second quatrain of, 187–91; sestet of, 191–95
slant rhyme, 64, 66
Smith, Patti, 6; "Dancing Barefoot," 25–26
song: intimacy in, 130–36; meaning in, 213–15; meter in, 43–53; rhyme in, 73–84; structure of, 151; word painting in, 213–14. *See also* address; art songs; form; lyrics; popular music; rap music; *and names of individual artists*
songmeanings.com, 214

Springsteen, Bruce, 6; "Born in the U.S.A.," 196, 197; "Born to Run," 196, 197; *Born to Run*, 202, 207; circumstances surrounding "Born to Run," 197, 208–9; "Dancing in the Dark," 196, 197; "Glory Days," 197; "The Promise," 207–8; "Rosalita," 197; "Tenth Avenue Freeze Out," 197. *See also* "Thunder Road"

Squier, Billy, "The Stroke," 33

standard rhymes, 66

Stapleton, Chris, "Nobody to Blame," 38

Stein, Gertrude, 173

Sterling, Andrew, "Meet Me in St. Louis, Louis," 78

Stravinsky, Igor, 5; "In Memoriam Dylan Thomas," 132, 135–36

Swift, Taylor: "Blank Space," 50; "We Are Never Ever Getting Back Together," 213; "Wildest Dreams," 47, 48

syncopation, 37, 38, 44, 47; internal rhymes as, 80–83

syntax: and enjambments, 101, 104–5, 112; and lineation, 96–97, 98; in rap music, 102–4; rhythms of, 116–24; tensions associated with, 108, 113–14, 124–25; transcription of, 218. *See also* lineation

syntax-oriented reading (of poetry), 99–100, 104, 108, 110, 114

Tavener, John, "He Wishes for the Cloths of Heaven" (Yeats), 21, 22–24, 228n20

Temperley, David, 151

Thomas, Dylan, "Do Not Go Gentle into That Good Night," 132, 135–36

"Thunder Road" (Springsteen), 235n10; close reading of, 179, 196–208; enjambments in, 203, 205, 206; multiple versions of, 207, 236n15; rhymes in, 204–6; structure of, 196–98

Tortoise, 207

transcribing lyrics, 217–26; ambiguity in, 218; "Anything Goes" (Porter), 218–24, 226; challenges of, 225–26; end rhymes, 218; factors to consider, 217–18; lineation in, 220–21, 222, 225; and meter, 217, 222–24; parallel construction, 218; as poetry, 217–18, 226; syntax, 218; vocal caesuras, 217

transmemberment, 53

Tribe Called Quest: *The Low End Theory*, 14; "Scenario," 14

Trixter, "Road of a Thousand Dreams," 72–73

Turner, Frank, 207

Twenty One Pilots, "Stressed Out," 70

Twomey, Cathal, 230n18

U2, 25; "Pride (In the Name of Love)," 131

Vaughan Williams, Ralph, "A Poison Tree" (Blake), 152–55

Vendler, Helen, 9, 227n2

Verdi, Giuseppe, "Suona la tromba," 113

virtual accents, 36–38, 44, 59

voice, and modes of address, 139–43

vowels, 15–18

Wagner, Richard, *Die Walküre*, 15

Wainwright, Rufus: Sonnet 29 (Shakespeare), 161–67, 169; *Take All My Loves: 9 Shakespeare Sonnets*, 162

Warren, Rosanna, 128

Webber, Andrew Lloyd: *Cats*, 131; "Memory," 131

Welch, Florence, 162

West, Kanye, "Sanctified," 71–72

Whitacre, Eric, "Sleep," 4

Whitman, Walt, 97; "O Captain! My Captain," 138–39; "Out of the Cradle Endlessly Rocking," 14

Williams, William Carlos, 97

Wolf, Hugo, "Auf eine Christblume I," 110–13

word painting, in songs, 213–14

words, as sounds, 9–10, 12–18, 19, 31, 65, 66. *See also* rhyme

Wylie, Georgiana Augusta, 15

Yeats, William Butler: "He Wishes for the Cloths of Heaven," 20–24, 30, 164; "The Second Coming," 15